CW01329567

Defeating the Panzer-Stuka Menace

Defeating the Panzer-Stuka Menace

British Spigot Weapons of the Second World War

David Lister

With contributions from Thomas Anderson and illustrations by Andrei Kirushkin

AN IMPRINT OF PEN & SWORD BOOKS LTD
YORKSHIRE – PHILADELPHIA

First published in Great Britain in 2021 by
FRONTLINE BOOKS
an imprint of Pen & Sword Books Ltd
Yorkshire – Philadelphia

Copyright © David Lister, 2021

ISBN 978-1-52678-715-6

The right of David Lister to be identified as the author of this work has been asserted by him in accordance with the Copyright, Designs and Patents Act 1988.

A CIP catalogue record for this book is available from the British Library.

All rights reserved. No part of this book may be reproduced or transmitted in any form or by any means, electronic or mechanical including photocopying, recording or by any information storage and retrieval system, without permission from the Publisher in writing.

Typeset by Concept, Huddersfield, West Yorkshire, HD4 5JL.
Printed and bound by CPI Group (UK) Ltd, Croydon CR0 4YY

Pen & Sword Books Ltd incorporates the Imprints of Aviation, Atlas, Family History, Fiction, Maritime, Military, Discovery, Politics, History, Archaeology, Select, Wharncliffe Local History, Wharncliffe True Crime, Military Classics, Wharncliffe Transport, Leo Cooper, The Praetorian Press, Remember When, White Owl, Seaforth Publishing and Frontline Books.

For a complete list of Pen & Sword titles please contact
PEN & SWORD BOOKS LTD
47 Church Street, Barnsley, South Yorkshire, S70 2AS, England
E-mail: enquiries@pen-and-sword.co.uk
Website: www.pen-and-sword.co.uk
or
PEN & SWORD BOOKS
1950 Lawrence Rd, Havertown, PA 19083, USA
E-mail: uspen-and-sword@casematepublishers.com
Website: www.penandswordbooks.com

Contents

Acknowledgements vii
Introduction viii
Addendum ix

Part 1: Of Men and Spigots 1
  1. Products of Empire 3
  2. A New Model Mortar 14

Part 2: The Bombard 25
  3. 'Macerated' 27
  4. Defeating the Ordnance Board Menace 38
  5. The Bombard 45
  6. The Answer to the Maiden's Prayer 59

Part 3: The Hedgehog 75
  7. The Perceived Peril 77
  8. The Great Hedgehog Scandal 92

Part 4: Miscellaneous Naval Spigot Weapons – Mustard Plaster,
       Water Hammer and Hedgerow 103
  9. Mustard Plaster 105
 10. Water Hammer 108
 11. The Hedgerow 112

Part 5: The PIAT – Baby Bombard, Jefferis Gun and PIAT 135
 12. From Parthian to Production 137
 13. Defeating the Panzer Menace 154

Part 6: Engineering Spigots – Petard, Denny Gun and Buffalo . . . 175
 14. The Stolen Tank of Victory 177

Part 7: The Matilda Hedgehog *by Thomas Anderson* 191
15. Spigots in the South-West Pacific 193

Part 8: The World's Spigots – Tree Spigot, Ground Spigot, Plate Spigot Gun, Bigot, *Leichter Ladungswerfer* **and Type 98 320mm** 215
16. The Other Spigots 217

Part 9: The End 229
17. The War after Next 231
Appendix A: Blacker Spigot Weapons 237
Appendix B: Bombard Ammunition Stores 238
Appendix C: Companies in North and South Groups 240
Appendix D: PIAT vs Bazooka – Comparative Trials 241
Appendix E: Matilda Hedgehog Serial Numbers *by Thomas Anderson* . . 242
Bibliography and Sources 243
Index 247

Acknowledgements

My thanks go to:
- The contributors of the ARRSE.co.uk PIAT thread
- The Blacker Family
- Alison Flowers, editor
- Andrew Hills
- Matthew J. Moss
- Ridgeway Military & Aviation Research Group
- Jeremy Rosenblad

And all those who have lobbed the odd document in my direction.

Introduction

In 2013, like the vast majority of historians, I considered the PIAT as a stand-alone development, which was a bit of an anomaly. I knew of the Bombard but lumped it in with the rest of the Heath Robinson contraptions of questionable usefulness that were given to the Home Guard in a hurry to face the threat of invasion. The sort of weapon seen in an episode of *Dad's Army*.

Around July 2013, I was at The National Archives at Kew looking for information on tank guns. I found a document listed in their catalogue as simply '23-pounder', and I requested it. My initial thoughts were that I was probably about to see an early version of the 20-pounder tank gun, although the dates on the document seemed to be too early for that. Or maybe it was some other experimental weapon, perhaps similar to the 8-pounder. Skimming through the rather thick file I quickly worked out that it was related to the Bombard. As this was of no use to me at the time, I was about to return it to the archives when I spotted a small, brown envelope as the next page in the file.

In UK files, such envelopes are usually filled with photographs or plans, items that cannot be bound together like normal sheets of paper, usually due to the size of the item. I opened it, and out fell seven tiny, aged, faded photographs (three of which can be seen on pp. 30–1). They showed the utter devastation caused by a Bombard against a tank. This came as a shock, and devastated my preconceived notions as much as the tank had been. Reading the attached report, it confirmed what I thought I saw in the pictures, and I began to realize the importance of the Bombard. If it were not for the imprecise labelling of that document, and me opening that envelope, this book would not exist, and history would be well on its way to forgetting the importance of spigot weapons to the British war effort.

Over the intervening seven years, I have been following the trail of Britain's spigot weapons, and it has had many surprising twists and turns. Facts that would have been front-page scandals if they were known about, stories that come right out of a spy novel and finally the realization that the effects of the Bombard are still being felt by the British military today.

So, please let me lead you on a trip through this odd world and a weapon that owes its life, development and effectiveness to a handful of very talented men.

Addendum

I sit here, some seven years after I started this project, and things have not gone smoothly. I write my books, then find pictures for them. The last three months have been taken up entirely by the 2020 coronavirus pandemic. The resulting lockdown has caused considerable problems in acquiring pictures, as many archives have, justifiably, sent their staff home. In my particular case the inability to obtain pictures relates to the Imperial War Museum.

There are a number of images that I wanted to include, but could not obtain from the IWM. The most critical of these would be of the Clarke Tree Spigot Gun. The image on p. 220 shows a US modified Tree Spigot; the IWM picture shows the weapon in its original form.

To that end I will list the reference numbers for those images that I feel are important to the spigot story, and the pages that they are relevant to. Please follow these steps to view them:

- Visit https://www.iwm.org.uk/.
- Under the 'Objects and History' tab select 'Our Collections'.
- Enter the relevant reference number in the search bar.

Alternatively:

- Search the web for 'IWM collections'.
- Use first link on Google – 'Our Collections | Imperial War Museums'.
- Then enter the relevant reference number in the search bar.

Important Images

Page	IWM Ref.	Reason for Inclusion
50	H 12300	An oddly shaped projectile, which may be the 20/15lb practice projectile. It is rarely pictured.
71	H 21581	The image, mentioned in the text, of a wheeled carriage for the Bombard.
90	A 30998	The original test equipment at Whitchurch being loaded for its test firing in front of the prime minister.
220	MUN 5773	The close-up of a British Tree Spigot Gun for comparison with the US modified weapon.

There are a number of pictures on the IWM website which are of general interest to the reader, but, like the previous images, they are unavailable due in part to the pandemic.

List of Bonus Images

IWM Ref.	Description
H 18634	Bombard ammunition store.
H 22530	An ideal holdfast installation for a Bombard.
H 38007	Petard loading sequence showing the loaders hand in position after shoving the round into the loading trough.
H 25543	This picture was taken at the South Foreland battery at Dover towards the end of 1942. The Bombard base unit has been sited directly onto a sturdy frame. In turn, this seems to have been mounted directly onto a coastal gun position, which would normally accept a pedestal mount. The shell magazines around the position would make ideal receptacles for the Bombard rounds, although in this case none are stored.
H 28311	A curious picture, showing a bombard round being worked on by two RAOC staff. I believe that they are attempting to add the coloured bands that denote if the round is fused or not, as detailed on p. 62.
H 30103	A nice picture of a Bombard gunner in operation, although the firing lever has not been grasped so the weapon cannot be fired.
H 17736	A good picture of a Bombard with a 14-pounder anti-personnel shell in place.
B 5193	An AVRE advancing down a narrow French street, photographed two days after D-Day.
NA 15430	Fusilier F. Jefferson with his PIAT. Fusilier Jefferson won a VC after he blunted a German armoured attack by charging the German tanks and firing the PIAT from the hip, knocking out several tanks. It is often joked that he won the VC for firing the PIAT from the hip due to the recoil, not the charging of the panzers. Oddly, when standing you would have less felt recoil than when prone.
B 8743	A Churchill advancing past a soldier in a foxhole with a PIAT somewhere in Normandy.
B 6899	A PIAT team in Caen.

PART ONE
OF MEN AND SPIGOTS

Chapter One

Products of Empire

Before we can talk about spigot weapons, and their use in the Second World War, we need to cover some background subjects. The first, and most important of all, are the people involved. By and far the most significant of these is Latham Valentine Stewart Blacker, OBE. He was a prolific inventor, who produced ninety-two designs for assorted weapons between 1935 and 1943. He was responsible for the introduction of the spigot mortar into British service during the Second World War, and thus all the subsequent events throughout the conflict.

Born at the height of the Empire in 1887, Blacker had a close interest in artillery even at a young age. His father, Major Latham Blacker, commanded a pair of guns at Gibraltar. Later, on HMS *Himalaya*, when moving back to the UK as a pre-schooler, he paid special attention to the Armstrong guns the ship carried for protection. When at boarding school, he entertained himself with ballistics, and along with a small group of boys managed to construct an improvised mortar that fired a croquet ball propelled by charges of black powder. The first and only target of this weapon was the headmaster's greenhouse, on which they scored a direct hit at a range of some 300yd. From boarding school he went to Sandhurst, and eventually in 1907 entered the Indian Army, and began serving on the lawless North-West Frontier, where he started learning about the local culture. Every four years British members of the Indian Army were given a prolonged period of leave allowing them to return home. Blacker's first leave fell in 1911, and he used the opportunity to return to the UK and begin to learn how to fly. The cost of his flying lessons was some £75, a rather princely sum. However, Blacker was gifted this amount by Ramji Lal. Blacker succeeded in qualifying as a pilot, being awarded certificate number 121 from the Royal Aero Club.

Later in 1911 Blacker returned to India, and the Royal Corps of Guides and began further adventures in the North-West Frontier. It was on one of his long patrols in the area in August 1914 that Blacker heard of the outbreak of the First World War. He came back to the UK and was immediately posted to the Royal Flying Corps (RFC). His first task was to try and tackle Zeppelins, with assorted early aircraft armed with eccentric weapons of war that every inventor in the UK put forth, claiming his contraption as the answer to the Zeppelin menace. One such device was named the Fiery

4   *Defeating the Panzer-Stuka Menace*

Stewart Blacker in his flying gear, possibly ready for his flight over Everest, 1933.

Grapnel and consisted of a TNT-filled tube with spikes, and the most absurd means of detonation ever devised. The tiny planes of the RFC were to hook the device into the fabric of the Zeppelin and await the explosion that would destroy the target. As usual, the inventor obviously failed to spot the main problem, that the underpowered aircraft would find it utterly impossible to reach the Zeppelin's cruising altitude. In the first months of 1915 Blacker was posted to France, where he had several aircraft shot out from under him.

Products of Empire 5

After the Battle of Neuve Chapelle, where the Indian Army sustained heavy casualties, Blacker had a crisis of conscience, and thus decided to leave the RFC and re-join the infantry in the trenches. He reached the front in the wake of the first German gas attacks, and with no defence against such a weapon, he led the battered remains of Indian infantry in counter-attacks. During this period he was wounded by artillery and spent some six months out of action.

It is at this time, at the end of 1915, when the story of the spigot mortar really begins. On the German side of the line a Hungarian priest known only as Father Vécer, or so the story goes, designed a spigot mortar. When the first weapons reached the front line, the troops initially called them the *Priesterwerfer*. It seems there was a previous design of spigot mortar, firing a similar round of ammunition, however the *Priesterwerfer* is the most famous. It was later standardized as the *Granatenwerfer* 16. It was a frame contraption with a spigot mounted on it. The entire frame could be traversed to provide an arc of fire, and the spigot could be raised or lowered to alter the range. It fired a projectile of about 5.5lb out to a range of roughly 330yd.

The British answer was the much cruder Hay Pocket Howitzer. Designed and proposed by Lieutenant Commander J. Hay of the Royal Navy, this was

A *Granatenwerfer* 16 set up, ready to fire, in a trench, belonging to the 6th Company of the 3rd Grenadier Regiment. One wonders how close to the front this position is as the Germans are exposing rather more body than seems prudent. (*Bild*)

6   *Defeating the Panzer-Stuka Menace*

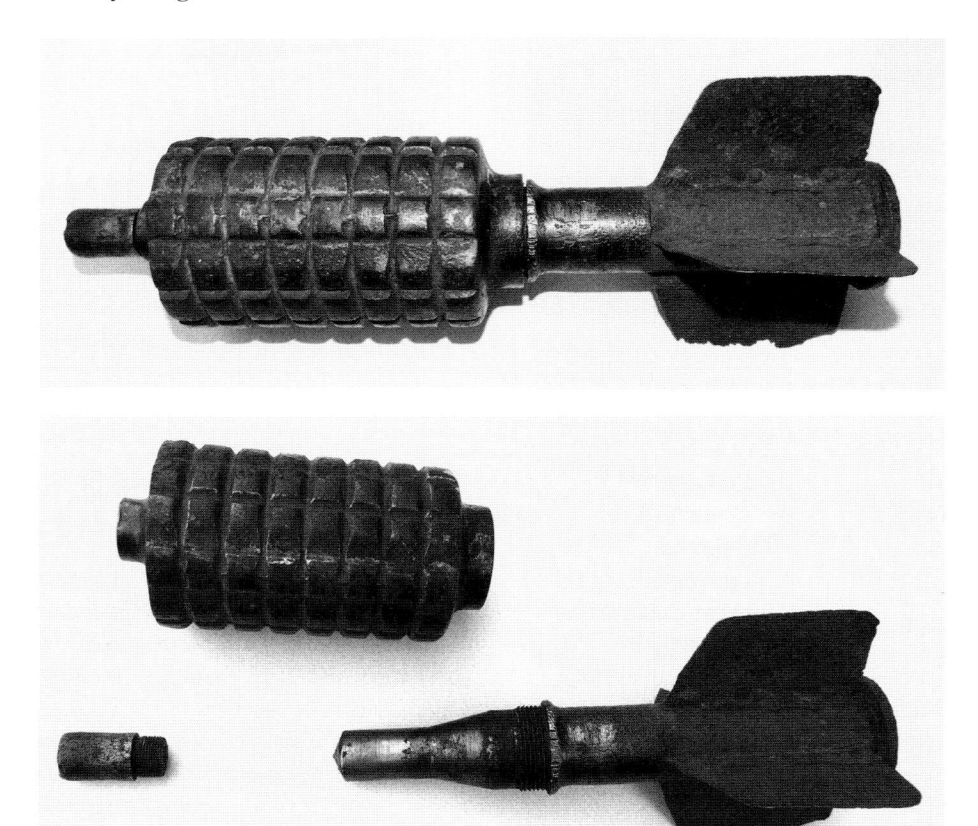

A *Granatenwerfer* 16 projectile, both complete and disassembled. The bomb was propelled by a blank 7.92 × 57mm Mauser bullet, and the tail tube was formed around that, hence the step-down. The tail tube calibre was 1in, which is a rather curious choice considering both Germany and Austria were metric countries.

essentially a large spike and baseplate that was driven into a bank pointing in the direction you wished to fire. Earth could be banked under the plate to slightly alter the angle. Range was achieved by different sized charges. Each was rammed down the fixed barrel that stuck out of the baseplate. This barrel was the spigot over which the projectile was fitted. A pull ring, to which a lanyard was attached, was provided. Pulling on this fired the charge and sent the grenade, which weighed just over 1lb, on its way. A maximum range of 450yd was achieved with 5 grains of gun cotton and 35 of ballistite, whereupon the grenade left a distinctly unimpressive 30in crater. This contraption was tested by the Ordnance Committee on 25 November 1915. Later, after the Second World War, Millis Jefferis, whom we shall come to in a moment,

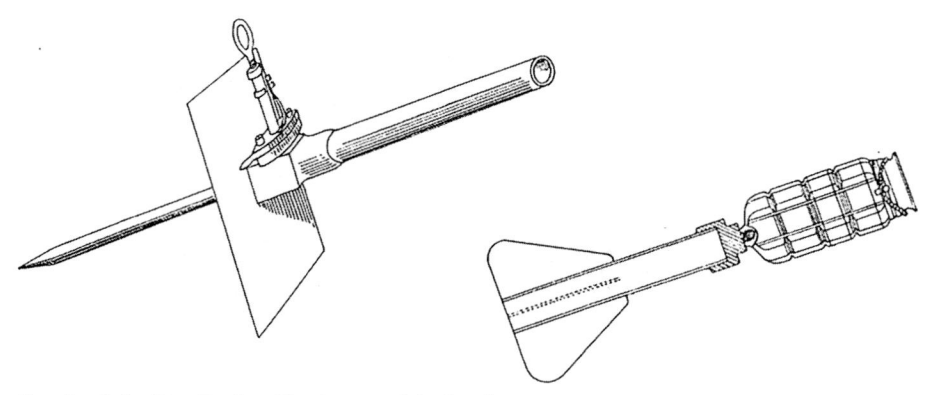

Sketch of the Hay Pocket Howitzer and its bomb.

stated that Blacker first proposed a spigot weapon in 1915, however there appears to be no record of this proposal, and Blacker himself does not make mention of it.

Blacker, when recovered, returned to the RFC. By a stroke of luck, his spell in the trenches meant that he had missed the Fokker Scourge. Blacker was a doer, and would instantly and ferociously attack any mechanical problem. In this case, interrupter gear had been designed but used a mechanical linkage. Blacker felt that he could improve on the system in a way that would not be affected by wear and temperature changes like the existing device. With the help of a Romanian engineer, they developed a hydraulic system which Blacker states was used for decades. During related trials on a machine-gun mounting, Blacker managed to shoot himself down, breaking his neck and ending his flying career.

At this point he returned to India and was involved, once again, in the 'Great Game' on the North-West Frontier and several campaigns in the Russian Civil War. In 1922 he was promoted to staff college at Quetta. From there he returned to UK, although he experienced quite a few adventures in Eastern Europe.

In 1932 Blacker's inventiveness turned to peacetime pursuits after he designed a new and improved aircraft machine gun. He began to work on a project to fly over Everest, and more importantly to film the passage. Both crew and cameras needed to be heated, and special devices were designed and constructed by the team to this end, the project taking place in 1933. Blacker himself was on one of the planes as an observer.

Following his return to the UK, until his death in 1964, Blacker began to invent and design weapons. His fertile imagination created a great mass of ordnance for reigning destruction upon the enemies of the king. The scope of this can be seen from the designations of his inventions. At least for a time, he took to numbering each weapon he designed sequentially. In 1935 he produced a weapon he called the 'Arbalest', which carried the title of Gun Number 8. In 1943 there are records indicating he had reached number 100.

Blacker beat several other designers to ideas, although he failed to patent these designs, and so lost his protections. In 1947 he designed a small, lightweight, bull-pup carbine that fired 9.5mm rockets, beating Robert Mainhardt and Art Biehl of Gyrojet fame to the idea by thirteen years. In 1937 Blacker designed a new type of magazine, although what gun it was intended for is hard to work out. It consisted of two drums feeding into a single-stack magazine. This was fifty years before the Beta Company brought out their C-mag. Blacker's design is all but identical to the modern equivalent.

At the time of the Dunkirk Evacuation, Blacker had been serving as a colonel in a Territorial Army artillery unit. He was hurriedly ordered to report to Woolwich barracks. Once there he found himself without a job as the original scheme the army had in mind for him was altered by the fast-moving situation in France. As luck would have it, he then bumped into General Hastings Lionel Ismay, an acquaintance from his time at Quetta. General Ismay sent him to the Military Intelligence Research Section C (MIRc), a research and development department of the army, which, in Blacker's own words, 'improvised infernal machines', and it seemed the ideal place for someone with Blacker's talents.

While an undoubted genius at weapon design, Blacker had a strong dislike of bureaucracy and was very much a man of action. This meant he often suffered reverses in the corridors of government. He wrote a letter on 3 September 1941 that perfectly demonstrated his prickly nature. Henry Mond, the 2nd Baron Melchett, often referred to as Lord Melchett, was in control of Imperial Chemical Industries (ICI), the producer of the Bombard. As we shall see, there were production difficulties which meant that just 15 bombards had been produced, against a forecast number of 3,600. Blacker wrote to Professor Frederick Lindemann, Churchill's scientific advisor, about the situation, protesting loudly in just five terse sentences. He closed off the letter with, 'He has his choice between murder and suicide.' Equally, Blacker kept a file he labelled 'Official Obstruction' where every rejection or similar reproach was stored like a book of grudges.

Having such a loose cannon rolling about in Whitehall was an unappealing prospect, and in about May 1941 Blacker was politely retired. He officially retired in October 1942 leaving the army for good. However, at some point between these two dates, Blacker set up his own company, Blacker Developments Ltd. He employed a small team of draughtsmen, who would turn his sketches, plans and ideas into complete and finalized drawings. It appears that Blacker Developments Ltd ceased trading shortly after the war, although exact dates are difficult to find. From then on, until his death in 1964, Blacker spent his time tinkering and experimenting. This was mainly with rocketry, although he did expend quite some effort on a new type of recoilless rifle. This was designed to fire a counterweight at an angle, up and to the rear of the projector. The idea seems to have been to remove both the massive firing signature and the danger zone that normally accompanies recoilless rifles.

Shortly after his death, Blacker's wife, Lady Doris Peel, contacted the local Royal Engineers bomb disposal team and asked them to attend and make her husband's laboratories safe. It took the bomb-disposal team an entire day to remove all the explosives, which ranged from simple black powder to modern shaped charges. The following day the engineers began to carry out controlled explosions on the recovered explosives, and this alone took several hours. There is a tale that many years later after the Blackers' home had been sold, renovation work was being carried out in the basement. During the work, the builders knocked through a false wall and found themselves confronted with Blacker's emergency supplies, which he had obviously secreted away against future need, perhaps if the Germans, or later the Soviets, had invaded. This store of explosives had been mouldering in the basement uncared for and was more than enough to replace the fine country house with a very large crater. This collection was also made safe by bomb-disposal personnel.

The other name often associated with British Second World War spigot weapons is Millis Rowland Jefferis. At first glance, there is a strong biographical resemblance between the two men. Jefferis was just four years younger than Blacker. However, during most of the First World War Jefferis was completing his studies at the Royal Military Academy in Woolwich, and only saw action with the Royal Engineers in the dying days of the war. From there he travelled to India and served on the North-West Frontier, where he took part in the Waziristan Campaign. For his actions in this operation, he was awarded the Military Cross. After more schooling at Cambridge, he returned to India in 1925, where he remained until 1936, and again like Blacker became fluent in Pashto. During his entire time in India, he was part of the Royal Engineers, and one of his principal roles was bridge building. From there, his interest in bridges morphed into an interest in explosives and how to blow up bridges and structures.

While in Britain Jefferis remained part of the army and when the Second World War broke out he was running MIRc. It suddenly became clear during the Norwegian Campaign that there were several bridges that needed demolishing. The army cast about for someone to do the job and settled on Jefferis. While there he was ordered forward to help with demolitions on a railway bridge, which the now Allied Norwegians refused to allow to be blown up. Now in the front lines, the unit Jefferis was with was surrounded and overrun. Jefferis linked up with three soldiers, whom he led to safety through the German lines. On his way, he blew up a pair of bridges to hinder the German advance. For his actions, he was mentioned in dispatches. From there it seems he returned to MIRc.

Jefferis, like Blacker, hated bureaucracy and officialdom, referring to them as 'abominable no-men of Whitehall'. However, instead of giving both men a common enemy, it seemed they disliked each other equally. Documents do not mention any interaction between the two, even minutes of meetings with both men, it is an utter void, almost as if both men tolerated the other's presence by ignoring them, lest they were impolite. Part of the problem seems to have come from their differing attitude to design. Jefferis was highly educated, and a capable mathematician. Blacker, on the other hand, came from the school of 'let's build it and see what breaks!' Jefferis saw the lack of learning in Blacker as a huge flaw, and it is possible that Blacker saw Jefferis as just another bureaucrat in uniform. Blacker does, in his autobiography, accuse Jefferis of stealing the idea for the Projector, Infantry, Anti-Tank (PIAT). Matters were possibly not improved by Winston Churchill repeatedly calling for the PIAT to be renamed the 'Jefferis Gun', citing the presence of Smith Guns, Hawkins Mines and even Blacker Bombards. It was not until the War Office sat down and explained the facts in detail, and pointed out that it was not current policy to use officers' names for weapons, having hurriedly renamed all the weapons listed to much more military sounding terms, that Churchill ceased his requests.

After the Second World War Jefferis remained in uniform rising through the ranks until he retired in 1953 as an honorary major general. Jefferis was to die just seven months before Blacker in September 1963. Unlike Blacker, Jefferis never wrote an autobiography, and, indeed, he seems to have been far more discreet about his life and as a consequence less information about him is readily available.

With both inventors at loggerheads with each other and the surrounding Civil Service, it is a miracle that any of the projects that emerged from MIRc ever came close enough to a German to blow him up. Much to the chagrin of the Germans, and the good fortune of Britain, MIRc had such a miracle in the form of Robert Stuart Macrae in the role of administrator. Macrae also took part in the weapons design process. It is likely that Macrae's input combined with Churchill's direct interest and support meant that the 'infernal machines' from MIRc caused such widespread mayhem for the Germans.

If it is difficult to find information on Jefferis, Macrae is all but invisible. Macrae had started his working life as an engineer, but by the late 1930s was the editor of *Armchair Science* magazine and an unnamed gardening magazine. He was recruited to MIRc when Jefferis was looking for information on strong magnets for the limpet mine project. He also worked on 'poulticing explosives', which as we shall see was quite an important concept. Macrae remained in the army until 1955 when he retired with the rank of honorary colonel.

Blacker's and Jefferis' views on bureaucrats were, probably, largely down to the misguided belief that it was simple to do something. Throughout 1940 Blacker was often heard to say that if the War Office had listened to him then the British Army would have been equipped with a weapon that would have enabled it to defeat the 'Panzer-Stuka menace', which was Blacker's term for *Blitzkrieg* in a time when the German word for this form of warfare was not in common use. How his prototype bomb-throwers were to have changed the strategic situation on the Western Front, or in Norway, is not entirely clear, but Blacker was very sure of the fact. A lot of Blacker's and Jefferis' obstructions were down to the War Office moving at the 'Speed of Government', which is never fast. To compound matters, MIRc was also faced with the Ordnance Board, controlled by the Director of Artillery (D of A) Major General Edward Montagu Campbell Clarke.

Both the Ordnance Board and MIRc came under the Ministry of Supply. Major General Clarke was promoted to D of A on 22 June 1938. The post of D of A was chair of the Ordnance Board, which advised and controlled all aspects of weapons development. This meant that all of MIRc's inventions would have to gain approval from the Ordnance Board. Major General Clarke had been a staff officer for a great many years, having the lofty and concise title of 'Officer-in-Charge, Danger Buildings, Ordnance Factories and Assistant Superintendent, Design Department, Royal Arsenal, Woolwich (temporarily)' prior to his promotion to D of A. This was likely precisely the sort of officer that both Blacker and Jefferis despised. There was a very real feud between the two departments, and the Ordnance Board would often outright lie or exaggerate flaws, perceived or otherwise, that they could find with the submitted weapon, to prevent MIRc's devices from achieving any success. A perfect example is Macrae's sticky bomb, officially called the ST Grenade.

The ST Grenade works by having a frangible case filled with a sludge-like explosive. When smashed onto a tank the case would break, and the explosive would settle downwards. The entire mass was held in place by an outer cloth covering that was impregnated with glue which, after a short delay of about 3–5 seconds, allowed the explosive to spread out a bit and the entire mass detonated.

The only reason that the ST Grenade was given a fair hearing by the Ordnance Board was that Churchill was present at the first demonstration, and had personally pushed it through to completion. This was in summer 1940, just weeks after Dunkirk, when the army was woefully short of any anti-tank weapons, irrespective of type. Instead of grabbing a cheap, easy to

A sticky bomb being assembled. The glass sphere covered with the cloth sock and glue can be seen on the left. The packing sphere is then fitted around this and fastened together. The person assembling the case is demonstrating how the cases are fastened together by a simple metal tag linked to a ring pull. When the time comes to tackle a panzer, this ring pull releases both halves of the packing sphere which fall away. The fuse is in the handle.

produce weapon, the Ordnance Board dragged its heels. Later they claimed that they had only been given details of the ST Grenade two days beforehand. Churchill summoned Jefferis, who provided Churchill with documentary proof showing that the sticky bomb had been submitted well before.

When Churchill became aware of the delays, in November 1940, he described the situation as 'most vexatious to encounter this obstruction', and pointedly demanded matters be resolved, saying of Major General Clarke, 'This is the same D of A that is always trying to crab this sort of thing.' Major

General Clarke did have some friends, as the Secretary of State for War, Anthony Eden, defended him suggesting this was not the best time for recriminations.

Amazingly the Ordnance Board would not leave the ST Grenade alone. In March 1941, the board arbitrarily ordered the discontinuation of filling of the grenade. Citing that the grenade's explosive was hard to detonate, that there had been some minor leakage on a couple of the first pre-production versions that they had inspected, and finally a case of bombs had broken when dropped from a height of 4ft 6in. The frustrated response from Professor Lindemann was that of course the bombs broke from that height, it is how they are meant to operate. Equally, ICI, who had fifty years of experience with this type of explosive, thought that it was safe. In a final retort, Professor Lindemann asked that if the explosive was as difficult to detonate as the Ordnance Board was complaining, who cared about a minuscule amount of leakage?

In truth, the Ordnance Board's schemes were for nought. The ST Grenade had done its part in the war effort and scored several successes in North Africa. However, the sticky bomb needed to use a gun cotton primer, which was in short supply. As other anti-tank weapons appeared, and the threat of invasion receded, the need for the ST Grenade vanished. The initial order for the grenades had been 1 million. By early 1941 around 100,000 had been produced and production was running at 7,000 per week. To achieve the 1 million requirement in any sensible time frame a massive upgrading of production facilities was needed. Thus, the War Office suggested that the order be lowered to 200,000, which was achievable and would save significantly on the rare primers. This reduction was approved.

The cabal of the Ordnance Board led by Major General Clarke would continue to bedevil Jefferis and Blacker, so in about late 1940, MIRc was moved, by Churchill, from the Ministry of Supply to the Ministry of Defence. Major General Clarke stayed in post until 1945, although towards the second half of the Second World War relations between Blacker and the Ordnance Board seemed to have mellowed. It may be that the Ordnance Board had its main enemy in Jefferis, or that Blacker's inventions were just too good to be ignored. But the first of Blacker's spigot weapons were very easy to dismiss.

Chapter Two

A New Model Mortar

Spigot-based firearms work differently to normal weapons. The spigot in the weapon's title is a long rod. The projectile has a hollow tube at its base, forming the tail tube which is slipped over the spigot. Between the spigot and the tail tube is a propelling charge. When the propellant is fired, the released gas acts in a manner identical to a normal firearm, only the tail tube, and thus the projectile, is thrown off the spigot towards the target. This action is similar to a piston. Imagine if you will what would happen on a piston if the arm and the case are not fixed together. The piston arm would be equivalent to the spigot, and its case the tail tube. This inverting of the firearm principle gives a spigot-based weapon certain unique technical characteristics.

The most important feature is that any shape or size of projectile can be used from the same mortar, which can provide flexibility. Equally, the weapon required to fire the shot is much simpler and compact. A perfect example of this is the famous Projector, Infantry, Anti-Tank (PIAT). This actually fires a 3.25in (82.55mm) shell. Consider the size of the smallest conventional guns of near that calibre and you will instantly see how much smaller and lighter spigot weapons are.

Another technical peculiarity of spigot weapons, one that has beset spigot weapons throughout history, is that it suffers from the same issues as 'muzzle-loading' weapons. Such as old muskets being loaded with lead ball. This method of sliding the two parts past each other during loading means that the spigot has to be slightly thinner than the calibre of the tail tube into which it fits, otherwise loading is all but impossible. This small gap means the seal between the tail tube and spigot is not very efficient, which can let propellant gas leak past. Creating a tight gas seal is termed as 'obturation' in ballistics. The gas leakage causes varied pressure and thus differing muzzle velocities between shots, as well as instability of the projectile. Both of these aspects affect the range and accuracy. Lack of consistent performance is always considered negatively in military firearms and is why spigot weapon use throughout history has been more of an anomaly. In almost all cases, better, more consistent results could be obtained from conventional weapons.

There were two types of spigot weapon from the 1930s and 1940s. These were the 'recoiling spigot' and 'fixed spigot' types. A recoiling spigot has a spigot that is mounted attached to a strong spring. At the end of the spigot is

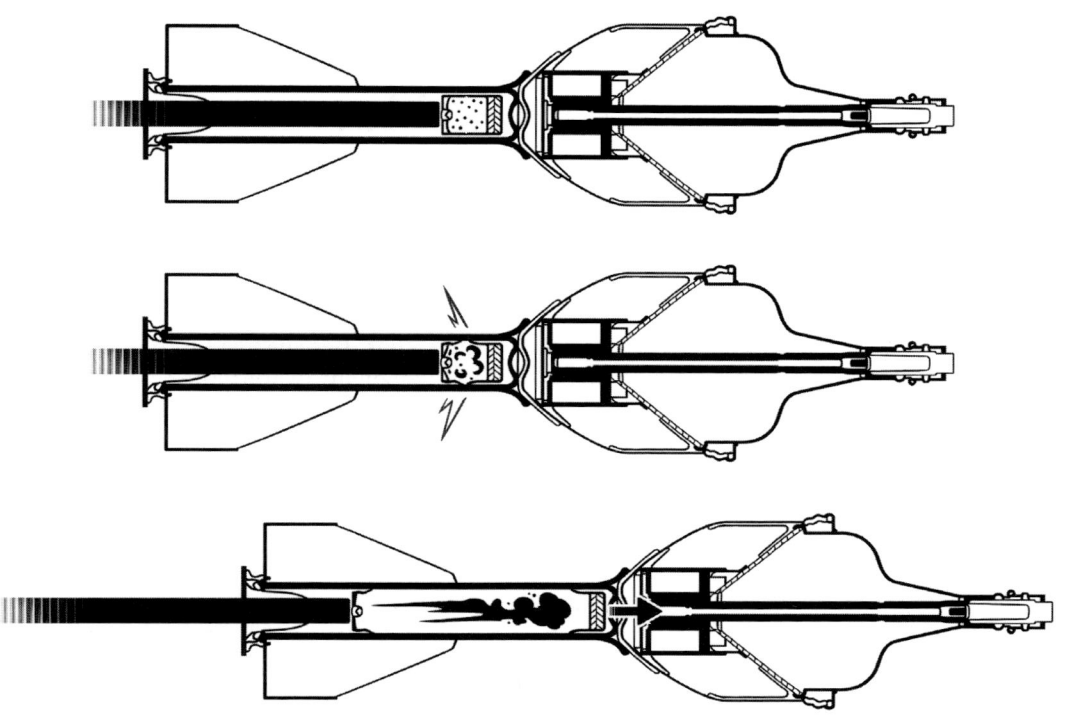

An illustration of how the spigot principle works on a PIAT. It shows the working of the propellent case expanding to form the obturation and using the gas bubble to launch the bomb.

a fixed firing pin. When the weapon is cocked, the spring is compressed, retracting the spigot. When the tension in the recoil spring was released, it would slam the spigot forward into the tail tube and the firing pin would detonate the primer at the base of the cartridge. The recoil from the shot forces the spigot backwards, and the spring acts as a recoil buffer to absorb the recoil. Hopefully, the recoil will have enough force to re-cock the weapon. Thus, all that is needed is a new bomb to be loaded, and the weapon can fire again. This action was also sometimes referred to as a dynamic spigot because the spigot is in motion.

In a fixed spigot the spigot does not move, and some other function is needed to detonate the propellant. This type of design is even simpler than a recoiling spigot type to build, as it is essentially a long stick with a trigger. The downside is that the considerable recoil is not absorbed by the gun and needs to be dealt with somehow.

The field of obturation is where Blacker's first and most vitally important innovation occurred. He made spigot weapons perform in a consistent manner by achieving sufficient obturation. He achieved this by creating a specially designed cartridge that contained the propellant. It was a simple tube, made with a line scoured around its middle on the inside of the case. Upon detonation, the case would split in two, with the bottom half expanding inside the tail tube to provide a tight gas seal. This was the invention that would enable the spigot weapon to play such an important role in the Second World War.

Blacker's road to spigot weapons started sometime in the early 1930s. In late 1933 he submitted a patent, that was approved, for a bomb-thrower. This was an attachment on top of a service revolver, which would use the mechanics of the revolver to provide the means of firing the bomb out of a barrel. This early patent is more of a statement of intent than a solid design and incorporates all conceivable ideas into the patent application. For example, Blacker states that it is possible to reduce the bomb barrel down to a spigot-like design, although such a device was not sketched. Equally, he suggests that there are three possible ways to trigger the firing pin in the bomb discharger part of the weapon. These would be to tap some of the gas from the weapon, after the bullet had passed out of the revolver, or to use the impact of the bullet as it travelled down the barrel on a mechanical lever. The final suggestion was to use the action of the revolver's hammer onto some other part of the device. It was this last design that Blacker pursued after some critical thinking. In 1934 he applied for and was awarded a patent for this new weapon. It was two of the ideas from his first patent boiled down and improved.

First, he shrunk the barrel down to a fixed spigot, it would seem to save weight and simplify. Through this spigot ran a long rod, with the firing pin on the end. This rod was under spring tension to be forced backwards, thus the firing pin would be retracted for most of the time. At the base of the rod was an extension at a right angle to the line of the rod. This meant the rod became the stalk of an L-shape. The base of the L could be swung into the space between the revolver's hammer and its body, thus when the hammer was released as the trigger was pulled, the hammer struck the rod, and forced it forward. This, in turn, pushed the firing pin into the tail of the bomb detonating the charge and sending it on its way. Such an action would also prevent the bullet in the revolver's cylinder being fired as the hammer would not strike the primer. Blacker designed the device with a toggle lever, that would move the rod in and out of firing position. Thus, if the grenadier armed with this weapon was surprised by infantry and needed to use his close-defence weapon, he just needed to flick the lever to 'bullet' mode, and he had a stocked pistol in his hands. For use as a mortar, the stock had a hinge along the top of it, which allowed the butt plate to fold into two halves to act as some form of bracing for use in indirect fire.

Blacker also thought about the ammunition. He realized that instead of adding a new logistics burden he could adapt the No. 36 Mills Grenade to his needs. On the base of the grenade was a metal plug to hold the detonator in place. This was a simple metal disk screwed into position and had no purpose other than to hold all the grenade's components together. Blacker proposed that a tail be manufactured which would screw into the same opening. Thus, the grenadier just needed to carry a supply of tails, and could switch out a plug for a tail from any spare grenades the unit had. Equally, if he needed to, the grenadier could use the bombs as grenades without removing the tail. In addition, there was the suggestion of a fairing that could be included and pressed over the top of the grenade to improve aerodynamics.

In 1935 Blacker started work on a new spigot weapon, one he called 'Col. Blacker's No. 8 "Arbalest" bomb-thrower'. The Arbalest and bombs were made by Parnell Aircraft Ltd, and Blacker was working as a member of the company's managing board. The Arbalest was a recoiling spigot weapon.

An artist's impression of a Grenadier armed with an AEB bomb-thrower. In this particular case, the grenade has been fitted with the tail, although the possible nose fairing has been omitted.

18   *Defeating the Panzer-Stuka Menace*

An artist's impression of an Arbalest. The soldier's left hand is on the clinometer, and he would sight his eye to it before firing. Also seen is the traverse dial in between the bipod legs at the front of the gun.

It is highly likely that Blacker was responsible for the invention of the recoiling spigot, as no spigot weapons that pre-date 1935 have these features. The spigot was attached to a handle that ran through the body of the Arbalest. Both components formed a T-shape, with the spring behind the crossbar. Interestingly Blacker included a provision for a cable to be attached to this assembly, presumably to make cocking easier. The weapon had a small baseplate and a bipod. The bipod was mounted in a slot several inches long, under the body of the weapon. The bipod had two locations, either at the front of the slot, or all the way to the back of the slot. About two-thirds of the way down the body of the gun, away from the muzzle, there was a trigger bar that stuck out horizontally to the right. This was attached to a circle of metal that encased the body, and was described as the 'saddle' by Blacker in his plans. On the left side of the saddle was a clinometer, which in itself had three settings. The gun could be traversed by 4 degrees without moving the weapon. This was done by a small dial on the bottom of the bipod. The projectiles, each bomb was 2.375in across, looked like miniaturized aircraft bombs of the period, and the plans for the two of them have been discovered. One was obviously a HE round as it had a nose striker, the other was curiously devoid of a detonator, and had just an empty chamber at the front, with what appeared to be a two-part case. It is possible that this was a smoke bomb, and upon impact, the case was designed to split open releasing the smoke.

In 1937 the British Army held trials for a new platoon light-infantry mortar or bomb-thrower. The competitors included a 2in Ecia, 2.5in BSA, 47mm Brandt, 52mm Telmera (Scott) and 60mm Brandt mortars. Blacker submitted one of his designs, although at first glance it is not entirely clear which of his weapons he put forward, due to confusion over the naming conventions Blacker and the Ordnance Board used. All the bombs for the Arbalest start with the designation 'AEB', followed by a number. It appears most of the drawings Blacker submitted to Parnell Aircraft Ltd also have this nomenclature. The problems for the historian arise in the 1937 trials when Blacker's submission is listed as an 'AEB (Blacker) mortar'. The only source for this is the Ordnance Board report on the trials. From the description in the Ordnance Board files, it seems likely that the submitted weapon was a variant of the 1934 Patent, of the modified revolver design. It should be pointed out that this was before Major General Clarke joined the Ordnance Board, and so the board was possibly less biased against the weapon.

From the trials reports the AEB mortar seems to have been based around a .38 service revolver. The 2-pound bomb that was proposed caused such concern over its safety features that Blacker was asked to attend the Ordnance Board and discuss matters before his weapon was allowed into the trial. The Ordnance Board's main worry was that the two safety features included in the bomb were both removed before loading. These included a handle, similar to the one found on hand grenades, which kept the bomb safe until released. This was added so the bomb could be used as a hand grenade, however, the handle was removed before inserting the bomb into the barrel. The other safety feature was a pin, which seems to have been withdrawn once the weapon was loaded and before firing. If the weapon operating drill was not followed and the pin removed first, then the entire weapon became very dangerous. To add to the safety nightmares, the bomb was push to fit on the barrel and could be rammed down too far, which would force the bomb onto the firing pin, with predictably catastrophic results. After discussing matters with Blacker the Ordnance Board agreed that the AEB mortar could join the trials, but only with precautions in place.

In the trials, the weapon performed very poorly. Only four rounds were attempted to be fired before the Ordnance Board ordered the AEB trials to halt. The first round fired, but the mortar collapsed. The second round was a misfire, as the bomb had not been rammed home sufficiently. After a second go, round two was fired, but the selector lever jammed into the 'bomb' position. Round three was a misfire due to adaptors and primers from the previous round still being in the barrel. After clearing the barrel, the round fired, leaving the adaptor and primer behind again. More concerningly the hinges holding the weapon to the butt plate had begun to fracture. Blacker surmised that errors in manufacturing the charge had meant that the propellent was too powerful. In addition, the recoil spring, listed as a 'shock absorber', did not function properly to run out the mortar for reloading. Both the shock-absorber issue and the primer and adaptor being left in the barrel were found on round four. At this point the trial was halted.

From the above descriptions, it is likely that the weapon was at least close to the revolver design, as it does not match the Arbalest. It could well have been some form of spigot weapon, as in 1944 Blacker tried to re-sell the idea to the War Office, and his letter detailing the modification of a .38 revolver with a butt plate on a rod and spigot-like contraption survives. In this letter, he also mentions that the weapon was trialled in 1937. The barrel referred to in the Ordnance Board reports could well have been just a holder to retain the mortar bomb.

Further confusion was added to other Ordnance Board proceedings of the period with talk of the 'Blacker bomb-thrower', but it is not clear what weapon they were referring to.

The confusion continued, when in December 1938 the Ordnance Board agreed to give the Arbalest bomb-thrower a series of trials to assess if it would make a suitable light-infantry mortar. After the first set of accuracy trials, it was determined by the Ordnance Board to discontinue the trials. However, Major General Clarke decided to overrule the board, and ordered one last trial to be held, after which a conference would be held to discuss the idea of spigot weapons. The results of the meeting, which was held in May 1939, were turned into a report and submitted to the Ordnance Board for comment. The report took the form of a questionnaire that was given to the conference members. In the report, the Arbalest was directly compared to the 2-inch mortar then in service.

Things started off well for the Arbalest, as it weighed only 12lb, compared with the mortar's 22lb. Although there was a note of an investigation to build the barrels for the mortar from a light alloy that was just about to take place. Such a light alloy would reduce the 2in mortar's weight. For the Arbalest things went downhill from there. In the method of operation, the Arbalest could be fired by Bowden cable, lanyard or the trigger. The trigger was described as liable to be accidentally operated, while the Bowden cable was considered cumbersome and unsuitable for service use. Indeed, in a short while, the Bowden cable would be banned from use on the army's weapons. The final option of firing with a lanyard had the unpleasant side effect of yanking the Arbalest off its aiming line, making it utterly inaccurate.

While the Arbalest could traverse 4 degrees either side of the centre line, the 2-inch mortar could be traversed 10 degrees. The Arbalest could not be cocked by one man in the prone position either. It was also a vastly more complex weapon, which would necessitate more logistical spares and much higher production costs in man-hours as well as financial burdens.

During the firing trials, the Arbalest was clamped into position and used specially made bombs. The 2-inch mortar used service ammunition and was free-standing. The Arbalest did manage to get roughly the same range, of about 480yd, against the mortar's 500yd. It was also judged that the Arbalest was much harder to load, slower to fire and much more difficult to lay. Equally the 2-inch mortar was faster to bring into action. The Ordnance

Board also stuck a knife in commenting that they found the firing pin and arrangement of the propelling charge objectionable.

The report closes with: 'The basic principle of the bomb-thrower must put it out of court. The Arbalest depends for its performance on the chamber being incorporated into the bomb. This is considered impracticable and only a complete re-design departing from this principle could be a service proposition.'

With all in agreement, the army divested itself of the weapon. It seems that the weapon was returned to Blacker, who was somewhat perturbed by the results of the conference. Blacker claimed that Major General Clarke had told him only the concept of the weapon would be studied, not the actual performance. In the Arbalest's defence, Blacker also pointed out that the concept of a mortar was much more mature, having been around for many centuries and gained the benefit of development over that time, while the Arbalest was still only three years old, and had undergone little or no development work. To further prove his point, he began a series of his own trials.

These trials started on the 19th, when Blacker fired five rounds, with the gun elevation at 24 degrees. Blacker measured the weapon's '100 per cent

A 2-inch mortar team practising in Wales, 1941. The baseplate is just in front of the gunner's chest, and you can just make out the pivot above the crook of his elbow allowing him to traverse the weapon.

zone', which is the length of ground that all the bombs fell into. In the first trial, he got a zone of about 30yd and the range averaging about 367yd. This was extrapolated to a 40yd 100 per cent zone at 500yd. The use of this measure gave an indication of accuracy, and thus the number of rounds needed to achieve a hit. Blacker had in his mind a critical weight of 12lb. This seems to have been the desired weight for the light mortar stipulated by the army. Blacker was aware that any saving in weight of the gun would be wasted if the soldiers had to carry a large number of bombs. To illustrate the point a 45yd long by 8yd wide 100 per cent zone would require 240 bombs to ensure a hit. However, by shrinking the area down to 25yd by 6in the number of bombs needed would fall to 100. Blacker calculated the area of a machine-gun nest as about $4yd^2$. This would, he stated, require 60 bombs from a 2-inch mortar to obtain a hit or just 25 from the Arbalest. Equally, Blacker was able to claim his weapon could engage a pillbox's vision slit directly, something a 2-inch mortar could not. This was down to the arc of the weapon, which Blacker saw as another negative, especially in the amount of propellant each weapon needed. The 2-inch mortar needed 47 grains of Ballistite, while the Arbalest only used 32 grains. Blacker put his improved accuracy down to using drum tails which gave better aerodynamics than normal fin tails.

As the results on the 19th were the same as the Ordnance Board trials, Blacker was convinced that he could do better. He noticed that the gas check on the weapon was less efficient than it could be, and so he set to work improving the design. Just six days later he fired another series, this time of seven bombs. The bombs were all identical, although Blacker does note that one bomb had a small defect in it, and it landed shorter than the rest. The simple modification gave a 100 per cent zone only 19yd in length and an average distance of 451yd.

A further round of modifications to the gas checks led to trial three on the 26th, this time the gun was elevated to 30 degrees. Unfortunately for Blacker, the wind was very strong and gusty, and it scattered the bombs about, giving a 100 per cent zone of 36yd.

Blacker also suggested that with the improved gas check, a better spring and 5 grains more propellant he could achieve 700yd. However, all this seems to have been for nought, as the Ordnance Board do not appear to have taken another look at the Arbalest.

There is a question of how many Arbalests were built. One complete weapon certainly survived. After Blacker's death, the complete Arbalest was gifted to a museum, which would later close. This Arbalest was photographed and appears to be complete in all regards. There is an almost complete one on display at the Ridgeway Military & Aviation Research Group (RMARG) at RAF Welford, at the time of writing. The RMARG one is missing its baseplate, clinometer and parts of the bipod, and it is suggested that this one may

The one Arbalest that is known to survive at RMARG. The Arbalest is the middle weapon, a very early prototype of the PIAT is seen at the top and below is a mystery spigot that no one can quite work out what it is for.

be the one from the now-closed museum. Yet, residing in a private collection there is the very distinctive baseplate of the Arbalest. This could imply that at least two complete Arbalests were constructed. The one photographed and the component parts at two locations. Two weapons would also fit with Blacker's usual approach to experimental weapons, which seems to have been to have made two or three each. The only flaw with this idea is finding out where the complete weapon went. If it is the RMARG one, then the separate baseplate could still indicate a potential second weapon.

PART TWO

THE BOMBARD

Chapter Three

'Macerated'

Exactly what happened between 2 June 1939 and 6 September 1940 is a bit of a mystery. Documents from both those dates survive, with the 1939 document showing the final demise of the Arbalest at the hands of the Ordnance Board, and the 1940 dated ones revealing discussion about development work on the Bombard. To fill in the gap there is only one autobiography and secondary sources, neither of which provide exact dates or tackle the question of what people were actually thinking. We know from Blacker's autobiography that nothing really happened until just after Dunkirk, which takes us up to early June 1940. Blacker is then described as visiting Jefferis in his office and unwrapping a bundle, which contained 'a bizarre tube-like barrel'. From the description one could infer that the weapon was, in fact, the Arbalest, as one man alone would struggle to carry a Bombard, let alone place and unwrap it on someone's desk! It is likely that working on this weapon is what lead to Blacker being employed by MIRc.

What happened next is one of the more remarkable feats in weapon development history, as the Arbalest transformed into a newer heavier weapon. Jefferis and Blacker began to work on developing the weapon, before presenting it once again to the Ordnance Board. Unsurprisingly the weapon was rejected, with Jefferis being told that 'even if the weapon was sponsored by God, it would be rejected'. This statement is almost certainly down to the feud between Major General Clarke and Jefferis. Although it might have been influenced by the rejection of the spigot weapon in the previous year, and an element of frustration that this same idea kept coming back. When Professor Lindemann heard of this he stepped in and used his position to arrange a demonstration of the Bombard at Chequers.

This caused a bit of a surprise for MIRc, and the entirety of the department was brought in to work on the design. The offices were working 24 hours a day. Eventually, engineering drawings were produced and passed to the musical instrument makers Boosey & Hawkes Ltd. The Chequers demonstration is mentioned in the past tense, when the document trial resumes on 6 September 1940. The exact date of the Chequers demonstration is not recorded precisely, but between the Dunkirk evacuation and September there was a total of just twelve weeks. We know seven of these were taken for the design work, the remaining weeks including the time to actually build the weapon and bombs and then hold the demonstration. In that brief time period, the Arbalest had undergone a metamorphosis into an entirely new weapon, the Bombard.

This butterfly of devastation's first, and most important, flight was at the Chequers demonstration. Here, luckily, most of the accounts all seem to be roughly in line with each other. At the demonstration, as well as Churchill, there was a huge array of officers and observers, including General de Gaulle. There is some confusion about how many dummy rounds were fired that day, Blacker says two, another account says one. Equally, other accounts state that the Bombard was negligently discharged, and nearly decapitated de Gaulle, which may have been seen as a bonus by Churchill. It seems likely, as Blacker fails to mention a target but implies a shot fired off in general, that this negligent discharge was the first round of the day. The second round was aimed at a tree some 500yd (457m) away. The crew of the Bombard carefully laid onto the target, and fired. With a loud report, the cumbersome projectile whirled through the air, smashing into the tree dead centre. Later, on the service weapon, the accurate range of the Bombard was given as less than half the distance this round was fired. All accounts consider that lady luck was smiling on the Bombard that day by causing the round to hit that tree. The effect was immediate, barely had the splinters from the tree settled than Churchill ordered the weapon into service, and offered up funds of some £5,000 to ensure that it was delivered.

Another offshoot of this demonstration, and subsequent events, was MIRc changed departments. As we have seen Churchill was becoming frustrated with the Ordnance Board and Major General Clarke's stance on anything that was created by Jefferis' team. Here was the last straw, a weapon that was devastating, and cheap, and would never have seen the light of day if not for his office intervening. Thus, MIRc was moved to be under the direct command of the Minister of Defence, who was one Winston Churchill. The post of Minister of Defence was created when Churchill came to power. There were three service chiefs, one for each branch, who were equal, but with no overall person in charge of warfare. By creating a new position Churchill assumed full control. MIRc, formerly under the Ministry of Supply, was moved lock, stock and quite literally barrel to be under the control of Churchill and renamed Ministry of Defence 1, or MD1. As it was reporting directly to Churchill, it later obtained the nickname 'Churchill's Toyshop', although these name changes would all be in the future, in about November 1940.

This change actually caused some irritation in Blacker's life. At the time he was staying at the RAF Club in Mayfair, London. As well as nightly raids from the Germans, he was attempting to deal with questions from senior officers demanding that he 'clarify his position'. Blacker called this 'balderdash' and complained that it was delaying his work on the Bombard. There were even moves to post Blacker overseas to Singapore. Luckily Churchill, whom Blacker reached through Professor Lindemann, was able to keep Blacker in place.

Despite these interruptions, Blacker's mind was never far from developing new weapons. On 6 September 1940, the eve of the Blitz, Blacker wrote to Professor Lindemann again, this time requesting permission to embark on a new weapon, an anti-aircraft Bombard. This was to be constructed similar to the scaled-up Arbalest now under development, only to speed construction Blacker was suggesting that they use redundant stocks of oleo struts from Vickers Virginia landing gear to act as the launcher. According to Blacker, Vickers at Weybridge had hundreds of such components in stock, with no conceivable use for them. Blacker knew this as he had visited Vickers, of his own accord, and approached them with the idea. Vickers, possibly seeing the chance to unload a large pile of useless stock on the government, were quite supportive and keen. Blacker envisioned the bomb being identical to the anti-tank version, only with a time fuse instead. He was quite adamant that this weapon could project a bomb to the height of 1,200ft. It seems that this idea was not pursued any further. This letter is also the earliest document so far that the author has seen where the new weapon, under development, is named the Bombard.

This letter does highlight one thing that would change between the prototype Bombard, which was known as the 'Experimental Gun', and the production models. Blacker described the AA Bombard as being nearly identical to

Two more of RMARG's spigot collection. A Petard, possibly one of the versions for the 2-pounder mount, at the top. At the bottom is a large weapon that has a resemblance to the Arbalest. For example, the trigger mechanism is all but identical. It also has a curious mount that would attach it to a frame. However, this mount is not viable as a combat mount. Therefore, this weapon may be the Experimental Gun. Against such a possibility is the length, it appears to be a lot longer than the weapon that was described to the Ordnance Board, although the Experimental Gun went through so many re-builds this could explain the discrepancy.

the anti-tank version. Equally, there are documents talking about oil buffers from the period, and the displacement of air during firing. These almost certainly indicate that the Experimental Gun was of a recoiling spigot type, like a scaled up Arbalest. Confirmation comes from an Ordnance Board report where the particulars of the weapon are laid out. The recoil stroke is given as 8in, and the weapon is mounted on, presumably, a carriage which had two wooden trails 5ft long. This allowed the weapon some 60 degrees of traverse. The carriage was lacking a gun shield. Overall the weapon was 4ft long with a diameter of 4.5in. The Spigot diameter, and so the calibre, is 1.125in. There were two shells envisioned, a 23-pounder anti-tank shell, with a muzzle velocity of 256fps, and a maximum range of 580yd. The second projectile was a 14-pounder HE shell, which moved faster at 350fps and had a maximum range of 1,100yd.

On 20 September 1940, the Experimental Gun was sitting on a range. About 75yd away was an A.13 Cruiser tank. This Cruiser was slightly different to a normal tank, as it had an extra 1.25in (31.75mm) thick plate welded to the front of the turret. The armour was slightly sloped at 20 degrees, which increased the armour thickness closer to 34mm. On this plate, a postage stamp had been fixed as an aiming point. The small crowd of observers comprised four people from MIRc, including Blacker, a representative of the

A series of three poor quality photographs showing the results of the test firing on 20 September 1940. This first image is of the A.13 after the shot had been fired.

'Macerated' 31

The second is of the rear of the turret, showing where the armour plate had been ripped off.

The last photograph is of the rear of the turret, lying on the ground some distance behind, with a hole blasted through it by the scab from the front plate.

Ministry of Supply, an army officer and Gefforey Hawkes, from the weapons builders Boosey & Hawkes Ltd. The Experimental Gun fired perfectly, hitting the target, as best could be judged, within about 1in of the postage stamp. The 10lb of explosives detonated, the shockwaves reverberated through the British Army, and we are still feeling the effects of them today.

The front armour had a hole blasted straight through it, described as being 'about the size of a man's head'. Only a rough estimation could be taken, as the plate was crumpled and rammed inside the tank. In the process, it became intermixed with the structure of the tank and was impossible to recover. A large fragment from the front plate was blasted out of the backplate of the turret, creating a sizeable hole. The backplate was also torn clean off and hurled some 50yd from the tank. The fragment continued going and was never recovered. The official report states that the crew would have been 'macerated' (liquified, shredded, mashed, pulped). Upon inspecting the hulk, the Ministry of Supply representative exclaimed 'The buffer business is all right!'

To understand the excitement, and later scepticism, you need to consider the knowledge of the time period. To the modern tank enthusiast, the concept of a chemical energy shell, one that uses the potential energy contained within explosives, is well known and understood. However, in 1940, if you wanted to put a hole through an armour plate the only option was an armour piercing shot moving at high velocity, and all that it entails from a gun. Here was a low-velocity weapon firing a HE warhead that had done vastly more damage than a conventional anti-tank gun could.

Equally, you need to understand one important thing about the Experimental Gun, one that is clear to the modern person, it was firing High-Explosive Squash-Head rounds, known today as HESH.

Jefferis and Macrae had started developing the ST Grenade. Jefferis had begun the work before the war with a desire to create a weapon where the explosive would settle onto the surface, and thus increase the amount of explosive force in contact with the target. These 'poulticing' explosives, as they were called, had emerged from experiments at Cambridge University. As Cambridge is renowned for its bicycling culture it is no surprise that the initial attempts were made with bicycle inner tubes dipped in glue and filled with plasticine. To stand in for tanks metal bins were used. The experiments were largely unsuccessful. Later, after Dunkirk Macrae was given the task, and after receiving a suggestion of a glass bulb inside impregnated material which could be thrown, he developed the Sticky Bomb. There is one difference between the ST Grenade and HESH warheads. In the Sticky Bomb the nitroglycerine-based gel, which had the consistency of strawberry jam, was left to settle of its own accord for a few seconds before a timer detonated the charge. In the HESH round, the explosive is flung into the surface at great velocity splattering like a cowpat, after which the detonator hits the target triggering the explosive. For this reason, the fuses of HESH rounds were at the rear of the projectile.

The concept of poulticing explosives was thus known in MIRc when Blacker joined. There appears to be no evidence that he designed the 23-pounder projectile to be a HESH round, as that concept did not yet exist. Even so, to modern eyes that is what the Bombard anti-tank projectile was. Consisting of a thin-walled case, with a base fuse, the warhead was filled with plastic explosive. Blacker, however, does appear to have worked out what was happening with the explosive inside the warhead to provide such devastating effect against armour. On 28 September 1940, he submitted a patent, entitled simply 'Improvements in Bombs and the Like', and it clearly lays out the function of a HESH, even going so far as to detail the scab that is blown off the interior face.

As one might expect, in the current security environment finding details on explosives freely available to the public is rather difficult. We do know a bit about the explosive used in the 23-pounder bombs, it was called Nobels 808. Descriptions of the explosive differ as to the colour, but all describe it as feeling like playdough and smelling of almonds. One source suggests the consistency was the same as latex rubber. Handling Nobels 808 with unprotected hands would lead to a severe headache as it included nitroglycerine, which causes blood vessels to dilate. When the circulatory system in the brain swells this results in headaches. The explosive was invented when Alfred Nobel discovered that nitroglycerine could be dissolved in nitrocellulose. This caused the nitroglycerine to become desensitized, and less likely to explode when subjected to shock. Adding in some plasticizer and a small amount of ammonium nitrate created the substance that became known as Nobels 808. This explosive had a shelf life of about a decade. With the passage of time the plasticizer would break down and the explosive would harden up. Then the nitroglycerine would separate out in a process often called 'sweating'. This would leave the now useless 808 mass coated in a liquid that was highly sensitive to impacts and shock. Nobels 808 was at first called a 'cutting explosive' due to the very neat nature of the holes created. The detonation velocity was approximately 18,000 to 23,000fps, which was viewed very favourably when compared with the impact velocity of an anti-tank gun shell of the time, which was about 2,500 to 3,000fps. The detonation of the HESH round would also produce lethal fragments and pressures inside the tank, and if the armour was not breached, the mass of explosive would have an effect on mechanical fixtures outside of the armour, damaging tracks, guns and the like. As the war progressed the term 'plastique' or 'plastic' explosive was used more commonly to describe this family of explosives, due to the supple and workable nature of the explosive. The malleable nature of the explosive was later used by MD1 in their Kangaroo mine, where a wad of 808 was fired onto the underside of a tank and blasted a hole in the bottom. In late 1941 the ICI plant at Ardeer developed a new version of Nobels 808 which used less nitroglycerine, and this was termed 808B and seems to have become the standard throughout the Second World War. While 808 was less sensitive to shocks than nitroglycerine it seems that high-impact speeds could cause enough shock to prematurely trigger the explosive. During 1943 when ICI were carrying out studies on new demolition guns they tried projectiles filled with 808, which were fired at about 850fps. When the projectile struck the target, instead of achieving the pancake effect, the explosives spontaneously detonated. Luckily none of the spigot weapons in this book would be able to achieve such velocities.

In September 1940, the Experimental Gun had proved its destructive potential, but work was still needed to create a workable design. At this stage, it still lacked sights or a traversing gear, so no tests had been carried out against moving targets. The Experimental Gun had been constructed from off-the-shelf components to prove the concept, but for a service weapon this was seen as not feasible. The main sticking point was an adequate recoil buffer that was sufficiently cheap for mass production, and could be so arranged to create a shorter weapon. Work on this went poorly at MIRc, some disagreements about the work surfacing on the project team. This likely wasn't helped by Blacker's views. Over the preceding months, he had formed the opinion that the recoil buffer as designed was a mistake. He wrote to Professor Lindemann, on 25 November, outlining his thoughts. In his letter, he points out that the current design being proposed by MIRc (now MD1) had too many variables to its accuracy. Of particular concern to him was the weight of the recoiling parts. These were only twice the weight of the projectile. The lighter recoiling parts meant that they could begin to move sooner under gas pressure. However, at the time, all cartridge primers varied considerably in the speed of ignition. This, in turn, would affect the efficiency of the propellant burn. Thus, the rounds would develop different muzzle velocities as the recoil parts would start moving at different times. A heavier set of recoiling parts would remain in place until the propellant was completely engaged and thus the resulting velocity would be consistent. Blacker was concerned about consistent mechanical accuracy as the weapon had a rather high ballistic angle and low muzzle velocity, meaning that it could become wildly inaccurate if care was not taken. In his report to Professor Lindemann he outlined two possible solutions, the first was a complex, mechanical sounding nightmare, the other was a fixed spigot. In the fixed spigot all the recoiling parts would be removed, all the recoil would be transmitted through the weapon and into the ground. He estimated the weapon would weigh between 180lb and 200lb, which would absorb some of the recoil. Further, for handiness in action, the entire mass could be broken down into multiple man loads, and still retain the dampening effect once assembled. Blacker also suggested that the weapon really must have a gun shield. Blacker's views were fully supported by the Assistant Director of Artillery, Colonel Evans.

In November Boosey & Hawkes were issued a contract by MD1 to build 4 more guns along with 400 rounds of 23-pounder and 100 14-pounder projectiles. These were to be split evenly between fully functional filled rounds, and dummy rounds filled to weigh the same. One wonders how much of this order was fulfilled, especially with the constantly changing designs and the disagreements over what shape the Bombard should take. A month later, in December, this order was still listed as a proposal. There was also a proposal to produce some 500 rounds of each type of ammunition. It is questionable if more Experimental Guns were ever produced, however, it appears at least some of the ammunition order was.

The projectiles themselves were also undergoing a significant amount of testing, and development. Most of which was concentrated on the 14lb HE round.

The first 14lb HE round had a tail that was listed as 'dead weight' and weighed 3lb, which at first glance compared unfavourably with a 3-inch mortar's 2.25lb. However, the total weight of the 3-inch mortar round was 10lb, so the total percentages of dead weight was about the same. The body of the round weighed in at 7lb of cast iron, with grooves cut in it to assist with fragmentation. The HE filling was about 1.75lb in total. The explosive used was either amatol or baratol, again like the mortar shell. The main issue arose because the warhead was made of cheaper cast iron, not steel. When detonated the explosives had such force that they would cause the cast-iron body to over fragment, creating a lot of very small ineffective shrapnel. At the time the definition of effective shrapnel was pieces that would penetrate at least 1in of wood.

An alternative filling of ammonal was suggested. However, this was rejected due to the high aluminium content, which was sorely needed elsewhere in the British war effort. Other factors against ammonal were its short shelf life, tendency to cake in the warhead and its susceptibility to moisture and water.

With ammonal rejected, thoughts turned towards debasing amatol 80/20. The number indicates the percentage of the explosive mix that was TNT and ammonium nitrate. After consideration 80/20 was deemed the minimum, as it would cause problems filling the warheads to the correct density, and the explosive may fail to detonate properly.

It was at this point a new explosive was suggested by ICI, Nobels 704B. This was a modified version of Nobels 704, which in itself was very similar to ammonal. The main differences between 704B and ammonal were that the aluminium powder was ground much finer and it included paraffin wax, presumably as a waterproofing agent.

While it was expected that 704B would produce the required level of fragmentation, there were concerns that the same problems with ammonal would also apply to 704B.

Despite this, on 14 and 16 December 1940 a series of trials was carried out, with one 14lb HE round filled with each of the explosives mentioned. Each round was suspended with the nose touching the ground, and fused to be detonated electronically. Wooden boards, each 9ft square and 2in thick, were erected at ranges of 15, 30 and 45ft. Each target was in its own quadrant, so there was no overlap. The results confirmed the concerns about over fragmentation, although the 704B was not as good as expected.

The main reason that the 3-inch mortar had better fragmentation characteristics was the shell was made from cast steel. This had a much higher tensile strength and thus complemented the much more violent explosives. There was, of course, the question of what to do with the 14lb bomb now. The first answer was to accept a sub-standard shell into service, an option that had obvious reasons for being rejected. The army could try to find another explosive, but that would mean a separate specialist production facility, and extensive testing, both of which would mean further delays. Finally, they could make the warhead of the HE round out of cast steel, but this would drive up the overall cost.

In the end, a fourth option was discovered. There is no record of who or where this idea came from, but from the time period, it is likely to have been MD1, which was working on the weapon's development. The warhead had a chipboard box placed in it, and this box was filled with amatol which meant that the explosive content of the warhead decreased from 1.75lb to 1.66lb. The chipboard box and the space around the box allowed some of the explosive force to be absorbed within the warhead, slowing the blast enough to

Table 1. Fragmentation of Shells with Different Fillings

Shell	Filling	Hits at 15ft Effective	Hits at 15ft Non effective	Hits at 30ft Effective	Hits at 30ft Non effective	Hits at 45ft Effective	Hits at 45ft Non effective
14lb HE shell	Baratol	49	614	26	94	5	15
	Amatol	90	452	10	120	8	45
	Nobels 704B	117	295	96	97	18	44
3-inch mortar	Amatol	81	58	108	8	15	19

generate a good range of fragments. It is likely this is the design of round that Boosey & Hawkes produced along with a supply of the anti-tank projectiles.

In early December MD1 decided to try another test and cast around for a suitable target. They located an A.11 Matilda on Hangmoor ranges, which had been gutted with its engine and gun having been removed. A letter was duly drafted to the commanding officer of the range to see if the tank could be used for test firing. No rejection letter was received, and so on 7 December 1940, the Experimental Gun was shipped to Hangmoor and Blacker and a few others set about this much tougher target. In total eight rounds were fired, two hit the tracks of the A.11, breaking the tracks, and ripping bogies off the hull, one bogie being hurled some 10yd away from the tank. Four more hits made holes ranging from 8in to 10in in size. A seventh round struck on the turret ring, and ripped the turret off and sent it flying to land some 5yd away. For the last round, the Experimental Gun was repositioned to 45 degrees to the side, to crudely slope the armour. A hole about 5in was created by the hit.

The main scope for this trial was to see how different arrangements of the fuses affected perforation of the armour. The trials had tested striker travel distances. Originally 0.625in travel distance had been used, however, a longer travel distance of 0.75in, which created about $1/300$ of a second delay, increased the size of the hole created. It is now known that this is as result of allowing the plastic explosive more time to splatter onto the target before detonation. It is likely that this test proved the concept that the Bombard staff had considered.

The next morning the owners of the A.11 Matilda arrived to collect their tank, only to find it blasted across the ranges. The request letter had never been posted. This understandably caused a lot of ill will, which Blacker decided to deal with in his own special way by suggesting that if the tank had been so easy to destroy, it was not worth very much.

Chapter Four

Defeating the Ordnance Board Menace

You will recall Major General Clarke's stance on anything produced by MD1, and how the Ordnance Board had tried desperately to halt any project, no matter how beneficial, that originated from Jefferis' department. This scathing hatred had applied to the Bombard from the outset and lasted for the entirety of the eight or so months that the Bombard was being developed. What is all the more remarkable is that the Arbalest had transformed into the Bombard in that time frame, all this in the face of opposition from Major General Clarke.

The Ordnance Board started its fight against the Bombard with what they surely thought was a killer blow on 5 November 1940 when the first provisional characteristics for the Experimental Gun were submitted. The Ordnance Board's stance was simply that this weapon could not be tested for service as there was no official requirement for the weapon. At the time the way the British Army obtained equipment was by issuing a requirement that stated the minimum performance of the weapon. The proposed equipment was then tested against this to compare the performance to see if they matched, or exceeded, the written requirements. One of the flaws in this thinking, and one that plagued the Ordnance Board's response to the Bombard, was that there were only mortars, howitzers and guns as weapon types. The concept of a crew-served, man-portable anti-tank weapon was utterly alien at the time, although the concept seems quite familiar to the modern observer. No doubt this very bureaucratic response had Blacker reaching for his Official Obstruction file. The Ordnance Board very quickly found they were outgunned on the matter of a requirement. The Assistant Chief of the Imperial General Staff, Major General Laurence Carr, wrote back and very bluntly pointed out that there was, and would be, no requirement as Winston Churchill in his guise of Minister of Defence had ordered the weapon to be developed. Major General Carr concluded his terse paragraph by asking on what date the trials would be held so the General Staff could be represented.

On 21 November, the Ordnance Board returned to the fray with a very long list of technical complaints that seem to be utterly unfounded. These included citing the weapon as a scaled-up Arbalest which had been rejected previously. They also listed what they termed a fundamental objection to the idea of firing a highly machined and very expensive barrel at the enemy with every shot. They also added that the cost and difficulty in obtaining sufficiently strong tubes was the reason for the failure of the Hay Pocket Howitzer of 1915. The projectile was singled out for some dire criticism, such as not being suitable for large-scale production and that it had to be partly disassembled to fit a fuse. Finally, the fuse itself was stated to be extremely dangerous and would arm after a very short drop. They also suggested that if the tail tube fitted tightly enough around the spigot to create obturation there would be an air bubble between the tail tube and the spigot that would require a huge amount of force to squeeze out. This air bubble would severely reduce the loading time, which would be compounded by the need to remove the spent cartridge from the gun after each shot.

They did have one valid complaint about the Experimental Gun being very complicated and difficult to produce, one which, as we have seen, Blacker would deal with shortly. On top of all these complaints, they asked for the decision to carry out trials to be reconsidered.

In mid-December Major General Clarke, buoyed by the Ordnance Board's recommendations, launched a bid to get further trials halted, arguing that the Experimental Gun in no way met the standards used to develop normal anti-tank weapons such as the 2-pounder and 6-pounder. Then he reinforced the claim by declaring, 'There are no technical grounds on which I could recommend the pursuance of this weapon for Atk [Anti-tank] defence.' Once again Major General Carr stated it has been requested by Winston Churchill and asked when the trials would be held. His reply to Major General Clarke was just three, very blunt, sentences.

Over the next few weeks, this war of words raged. At some point MD1 must have used the tests against the A.13 Cruiser as evidence in support of the Bombard as Major General Clarke was stung to respond in a letter to Jefferis, stating there was no evidence the Bombard could penetrate 40mm of plate, and that the two plates that made up the Cruiser target would not be equivalent. In the same letter, he stated that, 'There are three types of ordnance, Guns, howitzers and mortars. It would be quite impractical to allow each inventor to suggest nomenclature e.g. a very similar weapon was called by the inventor an "Arbalest" only a few months ago.' Here lies one of the main bones of contention between the Ordnance Board and MD1. The Ordnance Board seemed unable to understand that a new class of weapon was available, one that did not fit readily into the usual classifications, which they were using to view the weapon. A lack of understanding of the concept of chemical energy anti-tank warheads is also shown by the response to the Cruiser trials. Here the Ordnance Board seemed think that the Experimental Gun had caused a small hole, much like a 2-pounder AP round. Despite the Ordnance Board's repeated protestations, MD1 had a winning hand in the form of the Minister of Defence, Winston Churchill, and the trials were held in late February 1941.

The first, 'Trial A', was held on the 23rd, and trials B and C on the 27th. The first series of Trial A seems to have been to determine the average ballistics of the projectiles, with shots fired at different elevations between 10 and 40 degrees. The first thirty-nine rounds were anti-tank rounds. These had shrunk a bit from the experimental rounds and now only weighed 20lb. Confusingly, they were still termed '23-pounders' in the reports. These were propelled by 14 grams of propellent, which was sufficient to give a muzzle velocity averaging 214fps. This resulted in the average performance detailed in Table 2.

During the firing of the 40 degrees of elevation series, one round became unsteady in flight. This fault was down to damaged tail assemblies. Several rounds used throughout the trial were damaged in transit, some had bent tail vanes, others dented drum fairings. Finally, a series of seven 14lb HE projectiles were fired. These were fired at 10 degrees elevation and propelled by 20g of propellent, which gave a muzzle velocity of 315fps. These had a 3.46-second flight time to reach a maximum range of 345yd.

The accuracy of the weapon was also tested with seven rounds fired at a target 150yd away. One round sailed clear over the target, missing by around 2ft, and was likely the result of a damaged tail. The other six rounds had a vertical grouping of 9ft 6in and a horizontal area of 2ft. In the Bombard's defence, after every round the weapon swung approximately 4 degrees to the left due to the new gun shield being unbalanced on that side. Such a movement would have required relaying the weapon and thus introducing a new variable to compound the damaged tails.

The mention of the gun shield shows that the Bombard was coming close to its final form after its months of development. This trial also touched on other features that would reach the service weapon. The gun of the Bombard was a complete unit, consisting of the gun shield, spigot, firing gear, range control and sights. To mount this gun you needed a single pivot. During the trial, most of the shooting was done from a pedestal mount. This was a pivot

Table 2. Trajectory of the Experimental Gun

Elevation (deg)	Flight Time (sec)	Range (yd)
10	2.39	162
25	5.69	366
40	8.59	457

for the gun, set into a large concrete pedestal. The pivot was the apex of a birdcage-like structure of steel bars set into the concrete base. This had been designed by MD1 and constructed specially for these firing tests. It is suggested, however, that the concrete had not been allowed to cure properly resulting in damage that would become disastrous as the trials progressed. By the end of the trials, the steelwork of the pedestal mount had considerable play in it, which may have affected the accuracy tests.

In the interests of balance two rounds were fired from the new 'field mounting'. This was a pivot mounted onto a baseplate, into which four legs were inserted to form a cruciform shape. These mountings would become known as 'mobile mounts', while the pedestals became 'static mounts', or 'holdfasts'. The two rounds fired from the field mount showed that further work was needed. As has been said, the recoil force was 6 tons, and this was fed directly into the mount. The shock of firing caused the baseplate to jump 1.5in into the air, and after each round, the front two legs popped out of their sockets and were found to be lying some 2in from the baseplate.

It seems likely from the description of the equipment, and its close similarities to the service weapon, that the Bombard fired during these trials was of the non-recoiling type of spigot, and Blacker had got his way with the design.

The following week, in light drizzle, trials B and C were held. First, the Bombard was compared with a 3-inch mortar. In this test, both weapons were fired as rapidly as possible. As the comparison was to be against a 3-inch mortar the 14lb HE bombs were used, with the propellent of a 12g half charge. Again, because of the different elevations possible the Bombard was fired in three series of seven rounds each. These elevations were the same as the previous trials. The first series had a disastrous start when the first round jammed on the spigot, about 3in from its fully seated position. The Bombard was simply picked up, and a replacement weapon slotted onto the pivot. The first series took 30.8 seconds to complete. Series two got its seven rounds away in 26.8 seconds, and series three in a blistering 22.9 seconds. The average time for all these series was then computed at 27 seconds. The 3-inch mortar then started firing to see how many rounds it could fire in the same time, which it turned out was seventeen.

A similar trial for the 20lb AT warhead was then planned. These would be fired with a full-sized propellent charge. After just four rounds the trial was halted for safety reasons. The pedestal mount had been constructed and then placed onto a platform. The massive recoil forces, slightly aided by the light rain, had managed to shove the pedestal 1ft 6in backwards. In the service mount, the pedestals were firmly dug into the ground and would not suffer from this effect. Then another three rounds were fired from the mobile mounting to demonstrate it to the observers, some of whom would not have been there the previous week.

Next came the tests of how deadly a Bombard would be compared with the 3-inch mortar. A field of forty-six dummies was laid out, with 10yd between each one. The total area of this target was 102yd long and 30yd wide. At a range of 540yd, the Bombard fired nine rounds. The first appears to have been a ranging shot, or otherwise missed. The other eight rounds hit the target area. The resulting storm of fragments 'injured' thirty-three dummies. A separate target, but with identical layout, was then used for the 3-inch mortar target, although the range was given as 787yd. The first two rounds fired missed or were otherwise not counted. Then eight rounds were fired, but only six landed on target. These caused injuries to twenty of the dummies.

Trial C was then undertaken to assess the lethality and perforation against armour plate with 20lb projectiles fired at a 40mm-thick armour slab, 5ft^2. The trials went badly, the first two rounds hit, but were 'blinds', which is a term used by the British to indicate a round that did not detonate. In an attempt to get a working shell the MD1 representative at the trials modified the fuse, but still got a failure to detonate. Finally, a fourth shell was fired with exactly the same result. Unsurprisingly at this point, the trials were halted and rescheduled for early March. The extra week gave MD1 time to work on the fuse, and at the resumed trial results were indeed impressive.

The trial resumed on 6 March 1941, and at a range of 50yd the Bombard was fired against several armour plates and reinforced concrete blocks. The first round was fired at a 40mm-thick plate at an angle of 40 degrees. One Bombard round blew a 7.5×8.2in hole through it. As this was a HESH projectile, the round caused a scab of about twice that size. Next, a 60mm thick plate was fired at, this was sloped to 45 degrees. The Bombard only just failed to penetrate. The hit caused a colossal cracked bulge on the inside of the plate. This was just over 20in in size. The bulge was raised to a height of 1.7in. Although there was no devastating scab, the report states the results would have been disastrous for the crew due to tiny fragments and splinters being blasted off the inside of the armour. Another plate of 60mm armour was fired at 0 degrees. The result was a 14×12.3in hole and a scab over 15in across.

The reinforced concrete blocks then took their turn. The first two rounds were blinds, however round three blew the corners off the blocks, and split one in two, bodily throwing one half of the block to the ground.

After this, the Ordnance Board demanded that a 20lb round be fired upon by small arms. It was hit twice by .303 bullets, but the explosive filling failed to detonate, proving it was safe. This would be the last attempt by the Ordnance Board to try to disprove the Bombard was a viable weapon and find an excuse to reject it.

These trials were the graduation of the Bombard. It had transformed from Arbalest, through the Experimental Gun into the weapon that would enter service and proved that it would meet the tasks asked of it. In the anti-tank role, it was more deadly than a 2-pounder anti-tank gun. While it could defeat roughly the same amount of armour, depending on the exact range, it caused masses more damage inside a vehicle that it perforated. With regard to the HE round, it should not be seen as a replacement for the 3-inch mortar, as it lacked the range and rate of fire. The HE round was more to provide the anti-tank weapon with a HE round that could provide a mortar like effect over a shorter range. Of course, this did not stop Blacker suggesting, as loudly as he could, and with the support of Jefferis, that it was a way to consolidate both anti-tank and mortar platoons into a single formation using Bombards. The anti-tank weapon Blacker had his sights on deleting was the 25mm Hotchkiss guns, which the British had purchased some 300 of, for use by the British Expeditionary Force. Why he selected this weapon, when the numbers surviving in British service would almost certainly be tiny, if they existed, as these weapons would have had to have been rescued from France first, is not recorded. Blacker's suggestion was a company headquarters with four platoons. Each platoon had three sections, each with two Bombards. These twenty-four Bombards would form a weapons company for each Home Guard Battalion, although with the variable and localized organization of the Home Guard it is debatable just how many formations like this were actually deployed.

The victory of the Bombard seems to mark the end of the Ordnance Board obstructionism, at least with regard to spigot weapons. As we shall see in later chapters, there seemed to be no attempt to end the PIAT project. Indeed, with the Petard, the Ordnance Board files are utterly devoid of documentation relating to its development. Major General Clarke served as D of A and led the Ordnance Board until 1945. It is difficult to see why Winston Churchill would leave someone in such a bad odour in position to continue their obstructionist ways for the entire course of the war. Perhaps Major General Clarke readjusted his views and realized that the entire nation was facing an unprecedented threat and it was no time to be obstinate. Or maybe someone high up had a quiet word about his potential future, or just maybe the Bombard situation forced him to realize that technology had moved onwards.

With the Bombard's design now sealed, Blacker's tenure with MD1 ended, although Jefferis and Blacker would later bump into each other over the PIAT. Blacker departed MD1 and retired from the army. He would very shortly found Blacker Developments Ltd. During this time he would continue to develop spigot weapons. Blacker was working on a fully automatic spigot weapon that was magazine-fed for use by ground-attack aircraft, primarily in the dive-bombing role. This weapon fired 6lb projectiles from a magazine in the wing. The projected muzzle velocity was about 400fps, which would be increased by the speed of the dive. Blacker envisioned a rate of fire of two rounds per second. It seems that Nash & Thompson, a subsidiary of Parnell Aircraft, were to build a scaled down version of the weapon, which fired projectiles of just 2lb. In May 1941 they reported to MD1 that they would soon have the scale version working and be ready to demonstrate it. However, like many of Blacker's inventions, it seems to fizzle out and disappear from the historical records after this date.

Chapter Five

The Bombard

The final design for the Bombard was now ready, and the drawings sealed. The main component was the gun itself, weighing in at 112lb. This remained fully assembled at all times, and needed two men to carry it. At the core of the weapon was the spigot. This had a casing around it to protect the loader from the blast of the gun. The spigot ran back into a pivot point that was mounted on the traversing block. The control lever for setting the range extended from the pivot point at an angle of about 150 degrees from the spigot. The range lever ran backwards through an opening on the gun shield. This lever was for quick setting of the range. On the right-hand side of the range lever was an engraved plate moulded to the curve of the shield. When the range lever was adjusted up and down, it would move a window along this scale, which indicated the range for the weapon. The left-hand side of the engraved plate was the 20lb projectile range and right-hand side was the figure for a 14lb projectile. When the desired range was reached the range lever could be locked in place by pushing the handle on the top of the range lever through 90 degrees to the right. For fine range adjustments, there was a range drum that both the commander and the gunner could adjust. This would raise or lower the angle of the rake sight.

   The gun shield was affixed to the traversing block by brackets. Unusually the gun shield was curved towards the front, this curve allowing it to mount the range scale. Other controls such as range drum, firing and gun-laying controls were welded directly onto the gun shield. On the Mk I version of the Bombard there were two spirit levels attached to the shield, and these would allow the gun to be placed level, one set for vertical the other for horizontal inclination. There was also a head guard or buffer, with a thick tube of rubber over it. This was a padded bar that stuck out from the gun shield above the sight aperture. At first glance, this buffer appears to be a forehead rest for the gunner. However, training material strongly emphasized that this was not the case. If a person's head rested against the buffer when firing the violent recoil would break their neck! Instead, this buffer was there to protect the gunner's skull should their head be too far forward during firing. The rubber would absorb some of the impact's force, and push the gunner's face away from the controls preventing severe injury.

Left-hand side view of the Bombard. This remained as a single unit and required two men to move. The opening at the top of the spigot chasing could also appear at the bottom and seems to have been entirely random. Some sources indicate that the placing was to allow the remains of the spent cartridge to fall away when on the bottom of the spigot casing.

The sights were a peephole rear sight with a rake sight on a bar that extended forwards until it was about the same level as the traversing block. This allowed the gun to be aimed at moving targets, with the individual foresight bars corresponding to a target moving at 10, 20 and 30mph.

The firing controls consisted of two handles, one on the left, next to the range scale, which was simply somewhere for the gunner to place his left hand and add authority and delicate control to pivoting the gun. The right handle, on the extreme right hand of the gun shield, held the firing mechanism, which consisted of a firing lever, extending downwards from the top of the handle. A trigger was fitted onto the firing lever, and caught onto a latch on the firing

Shot of the rear of the gun shield on a Bombard. On this particular model, the gunner's head guard is made of multiple rings of rubber, on others, it was a solid tube.

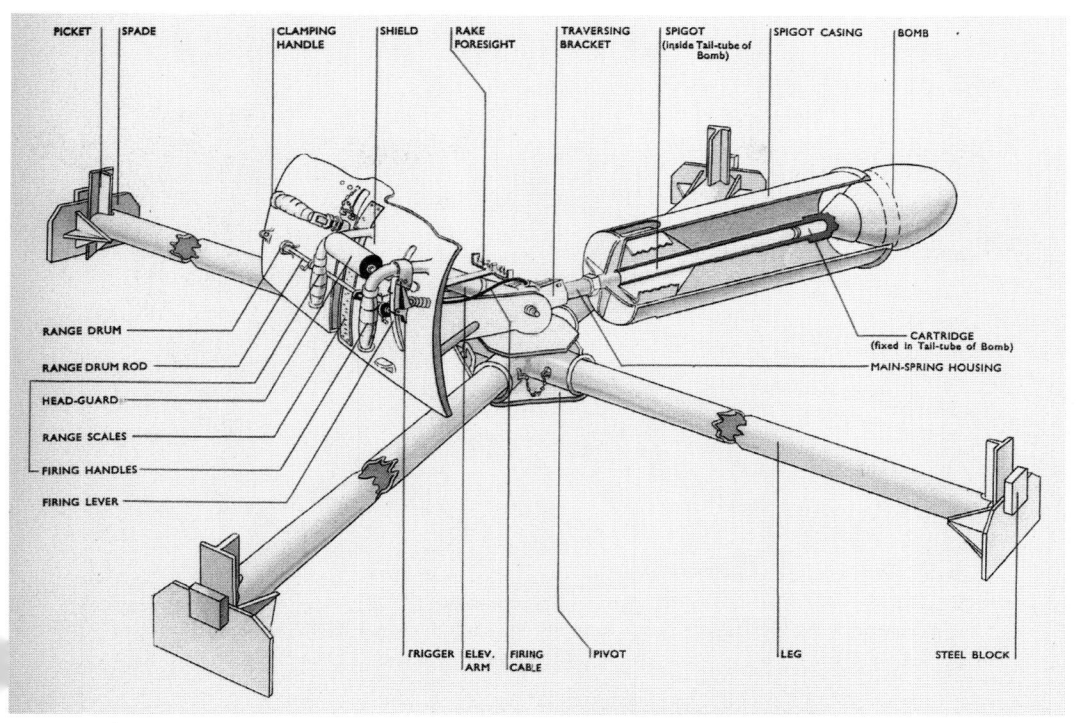

A diagram explaining all the component parts of the Bombard.

lever. The top of the trigger was attached to a Bowden cable which ran through the gun shield and into the top rear of the spigot. The Bowden cable connected to the back of the firing pin, which moved through a hole in the spigot. When the Bowden cable was tightened it would retract the firing pin, compressing a return spring.

Thus, when the firing lever was pulled, the trigger would be locked to the bottom of the firing lever. This would serve to pull the Bowden cable taut, retracting the firing pin into the spigot compressing the spring. When the trigger was pulled it would release the cable, and the spring would force the firing pin forwards, and extend it out of the spigot, striking the detonator on the propellent charge on the loaded bomb.

The mounting block at the centre of the gun's mass was to be fitted to a standard sized pivot. This pivot could either be in a static or mobile mounting. The latter was a quadpod, with a central base unit, weighing 56lb, with the pivot firmly attached. Each 44lb leg could then be inserted and held in place by substantial locking pins. The feet of the legs could also be seated into the ground better by the use of pickets, which weighed 5lb apiece.

The fixed mounting was similar to the one used in the Ordnance Board trials at the start of 1941, a birdcage-like steel frame set into a concrete pedestal. This pedestal was securely sunk into the ground with the top level with the surrounding terrain. In the ideal example of such a position, the trench and walls of the dugout position were reinforced by whatever was

The steel structure of a holdfast pedestal mount. On this surviving example at least four of the arms have broken off due to ageing, but one can see how the pivot is attached. (*dunkirk1940.org*)

locally available, such as brick or concrete. Into the side of the dugout that was expected to face the enemy four ammunition recesses were constructed, and these would each contain ten bombs. Their location towards the enemy might, at first, seem to be counter-intuitive, however, as the loader would have to be on the side of the trench facing the enemy it would mean he had a good supply of ready ammunition.

With regard to the ammunition itself, the two main types of projectile have already been briefly mentioned. The main one was the 20lb anti-tank round. This bomb had a diameter of 6in, with an identical width drum tail, and a length of 26in. The No. 283 fuse was inserted in the base of the warhead, which contained about 9lb of Nobels 808 explosive. The Mk I 283 fuse was a simple tube shape, which meant that it could be inserted the wrong way up in error. Thus, in January 1942 a Mk II version appeared, the main difference being the addition of three flanges on the base of the fuse to prevent it being inserted incorrectly.

The 20lb anti-tank round had a weight of between 18.75 and 20lb. It seems this was due to manufacturing inaccuracies. Each bomb was marked with an indicator which denoted how much variance that particular bomb differed from normal. These indicators were:

+2: Below 20lb 0oz, but above 19lb 12oz.
+1: Below 19lb 12oz, but above 19lb 8oz.
 0: Below 19lb 8oz, but above 19lb 4oz.
−1: Below 19lb 4oz, but above 19lb 0oz.
−2: Below 19lb 0oz, but above 18lb 12oz.

The mobile field mount without the gun fitted. This is just an illustrative set-up as each of the legs would have been seated firmly into the ground and the pivot should be resting on a solid surface. The furthest away leg has a picket inserted; this would be hammered into the ground to provide added stability.

Table 3. Trajectory of the Bombard

Range (yd)	Flight Time (sec)	Max Trajectory Height (ft)
100	1.3	6.5
200	2.7	26
300	4	72
400	5.7	130
485	8.4	285

It is not entirely clear why the bombs were so marked, especially as there was no conversion formula issued for the bombs. Equally, it seems unlikely that it would materially affect the accuracy, flight time or range to any great degree, the characteristics of which for the 20lb bomb are listed in Table 3. The data in this table illustrates why the tactical advice around the weapon was only to engage moving targets at a maximum of 150yd.

The 14lb HE bomb was, depending on the source, between 24 and 28in in length. This difference in published material is likely due to one source counting the nose and fuse, which was the same as the No. 152 fuse and nose assembly taken directly from the 3-inch mortar. The warhead and tail were only 4in in diameter. Like the 20lb projectile, the weight of the finished bomb could vary, and they used a similar marking system:

+2: Below 15lb 4oz, but above 15lb 0oz.
+1: Below 15lb 0oz, but above 14lb 12oz.
 0: Below 14lb 12oz, but above 14lb 8oz.
−1: Below 14lb 8oz, but above 14lb 4oz.
−2: Below 14lb 4oz, but above 14lb 0oz.

There were several other rounds, all for drill or practice. There was a 20lb drill round, identical to the live round in shape and size, however, the warhead was filled with sand, and so marked. A curiosity of this was the provision of a dummy cartridge, which was made with a soft metal cap. This was designed not to damage the firing pin when it struck the cartridge. It was also stressed that the Bombard should not be dry fired without something to absorb the impact of the firing pin, otherwise it would damage the firing mechanism. Should no drill round be available then a brass rod of at least 0.5lb could be used in the same fashion.

There was also a practice 20lb round, which was fully primed with a cartridge, but once again filled with sand, and could only be fired once, as the denotation of the propellent would cause damage to the tail tube. There was a very curious fifth round, the 'Practice Inert 20/15lb'. This looked like a 14lb projectile with its forebody extended forwards. It was filled with concrete and

A demonstration of the Bombard to Home Guard. There is a 20-pounder anti-tank round loaded and ready to fire, although with the location of the photographer one hopes it is just a drill round!

was designed to allow multiple firings, and up to a range of 200yd had the same flight characteristics as a full-blown 20lb anti-tank round.

The rounds described accompanied the Bombard through its service. However, there was a sixth experimental round developed. This was a 10lb hollow charge (HEAT in modern terminology) round. Work first began on this in August 1941 by MD1, with assistance from the Road Research Laboratory. Development seems to have been driven, at least in part, by the No. 68 grenade. This puny hollow charge round was designed either to be fired from a cup discharger on a rifle or even thrown by hand. Officially the No. 68 could perforate some 52mm of armour, however, MD1 saw some flaws in this claim. The main one was that conventional methodology had been applied, as would be applied to a high-velocity shell impact. No work had been done on the behind armour effect. Equally, the level of knowledge of hollow charge warheads was negligible at this time. The introduction of the MD1 interim report, in October 1941, even admits as such with the sentence, 'The hollow charge penetrates plate in a manner not yet fully understood ...'. Another example of the immaturity of knowledge is mentioned later in the report. It had been noted that static charges were performing better than identical warheads fired from a gun. MD1 had theories about why this might be so, such as difficulties of fuse design or insufficiently strong cases, which subsequently were not focusing the explosion properly. Today we know that the cause of this effect is down to the spinning of the projectile. MD1 worked out that a 20 per cent reduction in penetration was occurring due to this factor. By luck the Bombard and other spigot weapons would be immune to this effect, due to not using rifling to spin their bombs.

MD1 addressed their other concerns about the lack of post-armour effect with testing. They dug a trench, suspending a battery of pressure and fragmentation measuring devices along the side, and blocking the trench with a crossways slab of armour, against which they would fire their hollow charges. The trench was to recreate the interior of an armoured vehicle. The results of the test proved that the behind-armour effect from a No. 68 grenade was, after applying all modifiers, only lethal to the crew of vehicles protected by 19mm of armour. The modifiers applied to the No. 68 grenade included the penalty for spinning, so the armour thickness that the warhead would defeat, and cause a useful behind-armour effect, would be slightly higher than the calculated value reported. But this was still very much reduced compared with the

The No. 68 grenade. This particular round is a drill round, but apart from the colour, the only differences are the internals. The first obvious dissimilarity with what would be considered a conventional hollow charge weapon is the lack of standoff probe. Instead, the projectile relied upon a base fuse inside the forward half of the tail. Such a standoff probe may well have done good things for the weapon's performance. The hole (below the 'o' in No. 68) is the location of a safety pin, which would be removed before loading. The other striking aspect is how aerodynamically terrible the shape is, especially with the baseplate that allows it to be fired. This was likely done for simplicity of both manufacture and operation.

An utter mystery in picture form. This photograph was known to have been taken at MD1's research station at The Firs. The weapon is a heavily modified Bombard, however, the projectile being loaded matches no known design. The shape and the shell's construction strongly indicate this could be the hollow charge round due to the presence of what appears to be a standoff probe on the front.

maximum penetration. In the case of the Bombard hollow charge, MD1 tried a variety of charge sizes, including 5in and 6in. They found that the 6in charge would provide the best performance.

By August 1942 the final design for the new 10lb hollow charge round was complete. The testing had been carried out, and the weapon was found to be impressively destructive, one letter about it stating, 'and does make it [the Bombard] capable of tackling the biggest enemy tanks that the enemy can devise head-on ...'. Trials seemed to back up this rather startling claim, with the warhead containing about 2.75lb of explosive, which was about 70 per cent the explosive content of the 20lb anti-tank projectile. Due to the lighter weight, the 10lb had a higher muzzle velocity 300fps, compared with the 242fps of the 20lb. This increased speed would make the 10lb more accurate. Trials found that the 10lb could perforate 5in of armour sloped at 45 degrees, 6in at 30 degrees and 7in at normal. Another trial was conducted against spaced armour. The front plate was 75mm, with a 12in gap followed by a 25mm plate. The 10lb charge blew a hole right through it. Such performance would have enabled the Bombard to take on and kill any German tank head-on. Even against the colossal King Tiger the 10lb would have had a chance, although that would have been borderline, and down to the circumstances of each engagement, such as range. At longer ranges, the high ballistic curve of the Bombard would have negated some of the King Tiger's sloped front plate, although compound angle might have added to it. But in such a hypothetical engagement the Bombard's maximum rate of fire was given as twelve rounds per minute, although six was considered normal. Such a hail of shots may just have won the day.

The 10lb bomb never entered production, purely for logistical reasons. At the time the Bombard's production was coming to an end, especially the ammunition. Only about 750,000 rounds were left to deliver from the ammunition order placed the previous year. The Ministry of Supply considered what savings could be made if the hollow charge warhead was to take up the balance of the remaining ammunition to be produced, but this change would only save some 1,000 tons of explosive. Besides, there would have been the added expense of modifying the existing factory space to the new type of ammunition. Other considerations included the need to re-fit all Bombards with new range scales, drums and sights, which would have added even more cost. There was also the current state of the war. The German invasion of the UK was known as Operation Sealion. The operation was always going to have failed, even if the Germans had 'won' the Battle of Britain. At the time this change in ammunition was being considered, in late 1942, such an invasion was utterly preposterous. By this time Britain was beginning seriously to look at returning to the continent. There was the suggestion that the Bombard, perhaps with the 10lb hollow charge, could be useful in such an invasion, which would justify the expense of the new ammunition and sights. The concept was for a Bombard to be landed with the first waves on D-Day. This was because the weapon was man-portable, unlike the 6-pounder gun. Issuing the Bombard in such a way would give the assault waves a longer ranged anti-tank asset that could be landed by manpower alone, and used to halt tank attacks aimed at throwing the Allies back into the sea until heavier conventional weapons could be landed. With their primary role fulfilled, the Bombards would switch to protection of the line of communication and rear area security. Here its ability to function as a mortar would allow the weapon to be useful.

If it was decided to carry out this scheme, it was envisioned that a select number of the Bombards could be converted to accept the 10lb ammunition. About 5,000 such conversions were considered. The Bombard also had the added advantage that it was lighter than the same weight of mines needed to cover the same area. In the end, the difficulties in switching manufacturing along with the cancellation of the last part of the ammunition order, which freed up explosives and materials for the new Projector, Infantry, Anti-Tank, meant the 10lb hollow charge remained strictly an experimental projectile.

Back in mid-1941, with the drawings for the Bombard being sealed, work could turn towards organizing production. ICI would obviously be heavily involved as they were the main producer of Nobels 808. ICI took over control of production of the Bombard as well as filling the projectiles. Due to the simplistic nature of the weapon, when compared with a conventional gun, it was realized that production of sub-components and complete weapons could be parcelled out to smaller manufacturers. Although ICI remained the principal company, the sub-contractors were divided up into two groups based on location, and ICI was given oversight of one of these groups. These were the North and South Groups (see Appendix C), with ICI in charge of the North Group.

As the weapon was about to enter production it was quickly found that alterations to the design were needed. The result of this delayed production. With these setbacks, it was hoped that production would start in July 1941 with a forecast of 250 weapons, a target that ICI utterly failed as the company delivered no weapons. On the plus side, the Southern Group of companies had produced 112 mounts. It seems that this gave a false impression to some unknown person, who held a conversation with the owner of ICI, Lord Melchett. During this conversation it was stated there were plenty of spare mountings available. To that end it appears ICI focused on the production of the guns over the mountings, delivering just 400 mountings in August. Against that ICI claimed to have delivered some 1,132 guns. This claim was not supported by the War Office, and it caused an argument between various civil servants and ICI until Lord Beaverbrook stepped in. The reason for the disagreement was down to terminology. The Chief Inspector of Armaments (CIA) had 'accepted' 1,132 weapons from ICI, which ICI took to mean their work was done. However, 'accepted' was not the same as 'passed inspection'. The latter term means that all is in order, and the weapon was ready to issue to the front line. In August just fifteen Bombards had been passed. There were two main reasons for this failure to pass the final inspection. The first was with the range scale. Due to the speed with which the designs and production had been drawn up, there was an ambiguity in the plans for the production of range scales, and this caused delays with engraving sufficient range scales. Thus, ICI had hit upon the plan of issuing the Bombards with paper range scales, with the distances printed on them. Paper on a field weapon would be disastrous, as it would inevitably get damp and become useless.

Another pressing problem was both the lack of spirit levels and the design of the bracket to mount them onto the Bombard's gun shield. The bracket needed revision and was another item that had to be fixed on the drawings. There was plenty of time to sort this, however, as there were no spirit levels. ICI approached Cook, Troughton and Sims, the company that was making the spirit level for the 2-inch mortar, with the idea of using the same production. As Cook, Troughton and Sims was fully engaged with contracts to produce the spirit levels for 2-inch mortars on government placed contracts they refused. To sort out this bottleneck the Ministry of Supply became involved, and after a visit to Cook, Troughton and Sims to explain the situation, the company accepted an order for 4,000 spirit levels. At the time production was 3,200 per month, although Cook, Troughton and Sims thought that capacity could be expanded up to 7,000 per month. It is not recorded if this production increase took place. As later versions of the Bombard are missing their spirit levels, this would indicate it was either cheaper or production could not be increased and the feature was removed. From these shaky first steps production steadily increased throughout 1941. By February 1942 production was at about 3,500 guns per month. Table 4 details weekly deliveries.

In December 1941 Messers Thomas Broadbent and Sons Ltd, of Huddersfield, were working as one of the Northern Group. Broadbent's was one of the seven that were assembling completed Bombards. They encountered problems in the final assembly, mainly relating to the gun shield and its attachments such as the sight elements. At the time the gun shield was constructed

Table 4. Production of the Bombard and Mounts, 1941

Month	Week Ending	Guns	Mobile Mount	Pedestal Mount
July	19	–	–	–
	26	–	–	112
August	2	60	63	–
	9	20	20	–
	16	31	31	50
	23	400	163	44
	30	533	181	14
September	6	418	273	33
	13	500	670	141
	20	547	739	83

from two halves which were then welded together. Broadbent's felt this created manufacturing issues as there would need to be considerable finishing and working to get two halves to match. Besides, Broadbent's felt that the sight brackets were too difficult to fit, and the range locking handle could be improved. None of the other contractors remarked on the problems that Broadbent's did in this period, however, the manufacturing jigs did get upgraded around this time, so there may have been problems for all companies involved. Equally, Broadbent's engineers felt that the design of the weapon was extremely poor. To this end, they re-designed the gun shield, controls and attachments. Then they built one of their improved Bombards, before announcing it to the War Office.

Broadbent's changes included creating a new flat gun shield, which was gas cut, moving all the controls and gun sights over to the left of the gun shield. They also deleted the dual-range controls but left them for the gunner. Another change was made to the range locking handle. In the original design, the handle was locked into position and it would bite into the metal of the range cam to hold itself in place. Broadbent's felt this was an inferior design and created a lock that would not bite. Broadbent's claimed that this would save some 10–15 per cent in labour costs.

The appearance of the weapon, rather out of the blue, caused a bit of a stir in the War Office, and the modified Bombard was shipped to London for review. All the modifications were quickly rejected, as they had previously been considered during the design phase. The new range locking handle was rejected due to the fearsome recoil of the Bombard. Earlier trials had shown the only way to prevent the lock slipping was to have the lock bite into the metal. Equally, on the first variants, the range control was under the gunner's operation, however, it had been found that when engaging a moving target it was impossible for the gunner to estimate and set range while keeping the sights on the target. Thus, in the production weapon, the detachment commander dealt with range while the gunner concentrated on tracking and aiming.

During 1941 the total number of Bombards ordered had spiralled upwards. In March the production ordered was just 2,000 guns, in April it was increased by another 12,000. By June the total order was 24,500 guns. In December the order was increased again to 31,000 in total. By August 1942 the total order had crept up to 36,000, although later it was revised downwards to 32,500 guns, which was completed in about February 1943. Mountings were a slightly more complex situation due to there being two types. To confuse the situation a little more, in the second half of 1941 each Bombard fitted to a static mounting was to receive a mobile mounting as well. Documents are also not clear what they consider a single static mount. One would presume that it is an individual pedestal, however, some documents state that each static mount consisted of four pedestals sited around a potential ambush location. This was so the Bombard could be displaced to alternative firing positions if it was detected. In the end, holdfast mounts were overproduced with 18,162 being recorded as produced, against a requirement for just 18,000.

The number of rounds produced is also a confused picture, due to the combination of multiple natures of projectiles. Ammunition requirements sometimes changed from week to week. For example, on 1 May 1941, some 2,600,000 rounds were required. In the intervening eight days, until the 9th, this figure had been raised to 4,360,000 rounds of just 20lb anti-tank and then been reduced down to 2,175,000 rounds. Counting tail units produced offers no insight, as training rounds were issued with multiple tails due to each one breaking after a set period of use, indeed some tails could be used three times, while others just once. There is a final production figure for ammunition, though, and this was issued after the war, during the Royal Commission on Inventions, and based upon what records could be found. It is claimed that a total of 4,015,000 rounds of all types were produced. It is likely that this would be biased towards anti-tank production as that was seen as the priority. The total cost for this production of ammunition was £8,195,177. Regarding the figures for the Bombard, there is no definite mention of exactly how much a Bombard would cost. There is a document that mentions how much the December 1941 increase of guns would cost. Adding on an extra 17,000 guns would cost £1,100,000, which gives us a rough estimate of £64–5 per gun.

Chapter Six

The Answer to the Maiden's Prayer

Initially, the Home Guard was very enthusiastic about receiving the Bombard. Here was a weapon system able to obliterate any tank, and ideally suited to the defensive war the soldiers were expected to fight. There had been a morale problem caused by the perception they were getting cheap and shoddy guns. This stems from the main rifle that the Home Guard was equipped with, the imported P.17. At the time nearly everyone in the country was familiar with the .303 SMLE that equipped the regular army. It was iconic and embedded in the population's identity, the weapon that had won the First World War. The newly formed Home Guard was issued these guns imported from the USA, not proper battle rifles! In reality, the P.17s were often newer and perfectly well-made rifles, however, they were condemned because they were not SMLEs. Then at a time when the tank had created such devastation in the Low Countries and France, the Home Guard was expecting to face them in huge numbers. To defend themselves against these monstrous clanking machines they had been issued a series of Heath Robinson contraptions such as the Northover Projector, which was little more than a modernized black powder cannon. At this time the Home Guard was feeling that they were getting the dregs of the armament supply. Then into this situation entered the Bombard. A modern, deadly anti-tank weapon, designed specifically for the Home Guard. It also fitted into the curious class of weapons called sub-artillery that only the Home Guard was equipped with, and so was clearly for them, not the regular field army. One Home Guard officer described the Bombard as, 'The answer to the maiden's prayer'.

On 12 October 1941 a demonstration of the new 29mm Spigot Mortar Mk I, as it was officially known, was carried out at the Horam Brickworks in East Sussex. With this being on the south coast, it was seen as a priority to get the new weapon into service in these areas as they would most likely to face any invasion. The event was organized by the 55th Infantry Division. The local Home Guard Battalions also attended and were to show off their newest weapon. After familiarization lectures for assorted weapon systems during the first half of the event, in the afternoon the Bombard was to fire off a few live rounds to demonstrate its capabilities. When the trigger was pulled the 20lb anti-tank bomb detonated still on the spigot, fatally injuring one Home Guard, and possibly killing a second. Another lost an eye, while a third had to have his arm amputated. Three other Home Guard were lightly wounded. The army also sustained three very serious injuries and at least one minor.

On the 13th a court of inquiry was held into the incident. It ran for two days, and several witnesses, including Blacker, were called to give evidence. It concluded that a faulty fuse was to blame, but not in the way one might expect. It revealed that the rubber pad on the base of the No. 283 fuse had separated from the fuse body. This had been the main way of telling which way round the fuse was when it was inserted into the projectile. With the pad missing, a fuse had been inserted upside down, with deadly results. All the initial production of ammunition, with lot numbers one through to fifty, was immediately recalled. Instruction manuals from then on would stress the importance of inserting the fuse the correct way, but, as has been discussed, a Mk II fuse would be introduced very shortly and this was impossible to insert incorrectly. It was likely the Mk II fuse was a direct result of the Horam disaster.

However, the damage had been done. Most Home Guard now saw the Bombard as a dangerous and unsafe weapon, and shied away from accepting it into their units. This dislike was fuelled by rumour and word of mouth. In some interviews with Home Guard members they tell that a Bombard would kill its gunner if you pulled the trigger, and similar hair raising stories. For the best part of eighty years this has been the benchmark and the way the Bombard has been assessed by historians, and why its reputation has been so poor.

Seemingly by sheer coincidence, the best answer to this aversion was just beginning to be enacted. Schools were being set up across the country, and these would train and, more importantly, create personal enthusiasm for the weapon by demonstrating its capabilities. These individuals would then return to their units to pass on their knowledge. Buxton was one such school, and the final report issued by the school has been preserved. From it some useful insights into the Bombard can be gained. The school was based at Perseverance Quarries, and consisted of a single hut, along with some large cloth tents. Most of the equipment, and indeed the hut, were supplied by ICI, which also put any resources requested by the school at their disposal. The first course started on 17 November 1941, and the students in the final class were awarded their certificates on 23 December of the same year. Each course lasted just three days, and during this time the students would each get the opportunity of firing live rounds, and act as each member of the gun detachment. On two of the firing sessions, the targets would be moving. The first live rounds would be fired with an instructor as the gun commander, but thereafter the students would take over. On the moving target, the range was specifically arranged so that the target would shift from 180yd to 130yd. This was to force the gun crew to have to change range settings during the engagement. The total run of the target was 150yd in distance at a speed of 10mph, which gave an exposure time of about 30 seconds. The target itself was 9ft long and 4ft tall. On average, the students managed to fire three rounds, of which they would achieve a 66 per cent hit ratio. When the instructors tried the same moving target, they managed five rounds all of which hit.

Of note, the school at Buxton held a course on the tactical handling of the Bombard, which the other schools neglected. This was seen as the highlight and most interesting part of the course. The effect of the course could be measured as well. Of the 211 pupils who attended about 25 per cent had a negative view of the Bombard when they walked through the gates. By the end of the course, that view had been reversed. The final report cites one

Three Home Guard manning a Bombard at No. 3 GHQ school, 1943. Here they have access to a static mount pedestal, although the fighting position is rather poor. The position is not a fighting one as the lip of the trench is in a rather shoddy state of disrepair, and the sandbags would give the position away. Finally, there are no ammunition magazines in the wall.

particular case of a student who attended the school with negative views and had his colonel in support of those views. He left the school at 0900 after finishing the course. At about 1130 the student had returned to his colonel, had a detailed talk and then been on the phone trying to book places for the colonel and all company commanders in his unit. In total two independent Home Guard schools were set up in addition to Buxton, and another course was also held at Command Weapon Training Schools. Even so, despite the eventual acceptance and indeed enthusiasm for the Bombard, the views of that period remain to tarnish the Bombard's reputation, even today, as some historians take comments given from the last months of 1941 and apply it to the Bombard's entire life. Some even take the comments as the literal truth and mock the Bombard as a weapon system, when in fact it gave a devastating anti-tank weapon perfectly designed for the combat that the Home Guard was to undertake.

It seems logical to talk about the drills for the Bombard here, as they would have been exactly the sort of lesson the students of the Bombard courses would be learning. As well as official instruction, there were several small booklets produced by publishing houses. These were quite simply, and cynically, an attempt to make money from the keen Home Guard members. These books were invariably claimed to have been written by some retired officer, to lend an air of credibility to the instructions and tactical guidance given by the author of these works. Generally, the books do not contradict the official stance or suggest demonstrably unsafe drills. Although one booklet, produced by Gale and Polden Ltd, does issue some advice that borders on the risky. When talking about the No. 283 Mk I fuse the Gale and Polden booklet mentions the rubber pad. It states that if the pad is missing care should be taken to insert the fuse the correct way, and details some small holes on the base that should be towards the rear of the bomb. Official guidance was that should the rubber pad be missing the fuse was to be returned to stores.

The first thing to do to make the Bombard ready to fight was to prepare the bombs. The 14lb anti-personnel bomb needed no preparation as it was issued ready to fire, however, the 20lb anti-tank round needed to be fused. This was done by removing a strip of white adhesive tape from around the body, unscrewing the bomb, inserting the fuse, then reassembling the bomb. Then a khaki tape, supplied with the bomb, was used to mark the bomb as live. The bomb would then be replaced into the packing tube. This latter item was a compressed fibre tube each holding one bomb, the cap of the tube containing a wooden plug that was inserted into the bomb's tail tube to prevent dirt contaminating it. This packing tube was then held together by a strap. Transport was by whatever means the local Home Guard could arrange. One suggestion was a 15cwt truck could carry a five-man detachment, twenty-four rounds and the complete Bombard and stores.

The Answer to the Maiden's Prayer 63

Detachment Commander

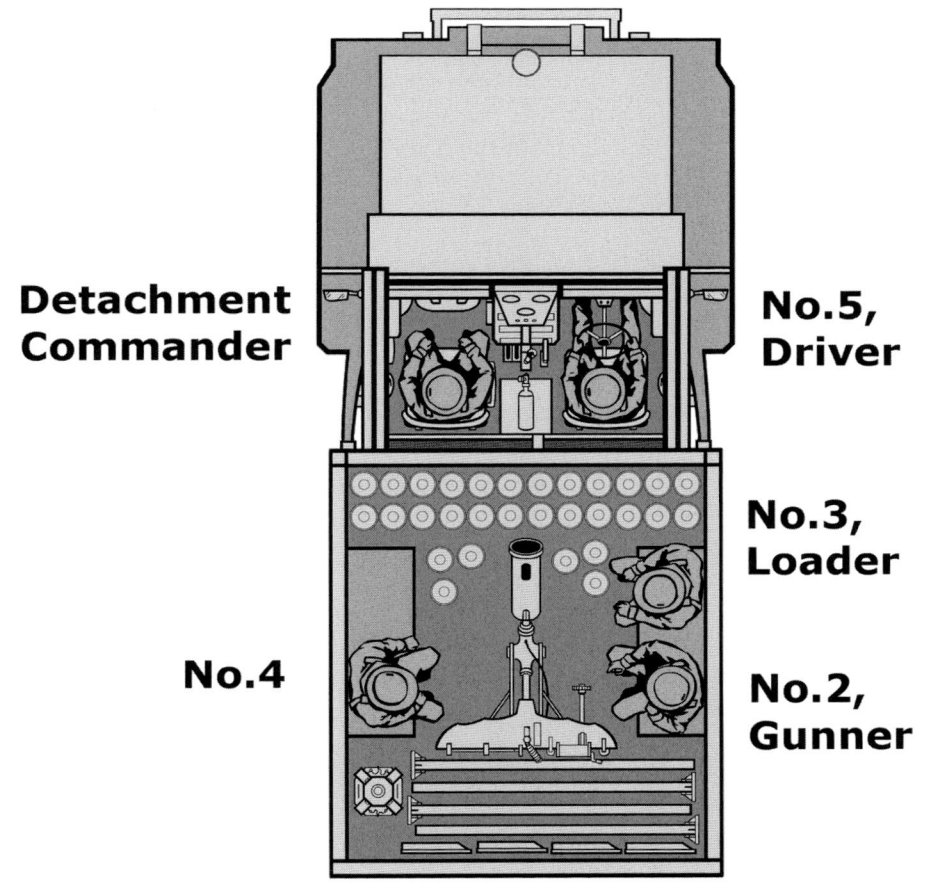

No. 5, Driver

No. 3, Loader

No. 4

No. 2, Gunner

The suggested 'ideal' layout for carrying the Bombard in a truck. This layout has been taken from E.W. Manders' 1944 illustrated book *The 29mm Spigot Mortar* on the Bombard. The space in front of the soldiers in the bed of the truck are for items such as sledgehammers and other tools.

When deploying the weapon the detachment commander would choose a suitable location for the weapon. Once he had selected the ground he wished to fight over, he placed the central base unit in the desired location. The rest of the detachment would then bring up the legs and assemble the quadpod, and brace the legs with sledgehammers and pickets as needed. The base unit had to be resting fully on the ground after the quadpod was assembled otherwise the legs would bend when the weapon was fired. With the mount in place, the mortar was brought up by two men. Once in position, the detachment commander would assume control of the gun, estimate and adjust range setting. The No. 2 will become the gunner and manage the fine aiming and

64   *Defeating the Panzer-Stuka Menace*

traverse of the weapon. The third man would act as the loader. First, he would remove the packing tubes from the bombs, but leave the cap, with its plug in place. When he wished to load a bomb he would remove the packing tube cap, check that the firing pin was not showing on the spigot and that the gunner had removed his hand from the trigger mechanism. If all these safety checks were passed he should place the bomb onto the spigot and push backwards until he heard a 'Chonk', the round now being seated. As the loader was often well forward of the gun shield he was exposed to the blast of the weapon firing, and for this reason, there was a sleeve around the spigot to offer some protection. It was found that the blast the loader had to endure was still rather potent, thus a portion of the protective sleeve was cut out on the top or bottom. This would allow the pressure to vent, making the life of the loader much more pleasant. Should the round misfire, the loader was to withdraw

Another demonstration of the Bombard. Here a tarpaulin is being used by the loader so he can ready bombs without the risk of contamination of the tail tube. While a sensible idea in a demonstration, one wonders if it could or would have been used in combat.

the round, about an inch up the spigot, rotate the entire bomb through about 90 degrees and reseat the bomb. If the round misfired again then it was to be unloaded and discarded.

A minimum detachment was three men, however, a fully crewed detachment comprised five men. In such a situation numbers four and five would provide local security and act as ammunition porters bringing up more bombs. It was estimated it would take around 5 minutes to fully unload from the truck. There were, on occasion, comparative demonstrations of time taken to get a weapon into action. These are somewhat misleading as the full circumstances of how far the equipment had to be moved before assembling is not known. However, with all the items to hand, one Bombard is recorded as taking just 25 seconds to be brought into action. Another, with a partially trained Home Guard crew, is recorded as taking 69 seconds. In the latter case, they then went on to fire ten rounds in 60 seconds.

There was a demonstration on 25 November 1941 to three Russian majors from the military mission. The British were more than willing to lend support to the Russians and a cheap mass-produced weapon like the Bombard would give quite an anti-tank punch to their forces. This was considered vital especially in the light of the Red Army units which had so recently collapsed in the face of German armour. The demonstration was a disaster. There were several miscommunications about when it was to take place, with elements of the government still trying to arrange the demonstration some ten days after the event. However, Major Macrae represented MD1 at the demonstration and, much to his horror, he noted several failures during the day. First, an utterly untrained gun detachment was used. This meant that they missed every shot, even at a range of 50yd. The ammunition used was some old rounds left over from the development period, and not service-issue standard. This meant the tails came off in flight. The impression given was so entirely negative that the Russians point-blank refused to attend any further demonstrations. However, as part of the massive amounts of British military aid given to the Russians there were at least 250 Bombards shipped by the end of June 1942. During the war, and even today, there persists a rumour that the Russians used the Bombard, although no evidence of it has been found, apart from the mention of the weapons being shipped to Russia. Some claim it was used in the defence of Moscow, others at Stalingrad. Use at Moscow is unlikely due to the British only just introducing it for the Home Guard at the time of the battle, but what of Stalingrad, or other battles? With the shipment of the Bombards to Russia it is possible these weapons were used. There is no information on the amount of ammunition supplied, which may have given us an idea of the likelihood of use. In addition, the number of guns was so small it makes one wonder if the Russians bothered to issue a tiny number

The Finnish Army conducting trials of a captured Soviet *Ampulomet*, 1942. On this particular weapon, they are using a log as the baseplate. There are other examples with more conventional metal baseplates. It seems that the baseplate for this weapon was made of whatever was to hand locally.

of weapons, with uncertain logistical support for the weapons. The claims of combat use could also be mistaken identification of a Russian weapon called the *Ampulomet*. Visually this looks very similar to a Bombard, with a short wide-mouthed tube on a mount of some form, and sometimes these are quad-pods like the Bombard. In function the *Ampulomet* acted almost exactly like the British Northover Projector, using a black powder charge to fire a glass projectile filled with incendiary fluid that would ignite on contact with the air.

Actual combat accounts of the Bombard in action are very difficult to locate. One theatre where the Bombard did see action was North Africa. The Middle East Command (MEC) learnt of the Bombard and asked to be kept informed about its progress in December 1941. By the end of January MEC had their hands on a sample of the weapon and some ammunition. They decided to carry out a trial on an abandoned Panzer IV they had spare. They set up the Bombard so that it was firing at the tank, at a rough angle of 30 degrees. The first round hit on the right-hand part of the vertical plate on the front hull that mounts the hull machine gun and driver's vision slot. The entire right-hand side was blasted backwards into the tank. The next round hit the left-hand side of the plate and had much the same effect. MEC closed off their telegram with, 'This appears satisfactory.'

It appears most of the Bombards that were delivered to North Africa were issued to Australian, New Zealand and Indian divisions. There are mentions of Bombards being used at Tobruk, although no account of their action has been found. Bombards were issued to the Australians for the defence of Tel el Eisa, but not fired. The 4th Indian Division stated it used the Bombard on several occasions, one of which was at Ruweisat Ridge during the First Battle of El Alamein, although no other details are given.

The use at Ruweisat Ridge brings forth one of those imponderables of history. The New Zealand divisions were issued Bombards at Mersa Matruh, but subscribed to the idea of the uselessness of the weapon after hearing the stories of the Horam disaster. The Bombards tended to be confined to the battalion transports, alongside the cookhouse, until about mid-June when

A New Zealand-owned Bombard in the box south of Ruweisat Ridge, 1942. There are supplies of ammunition below the netting, and a 14-pounder round has been partially uncased behind the standing soldier. Interestingly, this Bombard is set up with both the left and right legs being omitted. (*Durham County Record Office, D/DLI 7/762/1(46)*)

they were spiked by their crews as they retreated from Minqar Qaim. Comparing what happened to the New Zealand and Indian divisions at Ruweisat Ridge, both had similar battle experiences, but with very different outcomes. Both lacked armoured support, and were assigned to attack the same objective. The Indians fell short of their objectives due to stiff resistance, while the New Zealanders made it to their objectives. However, they had no secure line of communication due to bypassing several strongpoints. This prevented support weapons being brought up. Later both formations would be attacked by German armour. The Indians managed to hold on, and later withdraw voluntarily, but the New Zealanders were overrun and suffered heavy losses. While it would be a laughable misrepresentation to claim that this difference was entirely down to the presence of the Bombard, one does wonder if the New Zealanders equipped with the Bombard, which could have been man-packed up to the front, might not have been able to ward off the marauding German armour long enough to withdraw, and avoid being overrun and the heavy losses that caused.

The Indian Division also used the Bombard at Miteriya Ridge, and this provides a glimpse into the inventive ways the Bombard was deployed. The Germans had established an observation post, about 500yd away from the Commonwealth positions, and were using it to bring down accurate small arms and mortar fire. The position was well fortified and resisted all return fire. One night a Bombard was placed in a forward position in no man's land. The weapon's ability to be man-packed and its ease of concealment meant it was well suited to this role. The next morning, when there was enough light to see the German observation post, the Bombard obliterated the position with a couple of 20lb anti-tank bombs. The Indian report concludes with: 'Even if we had more inf A/tk [anti-tank] guns we would still use spigots in defence as they were so very inconspicuous, have a tremendous hitting power and are very simple to teach and learn.' The Indian Army seems to have been one of the major users of the Bombard, and they certainly appreciated the weapon. At the outbreak of the war against Japan some 250 Bombards, with 100 rounds per gun, were dispatched to Malaya. These would likely have been re-routed to India, where another 500 guns were also sent. The ammunition issue for the Indian batch was originally given as just 30 rounds per gun. Luckily this was seen as inadequate and was raised to 100 rounds. By May 1942 significant quantities of ammunition and weapons had been dispatched, as listed in Table 5. Red Card A and B was ammunition of uncertain quality. Red Card A referred to ammunition with faults that could be issued if circumstances required it. Red Card B was ammunition of doubtful quality that should not be issued until batches had been proofed by test firing.

The Commonwealth forces in the China/Burma/India (CBI) Theatre were to hatch a plan that could have taken the Allied use of the Bombard to a new

A three-man detachment manning a Bombard with a sand-filled inert round is loaded. In the grass around the crew are a considerable number of bombs ready to be fired. The projectiles still have the packing tube caps in place, onto which is marked the type of round inside. (*Enfield Local Studies & Archive*)

Table 5. Bombard Ammunition Availability

	Bombards	20lb Anti-tank	14lb Anti-personnel
Issued home	22,149	410,000	155,000
Issued abroad	2,815	235,000	71,000
Stocks available to issue	3,294	26,000	24,000
Red Card A	–	236,000	20,000
Red Card B	–	136,000	136,000
Unserviceable	–	13,000	–
Total	28,258	1,056,000	406,000

level. From 26–8 January, 1944 Commonwealth forces launched a series of attacks around Razabil in the Arakan area of Burma. In this area the low ground mostly comprised cultivated rice paddies, while any hills were covered in jungle. As these stretches of the jungle had been used for timber by the locals the undergrowth consisted of extremely dense vegetation. Japanese defensive positions were usually sited on reverse slopes and made of wooden log bunkers, with interlocking fields of fire, and the ability to cover each other. Often the firing apertures were cut through the undergrowth making the enemy position all but impossible to see. Even if the Commonwealth forces did manage to locate a bunker, they had trouble defeating it, without resorting to a costly infantry assault. Tanks were hampered by the terrain, and even if they could thrash through the mud to the required location, then the 75mm would often prove ineffective at destroying the bunker. To make matters worse, due to the extreme gradients, if the tank tried to approach the bunker it often lacked the gun depression to engage. Artillery could not be used due to the close proximity of Allied forces. To tackle these sorts of positions the Australians began to contemplate a way of defeating them and hit upon the idea of an assault tank. They did specify that any such tank should be able to be developed quickly, so as to get it into the field before the war ended.

Their first idea was to use a naval depth-charge launcher, fitted to the turret of a Stuart light tank. Spare depth charges would be carried on the rear deck of the tank, so the gun could be traversed and reloaded a few times. This idea matured over time, and eventually settled as an M4 Sherman mounting a Bombard by about February/March 1944. Calculations suggested that a 25lb bomb could be fired 190yd, and a 30lb round to 140yd. There was also discussion about creating an incendiary round that would spread oil and burn for approximately 5 minutes. Such a round would have two advantages, it would give smoke cover and suppress a bunker for the time taken for the infantry to close with it and would also clear undergrowth providing a chance to spot the bunker. In addition, removing the jungle cover would lessen the risk of Japanese tank-hunting parties getting into a position to strike at the tank. All such work was halted by several factors. First, the production of the tail tubes for the Bombard was beyond local capabilities and would require imports. Next, word of the Petard had arrived. Concerns were also raised about the number of weapons tank crews were being asked to operate. Finally, one argument that killed off even the suggestion of the Petard being used was that the Australians had started to produce Snake mine-clearing charges. These were 3in diameter pipes filled with explosives and could be coupled together to form a giant pole that was then pushed towards the enemy. When in position it could be detonated clearing all mines, barbed wire and undergrowth, and presumably crippling any Japanese bunkers.

The concept of a larger bomb for the Bombard was not new. When the Bombard was being developed in early 1941 General Andrew George Latta McNaughton of the Canadian forces was enthusiastic and supported Blacker in his work. Previously, during an argument with government bureaucracy, Blacker had requested General McNaughton have four of his junior officers size an intransigent civil servant and pitch him into a nearby horse trough.

The Canadians thought the Bombard could be improved in a number of ways. First, they mounted it on a 2-pounder, Mk IIIA carriage. This weapon was actually fired with a 20lb drill round on 13 May 1941. However, the Canadians considered even the colossal devastation of a 20lb anti-tank bomb was insufficient. Thus, they began to look at a 60lb bomb. To fire such a round everything would need to be upscaled, including the spigot. The Canadians then came up with the idea of an adapter or interchangeable spigot, that used a common firing system. If the gun crew had decided on a 60lb bomb they just needed to change the spigot quickly and load. This 60lb spigot was to be tapered for a large portion of its length to make loading easier. It appears that the idea of the increased size bomb was dropped due to the problems with producing an utterly new line of ammunition, and obtaining sufficient quantities of HE filling.

The idea of a wheeled carriage would find some use in later years with the ever keen Home Guard having a crack at the problem. Two examples of wheeled mounts are documented. The 26th Platoon, F Coy, 5th Battalion, Cambridge Home Guard designed a wheeled carriage with a pole trail. Ingeniously, the wheels were mounted onto arms at either end of the axle. These could be locked downwards lifting the Bombard off the ground to about waist height. This would give a decent cross-country performance. For firing the arms could be rotated through about 110 degrees which would place the base of the gun flat on the ground giving the necessary recoil absorption. The presence of the wheels would mean that the gun's arc was limited to the front 120 degrees or so, but was much faster into action. It may be that this mount was actually built by the Home Guardsmen employed by the Gas Light Company Ltd. In 2015 a pair of pictures were sold to a private collector, and they show a carriage that looks identical to the plans. This Bombard carriage is towed by one of the improvised armoured cars that the Home Guard often converted. Oddly, a second picture exists in the Imperial War Museum archives that shows a Bombard fitted to a wheeled carriage that looks identical to the Cambridge plans, only it is in service with the West Riding, Doncaster, Home Guard.

Interestingly, in 1942 there is a very brief mention of a wheeled mount for the Bombard from government sources, and is used in conjunction with the plan to deploy Bombards on D-Day. However, it is unclear if this refers to the same wheeled Bombard carriage that is mentioned elsewhere.

The second style of wheeled mount dates from June 1943 and is from the pen of a gentleman living in Willenhall, Staffordshire. With the assistance of Rubery Owen & Company Ltd, he filed for a patent that showed a Bombard-style pivot mounted onto an entirely conventional split-trail carriage. One wonders how such an arrangement would have survived the rigours of firing as it lacked any way of transmitting the recoil to the ground. The previous version from the Home Guard at least included a ground anchor that could be seated when the weapon was dropped into position.

So far there has been no discussion regarding one of the main belligerent nations of the Second World War in relation to the Bombard. This is of

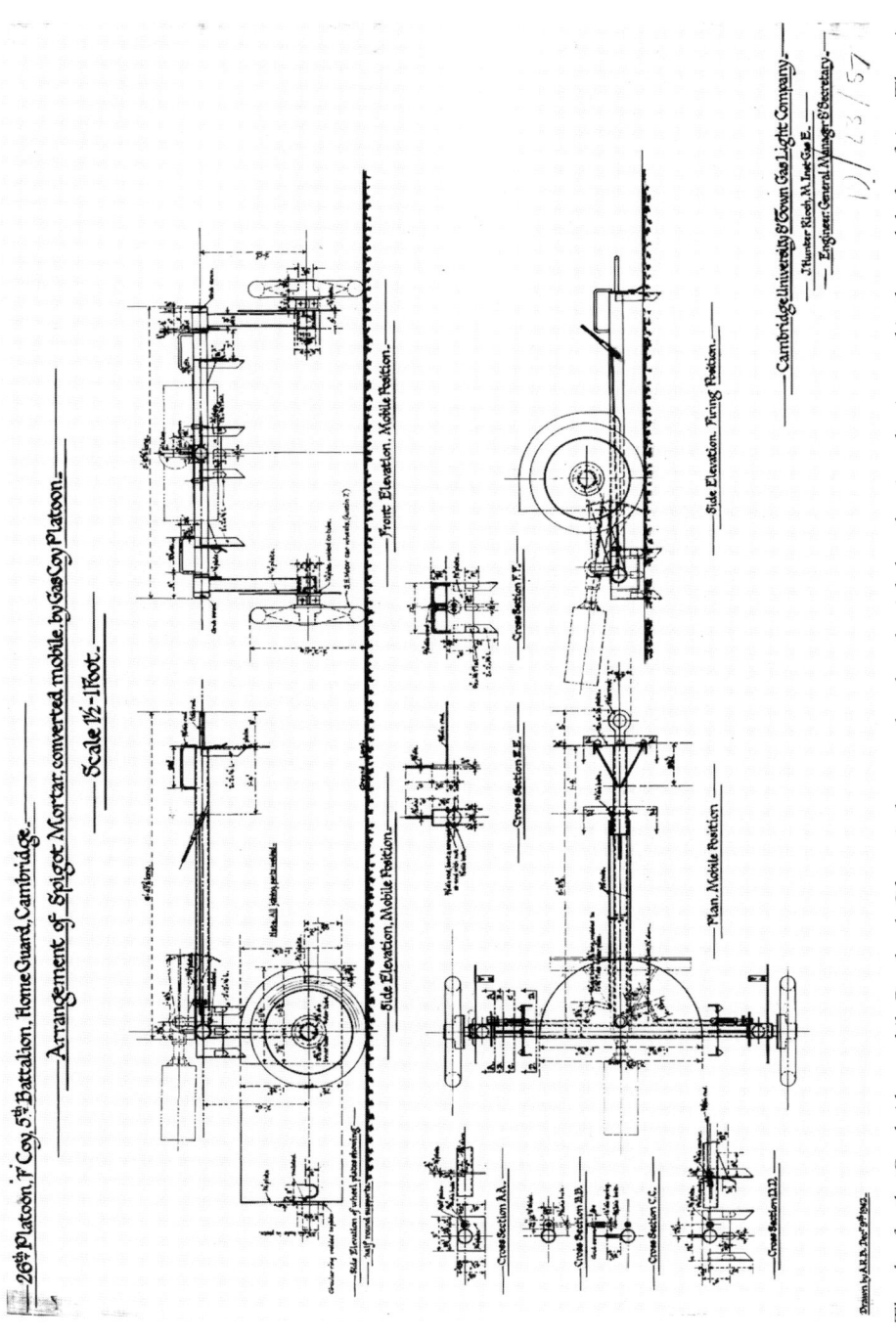

The plan for the Cambridge mobile Bombard. Of note is the ground anchor that is below the pivot that is seated in the earth before firing. There is also a picture of an identical mount in use with the West Riding Home Guard.

course Germany. What is stunning about the German response to the Bombard is that, despite facing it several times and likely overrunning Commonwealth positions which held the weapon, the Germans had limited information about it. In 1942 they identified the weapon and named it correctly, and also included a note that any samples of captured weapons should be sent for testing. It was not until about December 1944 that the Germans gave out particulars of the weapon, obtained from captured documents, to their frontline troops. One wonders how they obtained these documents. If they had captured them in North Africa, they would have published the weapon's characteristics earlier. One possibility is that the British were using documents that no longer held importance to the war in attempts to flush out spies and play other secret games, however, that is just speculation.

Even with these official documents the Germans utterly missed the main point concerning the Bombard. They saw it as a short-range grenade-thrower, and gave its armour penetration as just 50mm, entirely failing to appreciate the importance of the base fuse and the Nobels 808. The German documentation even goes so far as to say that the Bombard could possibly be improved with the addition of a shaped charge warhead.

The fact that the Bombard did not have a weapon-like appearance meant it was to be used in one further theatre of war, the war at sea. At first, there were trials of a Bombard aboard ship for anti-shipping work. This was thwarted by its terribly short range when compared with other naval weapons. However, Winston Churchill's love of special forces and cloak-and-dagger operations came into play. In August 1941 an unremarkable 65-ton wooden trawler, powered by dark-brown sails, was afloat in Poole harbour. She was called *Maid Honour* and was originally from Brixham. She was to be used as a raiding vessel by the Small Scale Raiding Force (SSRF). The original plan was that during the day she would appear as a simple sailing ship fishing at sea. At night, her shallow draught would allow her to slip in close to enemy installations onshore. From there the single Bombard mounted amidships could lob 20lb anti-tank rounds into the installation. The Bombard's lack of muzzle flash would mean her position was never given away, and HESH rounds were extremely effective against concrete fortifications. In daylight, the Bombard would look like part of her winching gear and be utterly inconspicuous. The question of how the boat would fare with the recoil was solved when a round was test fired. The one account we have suggests one member of the crew who was nearby was knocked overboard, and emerged minus his underwear, much to the delight of the rest of the crew.

Maid Honour left port bound for West Africa, with the objective of attacking U-boats reported to be using the rivers in Vichy controlled areas as rest and refuelling points. The concept of the operation was to slip up rivers and give the U-boats a massive surprise with the ship's Bombard. Upon reaching the area the force commander decided much more mischief could be had and launched Operation Postmaster, a plan quietly to steal two large ships from a Spanish port. For this operation, motor tugs were needed, and the SSRF left *Maid Honour* in Lagos, with her Bombard unfired.

The Bombard ultimately failed in its main role, of defeating German tanks in the stop lines of Kent, because it simply arrived in service too late. It was one of the first dedicated weapons for the Home Guard and likely boosted their morale, once the training regime had taken hold. Where it saw service it performed the jobs it was asked to do perfectly, although it could be argued that it was hampered in some circumstances by its short range. However, one should not view it in the same vein as a contemporary anti-tank gun, but maybe more in line with weapons like the modern Carl Gustav rocket launcher, giving the infantry a heavier weapon that could smash a tank at close range. The Bombard would have two long-lasting effects on the war, and beyond. The first was introducing the concept of chemical energy warheads in general, and HESH projectiles in particular, and establishing them in the military mind. In many of the documents and letters there is a sense of disbelief and even sometimes outright refusal to accept that a mere 'high explosive' round could cause such devastation to armoured vehicles. It is likely that a lot of the early resistance to the Bombard was down to mistrust of the data produced, which flew in the face of everything that had been previously established. But once the Bombard had bedded in the idea, it remained. The utter lack of hostility and interference from the Ordnance Board over the PIAT is a possible symptom of the chemical energy warhead being more accepted. The British Army has for many years kept HESH rounds in its inventory as the main chemical energy projectile of its tank fleet.

The other effect the Bombard would have, although less long-lasting, was to prove the idea of the spigot mortar. As will be discussed shortly, the spigot would play a key role in the defeat of the U-boats, a threat that Winston Churchill described as 'the only thing that ever really frightened me during the war'.

PART THREE

THE HEDGEHOG

Chapter Seven

The Perceived Peril

In October 1914 the German *Kriegsmarine* commenced U-boat operations against British shipping, although it was not until the following year, with the infamous sinking of the RMS *Lusitania*, that unrestricted U-boat warfare began to take shape. Due to the Germans not wishing to alienate the USA the unrestricted nature of the commerce warfare had several stops and starts. However, it signalled quite clearly to the British their vulnerability to attacks on merchant shipping. As the First World War ground on, in 1916, the British began work on a new way of detecting submerged U-boats. Named after the Anti-Submarine Division, this device would be called ASDIC and was an early form of what is known today as sonar. It works by emitting a pulse of sound and detecting the reflected echo. The emitted sound pulse was created in a directional 'beam', which is traversed about to search for the submerged object, much like a searchlight. In ASDIC's case, the 'beam' was similar in shape to a teardrop, and could be considered more of a 'slice' of the ocean. As the beam was traversed, it would be able to find a contact underwater and give a bearing, taken from the direction the emitter was pointing. Range to the submerged object was calculated using the time it took for the reflected sound to return to the receiver.

ASDIC missed deployment in the First World War, only entering service in 1922, but it gave a surface ship a way of detecting a submerged U-boat, albeit with some limitations. The shortcomings of ASDIC were, at first glance, quite substantial. The constraints on ASDIC technology were that as the ship approached the underwater contact the contact would reach the underside of the beam, and drop out of the bottom of the teardrop shape, thus becoming undetected. Depending on the depth of the submarine this could happen sometime before the ship was to pass over the contact. In the time between the loss of the signal, and the ship passing over the last known location, a submarine commander could have moved his boat, and thus be in a different location to the one that the attacking ship thought. To make matters worse for the attacking ship the nature of the weapons at its disposal for prosecuting the U-boat was rather primitive.

These weapons were depth charges. Simply these were large drums of explosive with a detonator which was set to trigger at a certain depth. Devices similar to depth charges had first been designed before the First World War, although it was only the inclusion of the hydrostatic pistol, which was invented in 1914, to act as a trigger that made them viable. The Royal Navy's first success with these weapons was in April 1916, and they remained the standard anti-submarine weapon for the rest of the war. If the depth and location of the submarine could be calculated correctly, and a rough clue on depth could be taken from when the contact was lost from the ASDIC beam, then the weapons could hopefully sink or force a U-boat to the surface. Of course, the chance of success in this regard was down to guesswork on behalf of the attacking vessel's crew.

Later in the First World War depth-charge-throwers were developed which allowed the attacking vessel to lay a pattern of five charges (one each at a corner of a square, and the fifth in the square's centre), hopefully, centred around the U-boat's last location. If the target had moved then the outside charges stood a chance of scoring a hit.

This situation was the state of the Royal Navy's anti-submarine methods at the outbreak of the Second World War. The only real change occurred in early 1940 when a heavier type of depth charge was introduced, and calculations were carried out that showed a ten-charge pattern was more effective.

Against this backdrop several factors were working in favour of the U-boats. First, the Royal Navy's crews were to become less experienced, with the increase of recruits and the loss of experienced pre-war ASDIC operators as casualties. Second, there were technical improvements to the U-boats, which allowed deeper diving and faster speeds underwater. Both of these would increase the chances of the U-boat being able to get outside the pattern. In addition, the increased operating depth would allow a U-boat to disappear off the ASDIC beam earlier, and then the slow sinking time of the depth charges would add an even greater amount of time to avoid the pattern.

With all these factors in play, it is hardly surprising that the kill rate from depth charges only reached at best 6 per cent. At the start of the war this was not as much of a problem as it sounds because the Germans hardly had any U-boats, and the ones they did have were extremely primitive and of short-range. Until the end of 1940, at most there were only ever ten U-boats at sea at any one time, so the chances of encountering one were rather slim. When a U-boat was detected the warships could stay to prosecute the target, laying multiple patterns down until they got lucky. Meanwhile, the convoy could continue with very little prospect of encountering another U-boat while unescorted. With the collapse of France and access to the Atlantic coast, this situation changed. Now there were more U-boats in the water, and convoys had to be protected all the time. No longer could a convoy escort spend hours attacking a submarine target and leave its precious convoy to continue alone.

Luckily, the Royal Navy was alive to this threat. Prior to 1939 the idea of ahead thrown weapons had been suggested but was not acted upon in any

Onboard the HMT *Stella Pegasi*, a Royal Navy Patrol Service trawler. The crew are loading a depth charge onto a Y-gun. The depth charge, once in place, would be on the cradle attached to a long rod, which extended down inside the gun. The cordite charge was burned in the combustion chamber which can just be seen on the top of the gun barrel.

meaningful way. These, as the name would imply, were anti-submarine weapons that could be projected forward of the ship. By doing so the attacking vessel could maintain ASDIC contact with the U-boat they were trying to attack, and the only margin for error was how deep the submarine was and how long the projectiles took to sink to that depth.

In 1940 the Royal Navy began to investigate the concept of ahead thrown weapons in much more detail. The first weapon was known as the Fairlie Mortar. It consisted of two banks, each of ten tubes on each side of the fo'c'sle. These would project a pattern of twenty bombs forward, each bomb was partially streamlined and contained a charge of 20lb of TNT. The pattern was created by some mortar barrels being longer or shorter to vary the muzzle velocity, and by some barrels being offset at an angle. The propelling gasses were generated by a cordite charge in a separate chamber, then piped into the base of the barrel.

In the summer of 1940, the newly renamed Department for Miscellaneous Weapons Development (DMWD), headed by the brilliant Edward Terrell, became involved. The DMWD was a research and development department of the Royal Navy, and it covered some of the same ground as MD1. The two departments had distinct flavours. Generally, MD1's inventions were of the sort that would explode, or fire something that would explode, while the DMWD had a much wider range of topics at its disposal. Some of its inventions were quite inert, such as the idea of using coal dust to camouflage rivers and canals to thwart German bomber navigation or camouflaged umbrellas that could be erected by coastal craft to mask their presence. The DMWD also initiated several other projects, not all of which bore fruit, while other ventures resulted in arguably some of the most important inventions of the war. The DMWD was also concerned with rocketry and this is how the unit became involved with ahead thrown weapons when the idea to use rockets to propel the projectiles was floated.

In December 1940 the Admiralty was still studying how technically to implement an ahead thrown weapon. Part of the problem was there was very little stretch potential in ship design, and the new weapon had to be arranged so as not to compromise other weapons. Thus, at a meeting at the Spa Hotel in Bath on 31 December the Admiralty looked at using the fore turrets on a ship to fire projectiles to lay a pattern. This was rejected simply due to rate of fire, as at best both turrets could get eight rounds off in total in the time it would take for an attacking escort to pass over the submarine's position. It was estimated twenty to thirty projectiles would be needed per pattern. At the same meeting, a number of new weapons were considered.

First to be reviewed were general ahead throwing weapons, which provided ways of projecting depth charges forward. The two mentioned were a long-range thrower developed by Thorneycrofts Ltd and the Vickers O Thrower,

The Parsnip Mortar, which was a scaled-up Fairlie Mortar with the charge size increased to throw a 60lb bomb. This photograph is really to indicate what the Fairlie Mortar looked like as there do not appear to be any pictures available of it. One presumes that to reload the barrels would pivot inwards and be reloaded when flat, much like the re-loading sequence on a Squid.

which fired an absolutely huge round with an explosive charge of 900lb and had a calibre of 13.5in. Such a weapon would have needed to throw the depth charge a significant distance to avoid sinking the firing vessel, which in turn would have resulted in a quite considerable mass of a weapon.

Under multi-bomb ahead thrown weapons, there were several devices of varying design, as well as the Fairlie Mortar. There are no details about the first one, and indeed it seems to have never been developed and disappears from the record almost immediately. It was some form of projector from Holmans Ltd and seems to have just been a rough paper design to fulfil the requirement. The next device was the rocket design, with the projector being designed by the DMWD.

The DMWD had another horse in the race. They had developed contacts with MD1, who had helped them with their design. This was given the designation Project 20. The design, however, came from the fertile mind of Jefferis. It consisted of a bank of recoiling 29mm spigots, with a reaction weight swinging below the mass. Although the basic principles were sound, there were problems with the design due to differences in the environments the weapon would be used in naval service and what Jefferis was used to on land. Thus, at the end of January development of the design was passed to Admiral Little (possibly Charles James Colebrooke Little), although Jefferis remained in contact with the project advising on spigots where necessary.

The final weapon presented to the meeting was a stick-mortar based design from the Chief Scientist of Devices (CS of D) and served as one of the main competitors, alongside the Fairlie Mortar, to Project 20. It featured slung beams, which were meant to flex under the recoil, and brace against the base of the launcher. This device might have carried the codename 'Porcupine'.

On the train back from the conference about ahead thrown weapons in December, Jefferis and the Project 20 design team were discussing their project entry and comparing notes on the other designs submitted. The team discussed their design, and came to the conclusion that a series of fixed spigots mounted to a beam would be more suitable. The firing mechanism was also switched to electrical means. One of the team, a Royal Navy Volunteer Reserve officer, Lieutenant I. Hassall, suggested the codename 'Hedgehog'.

Shortly after this the CS of D design was reworked into a spigot-mortar-style-weapon, but used mechanical means to fire the propellant charges. The CS of D design could also be trained left or right, however, the recoil force from firing was all transmitted through the mechanical linkages and into the controlling handle! Before too long it would become obvious that the two spigot weapons would produce an almost identical design, and so the CS of D design was merged into the Hedgehog.

The design for the Hedgehog was initially based around Bombard spigots. It had twenty-four spigots mounted in four rows. The forward five spigots of

Two US sailors loading a Hedgehog. The massive trunnions required to absorb the recoil can be seen in this view. Also of note are the rear bombs that are raised because their spigots are mounted directly onto the rear trunnion casings.

each row were mounted on beams that in part were copied from Porcupine. The beams were slung from two trunnions fore and aft. Such a mounting would allow stabilization to correct the roll of the ship, and, if need be, allow the pattern to be aimed off to one side by a few degrees. To save space the sixth spigots of each row were fixed directly to the top of the aft trunnion mount. When fired the bombs would land in a circle about 100ft across, with its centre roughly 220yd ahead of the ship.

The bombs would only remain on the spigots for a length of 12in, and to reach the required range they needed a much higher charge than the Bombard. This meant that the spigot diameter had to be increased to 1.75in (44mm) to improve stability and dampen vibrations. The other problem encountered was a large increase in recoil. The deck blow from a single Spigot firing was 14 tons compared with the Bombards 6 tons. As a full salvo, fired at the same time, would generate 336 tons of force, an amount that would smash through the deck of any ship the Hedgehog was to be fitted to, the answer was to

A group of sailors watch a pattern strike the surface ahead of HMCS *Kootenay*. The picture shows the slow speed of the attack run, usually recorded in single figures. This would give all hands the most response time to execute a successful attack. This salvo was fired on 18 August 1944 against the Type VIIC U-boat *U-621* in the Bay of Biscay. The operation would ultimately be successful with the U-boat being sunk with all hands by the ships.

ripple fire the salvo. Two spigots would fire simultaneously every 0.1 second. This kept the deck blow down to a manageable 28 tons of force. Even so, the weapon still needed to be mounted on a 4in gun position, necessitating the removal of the gun mount. The total space needed to mount the Hedgehog was kept down to just 30ft^2. This number seems high considering the mount itself was considerably less than this. The space requirement was to allow the crew to operate and reload the weapon. The gunner's station for the Hedgehog was directly to its rear, a large blast shield stuck up from behind the rear trunnions, onto which were mounted the controls. The controls were simplicity themselves.

First, the gunner had a handwheel to correct for the roll of the ship manually. As the crewman rocked the wheel back and forth it would slew the beams on their trunnions left or right, and thus keep them level. The ship's roll was displayed on a dial, the gunner simply chasing the needle keeping the roll lined up with the indicator. A buzzer was fitted, which was the command to fire the Hedgehog and was initiated from the bridge, which had the ASDIC set on it. Upon hearing the buzzer, the gunner turned a second crank handle, located to his right-hand side. This was the electrical ripple switch, and it rotated a live wire over a series of contacts. As the live wire touched a contact

The rear of the Hedgehog fitted to HMS *Westcott*. With the number of boxes on the rear of the blast shield, it appears this may be a Type A fire-control equipment.

it created a circuit to the relevant spigot in the sequence and the electrical primer was fired.

At the start of March 1941, a meeting was called by the Admiralty as they had revised the requirements for the weapon. Originally, the warhead weight of the projectile was to be 20lb of TNT. At this point, the lethality of such a warhead was questioned, so the Admiralty increased the weight to 30lb of explosive. All the project teams opposed this change, apart from the Hedgehog team. Here the versatility of the spigot design paid off, as all the Hedgehog team needed to do was increase the diameter of the projectile and alter the spacing between the beams. The other groups suffered badly, in the case of the rocket projector that was under design by the DMWD development had to be completely restarted from step one, and it is likely this setback crippled this design. The Fairlie Mortar team simply ignored the request and stuck to their 20lb warhead.

The original Project 20 round, designed by a Lieutenant Strickland-Constable, was based largely on a round created by Boosey & Hawkes Ltd. The new projectile for the Hedgehog was 7.2in in diameter, and this did harm performance. In the water, the rate that a projectile sinks is known as Terminal Velocity (TV). A higher TV means that the round will reach the depth of the submarine, whatever that is, faster, once again meaning less chance for the submarine to avoid the attack. The new Hedgehog round had a TV of 24fps, while the Fairlie Mortar had 30fps. The mortar achieved this by having a domed steel nose cap to improve its sinking rate and was fully streamlined. The Hedgehog projectile had a flat nose mainly to prevent rounds skipping off the water surface. The aft body had originally been planned to have a steel fairing to improve streamlining, but this was dropped to make manufacturing easier. The Fairlie Mortar round also had a drum tail and trials had shown this was perfectly satisfactory and so the tail design was adopted by the final Hedgehog round.

Tail tubes were initially welded in place, however, in the Mk I production round this was changed to being screwed into place to ease manufacture. The tail tubes also had another problem, depending on what was available for use at the manufacturer they would have a calibre of either 1.75in or 1.76in. These sizes were due to a standard and commonly sized tube produced by UK industry in large amounts, but it all depended on what was available at any particular time. Luckily, a spigot weapon could deal with such variance with Blacker's self-expanding cartridge design. To make the cartridges two 2-pounder cases were used. The case on the base was only about 1in in length, to cut down on the risk of splinters and shrapnel. To give obturation a rim was spun out of the base case, which was wider than even the 1.76in tube. These were inserted in the factory with a giant press forcing the charge into

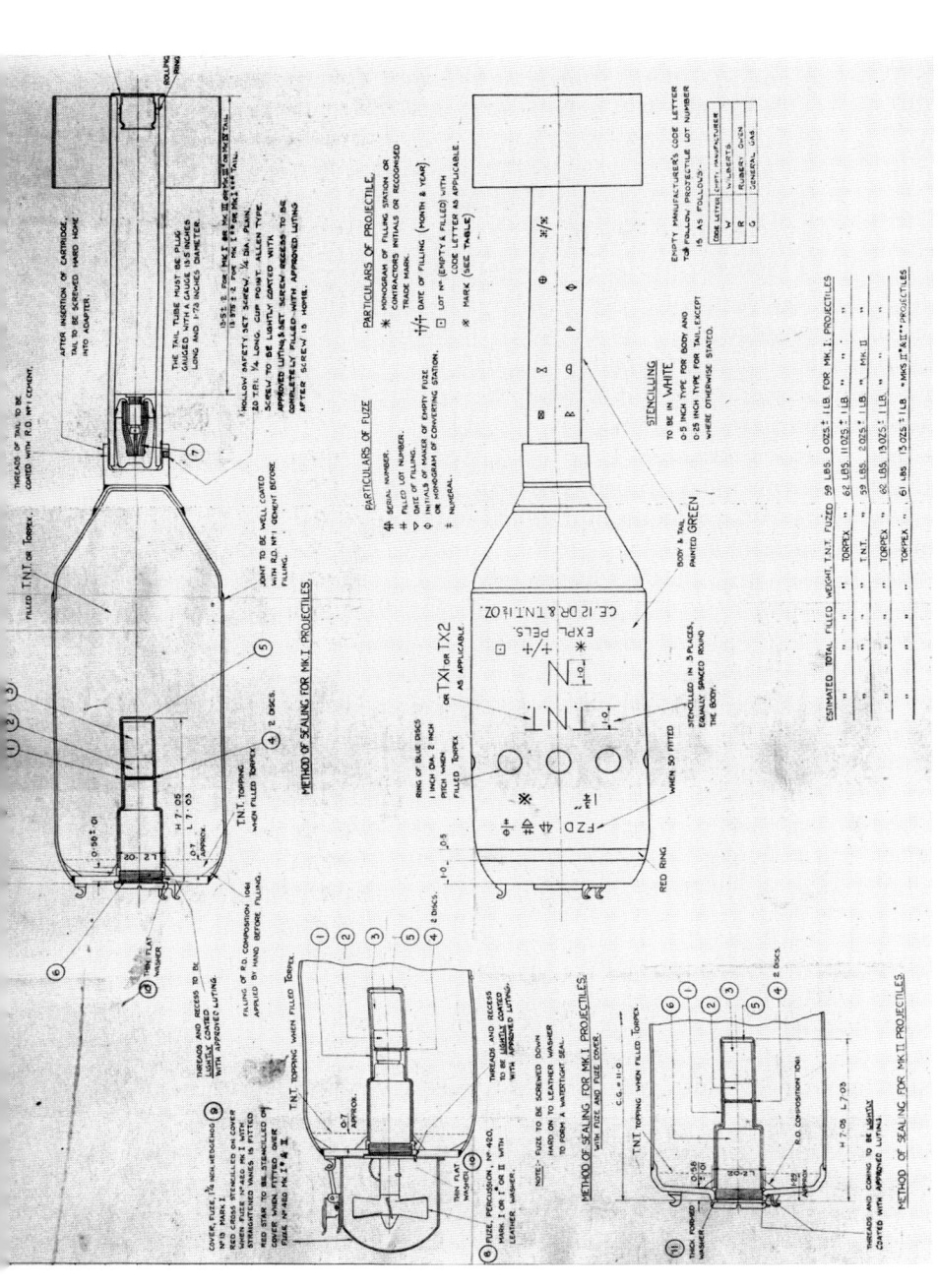

Plans of the Mk II Hedgehog round. Of note is the diagram of the nose with the fuse fitted, showing the domed fuse cover and the latch holding it in place.

position, and this meant that the Hedgehog was classified by the navy as a fixed round.

In February and March 1941 the issue of fusing was tackled. The principal problem was that the fuse had to work on contact with a submarine hull, but had to be inert when it impacted on the surface of the water, and had the requirement to arm itself at a depth of 10ft, so that the next impact would trigger the fuse. At the time there was nothing in the UK inventory that would come close to achieving this.

The Chief Engineer of Artillery Design (CEAD) was tasked to work on the problem and came forward with a design which had 187 parts, which proved to be utterly impractical. The DMWD collected all the ideas about solving the fuse problem and sat down with a technical staff to assess each in turn. Three were selected as the most likely to succeed, however, detailed investigations proved all to be unworkable. CEAD by this time had produced a fuse that had a large protruding ring that jutted out in front of the projectile. While this fuse worked, the trigger ring caused all sorts of problems with the trajectory of the projectile and so had to be cancelled. The DMWD consulted with a private individual, Mr P.H. Lindley, who had been working on a fuse for another project. Mr Lindley provided the details of his fuse, where a trigger weight was held in place by a series of balls. Captain Hawes began work with the Halls Telephone company to develop a fuse and they took Mr Lindley's design and modified the tumblers, this fuse becoming the Type H. On 3 March 1941 this design was presented at a meeting of all concerned, including a representative from CEAD. At the following meeting, on the 18th, CEAD produced designs of a new fuse, which worked identically to the Type H, although the small details were different. This fuse would become the No. 420 fuse and was adopted for service. The fuse worked by having a large weight held in place by a rod. This rod was linked to a propeller. As the projectile fell through the water the propeller unscrewed freeing the weight to slide to the front of the fuse. The weight pulled the striker with it, tensioning a spring. The striker was retained in place by the ball, which was pinched between the weight and the striker. Upon impact the momentum caused the striker to loosen the contact on the ball, which fell out of the way. The spring tension on the striker then asserted itself over the forward momentum and slammed the striker backwards, which triggered the primary explosive.

On 8 June 1941 a meeting was convened to decide which weapon would be adopted as the primary ahead thrown weapon. At this time there were only two still in the running, the Hedgehog and the Fairlie Mortar. The meeting broke down into a series of disagreements about the effectiveness of the warhead size, and if the Hedgehog's 30lb charge was needed, the Fairlie team asserting that it was not. This was countered with the accusation that the

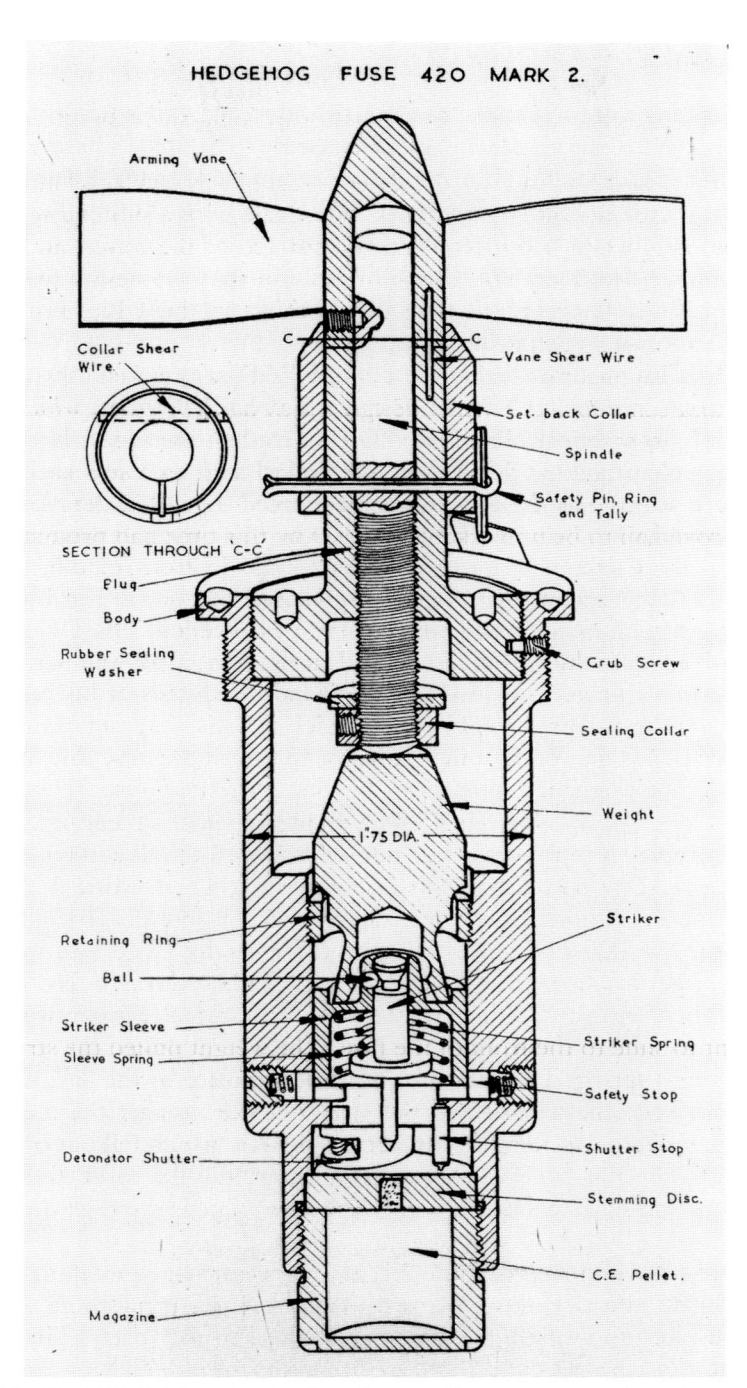

Plans of the No. 420 Mk 2 fuse showing how the propeller unscrews to release the weight. The ball bearing which is integral to the design is rather difficult to spot, but it is offset to the left and marked 'ball'.

90 Defeating the Panzer-Stuka Menace

Fairlie Mortar's solid steel nose would shield the target from the full force of the blast. To settle the argument asset trials were to be held. These took place on the Clyde against a 15mm plate, in addition to tests at the Road Research Laboratory (RRL), organized by the DMWD, to see if the steel nose would have the shielding effect. Both trials went against the Fairlie Mortar, although the champions of the weapon disputed the findings of the RRL. The Clyde trials showed that the Hedgehog would guarantee damage to the plate at a distance 6.5ft, while the 20lb charge had a radius of just over half that at 3.75ft. Thus, on 8 August 1941, the Hedgehog was selected as the preferred ahead thrown weapon. The final report on the matter would be issued a month later on 18 September. The Fairlie Mortar project would be ended. There were other factors in support of the decision, the Hedgehog project being much more advanced in its development despite the Fairlie Mortar having a significant head start. This was especially noticeable with regards to the fuse, as the Fairlie had not had any fuse work done on it at all, while the No. 420 was fully operational. As a curious side note, it was this report that also ended development of the colossal 13.5in Vickers O Thrower.

The first production equipment was produced later in September, and first fired from the land at Whitchurch, and subsequently fitted to HMS *Westcott*

View of HMS *Westcott*'s Hedgehog launcher. The salvo is armed with the protective caps removed and ready to be fired.

for demonstrations. The land-based firings were held in front of Winston Churchill and went perfectly. The equipment was then fitted to the destroyer at Liverpool. She was to be provided with several live rounds. But on the morning of her departure there was no sign of the truck carrying the projectiles, which had got lost overnight. Luckily, the truck arrived at the eleventh hour, and HMS *Westcott* was able to sail on time.

HMS *Westcott*'s first target was a wreck in Liverpool Bay. This provided a good ASDIC return for sighting and a solid surface that would cause the projectiles to detonate. Several single rounds were fired, followed by a full live salvo. All rounds functioned perfectly. Next HMS *Westcott* headed for the Clyde. There she met up with a British submarine, which provided a moving target. In eight attack runs against the submarine using dummy rounds, five hits were scored. After the last attack, the submarine surfaced with a projectile still lodged in its hull. The Hedgehog had proved itself without a doubt, and the decision to fit it to the entire escort fleet was taken.

Development of the Hedgehog and related items (described in one document as 'Hedgehoggery') would continue over the following years, while the weapon was in service. However, with introduction came a change in overseeing the deployment to service. The DMWD handed everything over to the Department for Torpedoes and Mining (DTM), and all the personnel involved with the DMWD were re-tasked to new projects. This led to what should have been one of the greatest scandals of the Second World War, but due to wartime secrecy no one knew of it until today.

Chapter Eight

The Great Hedgehog Scandal

To give some idea of the appeal of the Hedgehog one needs to compare the chances of scoring a hit on a U-boat. In the early days of development, a theoretically calculated 100 per cent hit rate had been claimed. However, this was widely regarded as suspicious even at the time, and later on a revised calculation produced a hit rate of 50–60 per cent. Other sources give an estimated figure as low as 48 per cent, but all these calculated figures are about the same, and this is several times the probability of a ten-depth-charge pattern. Equally, the depth-charge hit might not result in a kill, but a Hedgehog round had a good chance of sinking the U-boat due to being in contact with the submarine's hull when it detonated. Thus, the Hedgehog was a weapon that would massively increase the kill rate of the Royal Navy against the U-boats, just as the Battle of the Atlantic was beginning to escalate in earnest.

At the start of 1942 about ninety U-boats were assigned to the Atlantic. Later in the year around 140 U-boats would be operational. Despite this small number Allied ship losses rose significantly in the first quarter, forty-eight in January, seventy-three in February and ninety-eight in March, with the total tonnage lost doubling. Most of this was due to the U-boats operating off the coast of the USA which was largely unprepared. However, during the rest of 1942 Allied losses seem to remain at just over 100 vessels, equalling around 540,000 tons, each month.

During the first quarter, only six U-boats were sunk by Allied warships, and later in the year the number would average about four per month and never exceed six. Most of those losses were caused by depth charges. If the Hedgehog had been used to its full effect the monthly U-boat losses to warships could have been up to a colossal twenty per month. This combined with the increasing losses to aircraft, the U-boats would have been hammered to the extent that the Battle of the Atlantic would have been over almost immediately, with significantly fewer losses to Allied merchants.

The reasons for the lack of effect with the Hedgehog are varied. One of the lesser reasons was the fire-control gear or rather lack of it. Two fire-control devices were designed by the Director of Naval Ordnance (DNO): Type A and Type B. The Type A, built by Vickers Crayford, had a control box fixed to the back of the blast shield near the gunner himself. This used mercury switches to control the gyro, and give out a reading of the ship's roll, the gunner then using a hand wheel to follow the pointer, which was linked to the beams to create roll correction. It was an entirely new design specifically for the Hedgehog. Type B, however, used a much more standard Evershed & Vignoles fire-control gyro linked to a powered follow-up drive. The gyro box was fitted below the deck and used a transmission to the controls. Type B had a bearing input, which was linked to the bridge, where any offset could be set, and then the system would automatically apply the offset to the roll display for the gunner.

Both systems were produced in roughly equal numbers as neither one nor the other could be produced in sufficient quantities. Indeed, only a few Hedgehogs were fitted in all of 1941, with the bulk being fitted the following year. By the end of 1942 about 250 Hedgehogs had been built, with 200 fitted, and the rate of fitting was a steady twenty per month.

But the lack of fire-control systems meant that many of the early Hedgehogs were fitted without this piece of equipment. It was not until May 1942 that sufficient production of both types meant that all Hedgehogs could be installed complete, and have enough spare to retrofit to the mountings that were missing this essential part.

Another problem with the Type B was that the vertical datum had to be set manually by the gunner. This involved a significant amount of training to be wholly accurate, and the lack of instruction was the main cause of the Hedgehog's problems. When the DTM took over the Hedgehog project there was a new crop of officers who had no idea of the weapon's capabilities now running the project. The only person on each ship fitted with a Hedgehog given any training on the weapon was the ship's Anti-Submarine Warfare (ASW) officer. This individual was given a short and inadequate course at HMS *Osprey* when his ship was being fitted with the Hedgehog. No maintenance or other training was given to the ship's company. In January 1942 a handbook on the weapon was issued, however, it was wrong in so many respects it might as well have not been produced. A supplement was issued in July, but only covered parts of the fire-control gear and even this was not widely available until November 1943. In addition, many of the shore-based officers did not even know of the existence of the handbook, and certainly did not know the weapon, which led to some Hedgehogs being fitted incorrectly. In some vessels, upon inspection, the Hedgehog mount was rusted solid due to lack of maintenance.

One can imagine a ship's company returning to their vessel after a refit, and in place of the forward gun mount was this contraption. Assuming the ship had a fully working Hedgehog system, the company had no idea how to operate it, how to maintain it or what it did and no way of finding out. Is it any surprise then that vessels stuck to throwing depth charges over the back, as that was well understood, limitations and all.

94 *Defeating the Panzer-Stuka Menace*

Thus at the height of the Battle of the Atlantic Britain had developed a weapon that would have swept the U-boats from the sea, but no one had any idea of how to use it, and the Royal Navy was left fighting the battle with First World War era weaponry.

The Hedgehog was so misunderstood and disliked the crews were just not using it. Part of this feeling was generated by the lack of explosions. With a depth charge, there was a very definite explosion and a colossal plume of water. With Hedgehog there was no visible sign on the surface unless a round hit and the U-boat was forced to arise from the depths. This lack of feedback led to negative feelings on behalf of the sailors. Up until November 1942 only sixteen salvos from the Hedgehog had been fired, all without a hit. Thus, in autumn 1942 orders were issued from the Director of Anti-Submarine Warfare (DA/SW) to use the Hedgehog.

On 12 November 1942, as part of the escort forces to Operation Torch, two Flower class corvettes were on patrol near Oran when they detected *U-660*. Both corvettes began to prosecute the hunt against this contact. After some time HMS *Lotus* (K130) had expended her entire complement of forty

A Hedgehog launcher onboard the Flower class corvette HHMS *Tompazis* of the Greek Navy. This ship was formally known as HMS *Tamarisk* before being transferred to the Greeks. Note the second salvo on the floor ready for loading, this is most certainly not official Royal Navy practice, however, the bombs are not fused so would present minimal risk.

depth charges against the submarine, to no effect. They still had the contact but had nothing else to fire at it, until someone remembered their Hedgehog. It is possible that several attacks were needed, considering the amount of guesswork that went into the use of the weapon, but eventually they scored a hit, and *U-660* became the first U-boat to be sunk by the Hedgehog.

The problems around the use of Hedgehog persisted throughout 1943. For example, in the second half of the year, a total of fifty-three Hedgehog salvos were fired, which resulted in a grand total of four U-boats destroyed. This comes out as just 7.5 per cent hit chance. During the same period, depth-charge patterns had dropped in effectiveness to about 3.3 per cent. The likely cause of this was that U-boats had become faster, more agile and with deeper diving depth. Equally, most of the German captains now had some experience of evading a depth-charge attack. Even though the Hedgehog had twice the chance of an effective hit, it was still woefully below the capabilities of the weapon.

In January 1944 the Admiralty realized that the Hedgehog was performing poorly and set up a Hedgehog analysis unit at Londonderry. The unit ran a series of tests in an exercise area with randomly selected ships of the escort fleet from 21 January–3 February 1944. Experts in all fields of every aspect of Hedgehoggery were present on board the ship to review every step of the attack. An H Class Submarine was provided to serve as a target and would be travelling between 2 and 6 knots, and the experts recorded every detail about the attacks. On some days, weather permitting, an autogyro was on station to photograph the exercises. Thirty-six escorts were visited, and these carried out a total of ninety-five attacks. Only a direct hit on the submarine was considered a success, and a salvo was discounted if more than six projectiles failed to fire, which happened some seventeen times during the trial.

Of the ships, only six had crews who knew of the handbook, which was still woefully inaccurate. This lead to incorrect drills and poor commands which often arrived late or were confusing. However, in twenty-eight attacks hits were scored, which translated to a massive 30 per cent hit rate. A further eleven (12 per cent) of the patterns were placed around the submarine, with no hits. Six of those salvos were down to distorted patterns. Two of the attacks were carried out on targets other than the submarine.

The analysis unit found the main causes of missing, although there were others, were down to errors mainly from the ASDIC giving a false range, or it being interpreted wrongly by the operators. The main culprit was the range recorder. This, as the name suggests, was used to determine the range to the target. If this was calibrated incorrectly then the range displayed would be wrong, and thus the pattern would be placed long or short. In every single ship visited the range recorder was set up incorrectly to some degree. In thirteen vessels every aspect of the range recorder was incorrectly calibrated, in the rest, only some parts of the system were out of balance. The analysis unit made several discreet enquiries and found that in 90 per centof cases the equipment had been set up incorrectly by base staff. Equally, about 50 per cent of the ships had crews who did not know how to line up the range recorders themselves, and the crews on two-thirds did not know why these settings were chosen.

When the results were compared to the ships companies, evaluations showed that the ships with a Good or in some cases Excellent rating tended to have better results with the Hedgehog. Twenty-one of the ships accounted for all hits in the test. These were the well-run ships with excellent drills and maintenance, as well as motivation to understand what they were doing. This led to the analysis unit concluding that a well-run ship would manage to land the pattern around the U-boat three out of five times.

These findings obviously affected the situation, as operational kill rates started to rise. Presumably, the problems uncovered were tackled incrementally. In the first six months of 1944 seventy-eight salvos were fired against targets, twelve (15.5 per cent) hit. In the second half thirty-two with nine (28 per cent) hits. Finally, in the first half of 1945, the Hedgehog reached its best performance thirty-five salvos with ten (28.5 per cent) hits. Lessons had been learnt from the introduction of the Hedgehog, and when the Squid was brought into service in 1943 and 1944 the crews were given extensive training at the time of the refit.

A typical prosecution of a U-boat contact is the encounter between *U-641* and HMS *Violet*, a Flower class corvette. On 19 January 1944, HMS *Violet* was in the outer ring of escorts for convoy OS.65/KMS.39. This was a joint convoy that was sailing together for added protection as they crossed the Bay of Biscay, then once on the other side, the two groups would split. *U-641* was the only U-boat in position to intercept the convoy, and it began to approach for an attack. At 1901 a possible ASDIC contact was detected by HMS *Violet*. This was listed as 'doubtful' mainly due to the inexperience of the crewman who was operating the ASDIC set. This particular crewman was trained to stand watches but was not a fully qualified operator. The corvette reduced her speed to 5 knots and started to close on the possible contact, while an experienced operator was summoned to the bridge. In less than a minute the new operator confirmed it was a U-boat, some 1,800yd away. HMS *Violet* continued to approach and at 1,300yd *U-641* started to turn away, moving at a speed of 2 knots. At 1912 HMS *Violet* increased to her attack speed of 8 knots, and the steering control was passed to the ASDIC operator. At 1917 (and 45 seconds) the U-boat was judged to be at 220yd, this uncertainty was due to the wake from the U-boat degrading the ASDIC return, and the Hedgehog was fired. After 16 seconds two explosions were heard, followed 2 seconds later by a third. As HMS *Violet* passed over the plotted contact position she released a floating flare to mark the position.

At 1921 the contact was regained by the ASDIC operator, although he would later describe the contact as 'woolly' due to the turbulence from the explosions. HMS *Violet* extended out to 1,500yd and turned back in towards the U-boat at 1928. By now the ASDIC had lost contact, however, the flare marked the position so the corvette made another attack run. She reached the flare at 1935 and a large oil slick was spotted. At this point, the captain of HMS *Violet* opted not to fire, and passed over the U-boat's position. As she passed over the attack site a large explosion was heard by the entire crew, followed by noises of U-boat breaking up heard in the engine room. The ASDIC operator could not confirm as the wake of the corvette was blocking his sensors. On the third pass, the oil slick was now 277m by 185m, and a sample was taken by dragging a sack through the water, although no efforts were taken to preserve the sample so it had degraded by the time HMS *Violet* reached port.

It is likely that in this case *U-641* was on the edge of the Hedgehog pattern and was hit by three bombs. She then began sinking until, 18 minutes later, she reached crush depth and imploded.

Although some of the reasons for the failure of the Hedgehog were due to training and other systems, there were also significant technical issues and further improvements of the weapon in service.

One of the first modifications made, in autumn 1941, was to increase the pattern size. The DMWD looked at the pattern and realized that it needed to be placed with an extremely high degree of accuracy to achieve an effect. Thus, it was considered that increasing the pattern size would increase the chances to hit and deal with any errors. The first fifty Hedgehogs produced were therefore Mk I weapons with the original 100ft circle. From Mk II the pattern became an oval 140ft in length and 120ft wide. It was desirable to increase the size of the pattern even further but the limits of the mount restricted the maximum distance.

In April 1942, after experiencing some terrible weather, which would later carry away the ship's radar, HMS *Keppel* was prosecuting an attack on a U-boat. When she fired her pattern a large number of projectiles failed and remained on their spigots. Earlier in the year, on 18 March, the same ship had fired a salvo, and one of the rounds had misfired and landed on the deck near the bow. This was found to be down to two reasons. First, water had entered the cartridges, and then the rough weather had bounced the projectiles off the electrical contact on the spigots. The solution to these problems was considered fairly simplistic, but worked. To prevent water ingress to the cartridges they had cement and luting applied during construction to seal joints. The base of the tail tube had a wad of cloth around it to prevent water

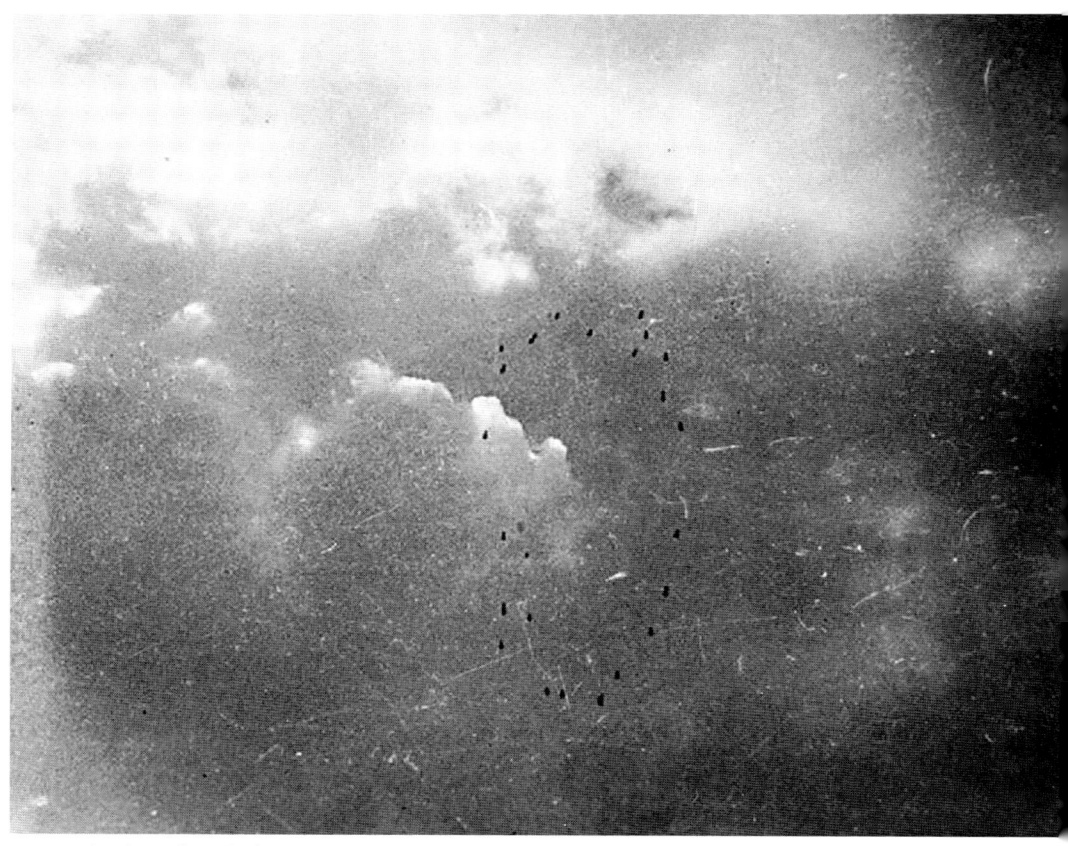

A salvo of Hedgehog rounds in mid-flight. The elliptical circle pattern forming can be seen.

entering via that route. To solve the bouncing problem the ripple switch was modified so that the length of the salvo was increased from 1 second to 2. This allowed the electrical contacts to receive current for twice the length of time, and so that any projectiles that had bounced out of contact were able to settle back into contact while there was still current to the spigot, and therefore would allow the charge to fire. Seawater entry also caused some problems with the Type A fire-control system, as the box was on the back of the blast shield it received much more of a deluge than the Type B which had a large portion of its electrical system below decks. This was not considered unusual and was seen as par for the course with electrical equipment on deck.

The last technical issue and the most concerning was a series of premature detonations in late 1942. Upon striking the water surface the rounds would instantly explode. This was attributed to the fuse failing. Thus, new propeller vanes were used which meant the bomb armed a bit deeper than before, and a weaker spring was substituted. This last change meant that the spring would not be affected by age as the older, stronger one had been.

As well as tackling technical problems as they occurred, the Hedgehog went through several technical improvements during its life. In several ships it was deemed important to retain the A turret. On vessels like the Flower class corvette, which only had a single frontal gun turret, the Hedgehog was mounted elsewhere, for example, to the right rear of the gun. On other vessels, such as the Bittern class sloop, this was not an option. For that reason, a split Hedgehog was designed. There would be two mountings on each side of the ship, each of which would hold two beams. The controls were on the starboard mounting. These were initially to be mechanically linked with cables, however, this quickly proved impractical. If the cables were too tight then the entire mount became locked up. If they were too loose then the beams would not track correctly and would overreact to inputs. The solution was to use a hydraulic system, using oil as a fluid. The mechanical power was provided by jacks normally used in aircraft control surfaces manufactured by Dowty Equipment Company. The first ship to be fitted with this equipment was HMS *Enchantress*. It was soon discovered that the jacks employed were too weak for the job, so stronger parts were manufactured. The first of these were fitted in April 1943 to HMS *Fowey*. A total of about thirty-five ships were fitted with the split Hedgehog.

On 3 October 1941 a U-boat slipped from the North Sea into the harbour at Barrow-in-Furness. *U-570*, soon to be HMS *Graph*, was unusually flying the White Ensign, having been captured in August. During most of September she had been in Iceland being sufficiently repaired to return to

A split-Hedgehog. One does wonder why the port mounting has a full blast shield when there would be no gunner standing behind needing to be protected.

the UK. Here the Royal Navy had a huge opportunity to study a Germans vessel, and every aspect of *U-570* was analysed. It also presented the opportunity of testing out the Hedgehog against a German U-boat, or at least a close approximation of one, as HMS *Graph* was too valuable to use as a target. Thus, the steel in *U-570*'s hull was compared with British steels, and while an exact match could not be found, one type was close. Using this they built several half-scale replicas of a cross-section from a U-boat hull. Twenty-nine trail firings were carried out against these targets in January 1942. The results were somewhat concerning for the Admiralty.

If the ballast tanks of the U-Boat were empty then the current Hedgehog round could get splinters through to penetrate the pressure hull, if they were filled then the round would have no chance of sinking the U-boat, but would likely cause enough damage to force the U-boat to surface. The production rounds for the Hedgehog were filled with 31lb of TNT. The absolute minimum to split the pressure hull was 36lb of TNT. Thus, it became clear that the efficiency of the projectiles had to be increased as quickly as possible.

The obvious and simplest option was to fill with a different explosive. The one that was immediately suggested was Torpex, which would have the same effect as an estimated 41lb of TNT. It should be noted that some other sources claimed Torpex was actually 50 per cent more effective, and one, a US ordnance manual, claimed it was 141 per cent more effective than TNT! In any case, it would significantly increase the explosive power and thus the damage the Hedgehog projectile could inflict. However, at that time the production of the explosive was just starting and current stocks levels meant it was unavailable for use. Comparative trials were arranged to see if Minol could be used instead and if Torpex would provide the required explosive punch. At the same time, discussions were held to consider simply increasing the size of the Hedgehog round, something relatively straightforward to do with a spigot weapon. The maximum weight projectile that the Hedgehog could fire was a round with a total weight of 100lb, which was one with a filling weight of about 53lb. The other consideration was the size of the ammunition lockers and other transport arrangements. This meant that the limit was about 92lb. There was the scope for a bigger size if a flush fuse like the Type H was fitted, and development of this was expected to be completed by about mid-1942. This target was not achieved as there were increasing technical difficulties until the Type H was abandoned in mid-1942. Studies were to be carried out for 42lb TNT in an 80lb projectile, as well as a 50lb warhead in a 92lb round. It was also later suggested to fill the bombs with a mix of TNT and RDX, however, this was rejected in March.

By the end of April, it became clear that alteration to a larger projectile would take longer than sufficient production of Torpex. Policy was set to continue with filling the current projectile with Torpex 2, although it would require a new body with a hole in the top to pour the explosive into. The existing projectile weighed 60lb and could carry 33lb of Torpex 2, although there may have been a layer of TNT at the top of the bomb, possibly due to problems with filling. Both Mk I and Mk II projectiles would be filled with Torpex, and the filling rate of 800 rounds per month could be achieved. As the Torpex-filled rounds became available they were issued in the UK, but stockpiles of TNT-filled rounds in the USA were to be used up first.

At about the same time as there were concerns on the lethality of the TNT-filled projectiles, the Admiralty began to consider countermeasures to the Hedgehog and how to defeat them. The most obvious defence to the Hedgehog in the Admiralty's mind was to fit armour plating to the tops of the U-boats. The answer to this was to develop a shaped charge Hedgehog projectile. Once the development was completed in about mid-1942 the weapon was not put into production. Instead, reports of attacks on U-boats were analysed, and if a sudden increase of hits with no effect was spotted in the data it would only take a few weeks to start producing the shaped charge rounds. One must question if the *Kriegsmarine* knew about the Hedgehog, and how it functioned. The lack of information available to the Germans would be due to the results on a hit or a miss on a U-boat. If the weapon hit, the U-boat was likely in trouble and would be forced to the surface or sunk, and thus unable to report back. If the Hedgehog salvo missed, then the U-boat crew would never know it was under attack as the projectiles would sink to the seabed or crush depth, and hopefully never be heard from again. This later point about projectiles being lost in the depth was sharply highlighted on 1 October 1942 when a report arrived at the DMWD stating that a number of 'bombs' had been recovered at Thornaby-on-Tees by No. 16 Bomb Disposal Section. The report stated that 'bombs' had been dropped by enemy aircraft. On inspection of the photographs of the 'bombs' it was found out that they were Hedgehog practice rounds used during development trials that had washed up on the beach. This was considered a security breach due to the projectiles carrying markings that listed them as anti-submarine weapons, in the form of an 'A/S' marking. Realizing that in the future a projectile could theoretically end up on a German-held beach, and give the game away, the A/S part of the marking was removed.

At the start of 1942, the US Navy adopted the Hedgehog for their escort fleet and produced a weapon called the Mk 10. Although it was largely identical to the British version, with the fire-control gear operated in exactly the same way as the British Type A, it was produced in the USA and manufactured differently. One of the changes was switching the roll correction handwheel for a double-crank design. This was applied in the British Mk III Hedgehog projector, but operational use showed no benefit to either method. Ammunition was modified to suit US manufacturing methods, and the

No. 420 fuse, slightly modified, became the Mk 136 in US service. The Admiralty advised the US Navy to make the frames of the projectors slightly wider, which they did. This allowed the US Navy to produce a Mk 11 weapon, which had a pattern with a circle of 180ft. At the time this was seen as a marked improvement, although there was no evidence taken from US operations in the Pacific to support the view.

With Victory in Europe, the Admiralty's thoughts turned towards Japan, and a number of vessels were to be prepared to join the current UK fleet in that theatre. For anti-submarine warfare, the Squid was seen as a much better option than the Hedgehog. But not all ships could be equipped with Squid in time. Thus, an improvement plan for the Hedgehog was devised. The first change was to modify the mount with powered roll correction. The ripple switches were all changed to the automatic type that had first appeared in 1944. In this design, a gramophone record motor would power the handle sweeping the arm over the contacts. The firing signal for this was linked directly to the ship's ASDIC range recorder. Manual backups for all these systems were provided as well. However, before long the Japanese surrendered and the war was over.

The Hedgehog was the best chance the UK had to win the Battle of the Atlantic a lot earlier than it did, but was let down by the means of its introduction (a fault that was not repeated when Squid was introduced the year afterwards). With the ending of the war, the Hedgehog had been surpassed by newer developments, such as the idea of fitting the Squid with a magnetic fuse, which was planned to come into service in the near future, and such plans were likely related to the Limbo anti-submarine weapon that entered service in 1955. But for a few brief years the Hedgehog gave sterling service around the globe, and once its teething troubles had been sorted out it became a weapon that helped conquer the U-boats.

PART FOUR

MISCELLANEOUS NAVAL SPIGOT WEAPONS

MUSTARD PLASTER, WATER HAMMER AND HEDGEROW

Chapter Nine

Mustard Plaster

It has been shown how the Hedgehog came about through the need for a more effective way of attacking a submarine. The problem had been tackled before the concept of the ahead thrown weapons emerged, and would in time be related to the Hedgehog, although fail to be more than an academic idea for several reasons.

In 1935 the Royal Navy became aware of a proposal for a connected wire device. This worked by two charges being connected together by a wire. As the warship passed over the submarine the device was heaved overboard. One would presume that first one charge and then when the wire was fully extended the second charge would be launched over the stern. The concept was that this wire would sink, and should it become draped over the U-boat the charges would be brought into close contact with the submarine and then detonate. It is interesting to note that the basic principles behind the Hedgehog were present in this device, such as smaller charges detonating in contact with the submarine, and a weapon that would comb the entire column of water on its way down. The smaller charge of the warheads would allow many more devices to be carried and therefore improve the endurance of the warship. Some tank tests were carried out, but the results showed too many negative features. First, the wire had a very low TV, and thus the submarine would have plenty of time to dodge the attack. But most crucially the tension in the wire actually drew the charges together as it sunk, meaning the deeper it went the smaller the area it was covering. With these results, all work on the project was dropped.

In 1941 the idea was revisited, and, furthermore, detailed quarter scale trials were held. The full-sized weapon would be a streamlined projectile 28in long, weighing in at about 100lb with a 40lb explosive filler. Two of these would be placed on racks at the stern of the craft and one would be dispatched over the side, then when the 60ft wire reached full extension the other charge would be dragged overboard. To minimize the shock of the second charge being dragged off the rack a closed coil untempered spring was used as a shock absorber between the charge and the wire. Various types of springs were tested, and it was found that bronze was superior to steel. A 18.5in-long spring could absorb some 2,500ft lb of energy. With one of these shock absorbers at each end of the cord, piano wire of just 15swg, less than 2mm thick, could be used. This was calculated to have a TV of 15fps. Trials found that where the shock absorbers were connected to the projectile had an effect on how the device performed. When the shock absorbers were attached to the extreme end of the tails the charges had an attitude of 60 degrees from the vertical with the wire taught, but a low descent speed. With the connections placed 12in from the tail end, near the centre of the projectile the previous behaviour of the charges being drawn together resulted. It was found that the best of both choices was to have the connection about 8in from the tail. If the later US trials were indicative, the sinking speed increase could be as much as 50 per cent, and the projectiles would be at about 16 degrees from vertical.

An estimated chance of success was calculated at 30 per cent with eight such devices located on the stern of a ship, if the U-boat was travelling at right angles to the attacking ship and quite shallow. This also assumed that a wire making contact would result in a kill, which was seen as doubtful due to the presence of wires and rigging from the conning tower to the ends of the hull, which would mean the wire would simply slip off the submarine. Equally, if the submarine was parallel to the course of the ship the probability of a hit would fall to near zero. This chance also applied if the submarine was deep due to the low TV. Because of these limitations, the idea was once again dropped.

The idea resurfaced again almost immediately when a serving Royal Navy officer came up with a scheme very similar to the one described above and forwarded it to the Torpedo School, HMS *Vernon*. The commander of the school rejected the idea stating that replacing current equipment would be prohibitively expensive and that there was a significant risk of fouling the wire during laying, and then the warship would be towing a live charge, with another on deck.

In January 1944 Lieutenant Kent of the Royal Canadian Navy Volunteer Reserve came up with a new take on the wire-connected device, which he codenamed 'Mustard Plaster'. It should be noted that all these suggestions from serving officers were utterly independent of each other and are examples of people coming up with what they think is a bright idea and being utterly ignorant of the previous attempts.

Mustard Plaster started life as a single Hedgehog round and spigot which was connected to a 210yd-long wire. At the other end of the wire was a 260lb lead weight. The Hedgehog projectile was fired ahead as normal, then when the full length of the wire was played out it would pull the weight overboard. If the line caught on a U-boat, the weight would continue to fall and drag the Hedgehog projectile into contact with the U-boat. It would require completely new fuse, which was never developed, and suffered the usual problems of connected wire devices.

Later in 1944, the USA started to carry out tests of air dropped connected wire devices, first at Morris Dam, then in 1945 at the Glen Fruin Research Station. These confirmed the findings of the Admiralty from 1941, but the inherent problems of connected wire devices and the ending of the war brought this avenue of research to a close.

Chapter Ten

Water Hammer

In June 1941 the DMWD started work on Project 11, which bore the name Water Hammer. At the time there was a requirement to fire anti-submarine projectiles of varying sizes ahead of the craft. However, on smaller craft, such as anti-submarine trawlers, the deck blow from these weapons would be far too high and do considerable structural damage should they be fired.

The concept was simple, to create a weapon where the recoil force would drive a plate through the water around the vessel, which would provide significant resistance and absorb some of the recoil. There would still be a deck blow as the weapon had to be attached to the ship in some way, but the reduced force might be manageable.

The theory behind the idea is that water can absorb the recoil in one of two ways. Either by setting up a compression wave between the recoiling plate and the body of water or by the simple viscosity of the water. In the Water Hammer there was never a compression wave formed, as it would require a colossal recoiling plate.

The Water Hammer ready for its trials. The device would be lowered over the side and attached to the pier before the testing started, however, one can see the sheer size of the springs needed.

Water Hammer 109

In essence, the design was that of a dynamic spigot, with a large plate at the base of the spigot, that rested in the water. There were a pair of springs involved to absorb some of the recoil force and to return the spigot to its firing position. This was mounted onto a heavy flame, which was then positioned attached to a jetty so that at high tide the recoil plate would be in the water.

The spigot was 1.125in in calibre, which is 28.5mm. It is possible this was used to allow the Water Hammer to use Bombard tails. Indeed, one of the shots fired from this weapon was listed as 14lb, and the projectile looks identical to a Bombard anti-personnel round. The other projectiles weighed 60 and 20lb, although interestingly the 20lb round was not the Bombard anti-tank. Each charge was fired by an electrical contact much like that of a Hedgehog, and the propellant charges contained either 15g of slow-burning

Plans of the Water Hammer.

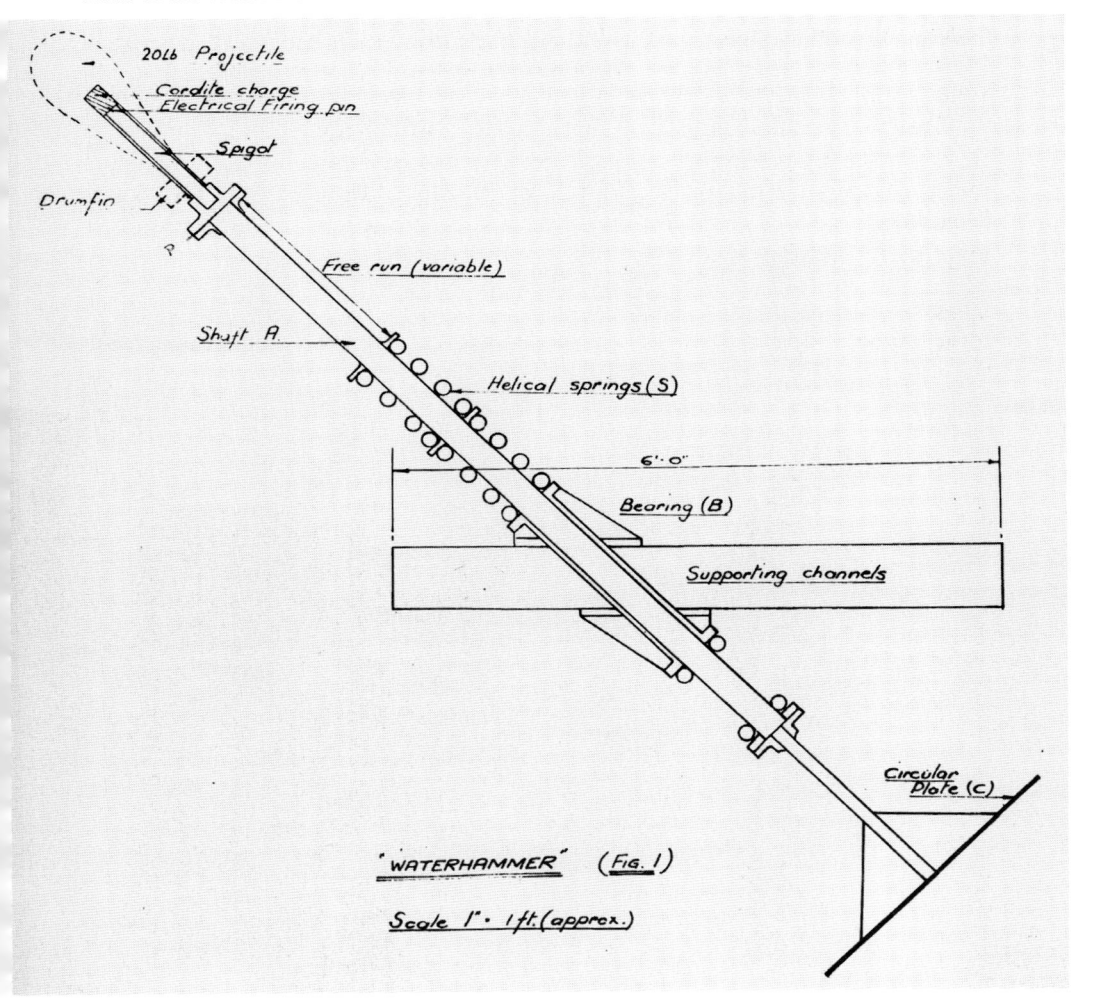

cordite or 17.5g of a mixture of fast and slow-burning cordite. There was also an interchangeable set of recoil plates, either 2 or 3ft, and springs that could be varied between lighter or heavier weights. The number of springs on the Water Hammer could also be varied.

Eight shots were fired with the apparatus. Two each of the 20lb and 14lb, with the remainder with 60lb projectiles. The 60lb rounds flew between 200 and 250yd, the 20lb projectile 700yd and the 14lb 1,000yd. Four rounds were fired because two sets of skirts were fitted to the recoil plate to see if they had any effect. One of the skirts was perforated. Both actually performed worse than the unskirted plate. The overall results were that the deck blow could be expected to be halved. This appears to be a rough average as some results only gave a 33 per cent reduction in deck blow, while others achieved 66 and 73 per cent reductions.

In the end, it seems that the project was abandoned because of the fixed nature of the weapon, as it could not be aimed or correct for roll in any fashion. To add these features would require considerable technical difficulties

Water Hammer ammunition ready for the trials, the smallest appears to be either a 14lb with no fuse or a practice round. The middle round at first glance looks like a Bombard 20lb, however, on closer inspection, it is a different shape. There is at least one photograph of an identical projectile being loaded into a Bombard during a routine demonstration so it maybe this is the 15/20lb practice round. The final round resembles a Hedgehog body mounted directly to a Bombard tail.

and development. Equally, to fit even a basic weapon would require the ship to be dry-docked and significant alterations made to the fabric of the craft.

A final clue might be in the earlier mention of the cancellation of the O Thrower in early August 1941. It seems likely that there was a large cull of existing ahead thrown weapon projects as the ideas fell out of favour, and the Water Hammer was abandoned at about this time.

Chapter Eleven

The Hedgerow

After the fall of France it was obvious that Britain would have to retake the continent and plans for this started to be laid very early on. These initial ideas and reviews spawned multiple questions about how to defeat obstacles to the successful invasion. It is a testament to the amount of preparation that it took the Allies some three to four years of planning and technical work before they felt ready to launch the attack, and even then it was a lot closer than they thought. These problems were assigned to committees to study the problems and come up with ideas to defeat their specified threat, an example would be the Anti-Concrete Committee with the scope to consider how to defeat the thousands of tons of concrete obstacles and bunkers the Germans were building. Another of these was the Land-Mines Sub-Committee, the scope of which was to consider how to defeat the minefields that the Germans would undoubtedly be laying in huge numbers along the Atlantic Wall. From this committee's work came vehicles like the Sherman Crab. The committee started looking at all the ways they could defeat landmines, and in the British archives was a set of notes on a series of experiments carried out in 1935 where the pressure wave from an explosive charge was used to detonate landmines.

Landmines of the time used the same basic principle. The fuse would contain a sheer wire and when the mine was tripped, the sheer wire would be broken, which would release the striker triggering a detonator. The countermining charge worked by the force of the explosion breaking the sheer wire and thus causing the mine to detonate itself.

The research into mines generally used British Mk II and Mk IV mines as well as a few samples of *Tellermine* 35 (TMi35). Later a few samples of TMi42 and 43 were obtained. The samples of captured mines were rare, and so in an odd twist Britain started producing *Tellermines* for trials. The original *Tellermines* had their firing pins removed from the detonators, and after the initial tests had their sheer wires replaced with British-produced wire. As per usual, British metals were of a better quality than the German variety but the trials managed to use a wire that was within 10 per cent of the German shear strength. This difference erred on the side of caution though, so the results could be considered an absolute minimum and the effect on live German mines would likely be greater.

During the period of early trials, indeed even after the Hedgerow project started, there were considerable disagreements between assorted departments each carrying out their own battery of tests. The usual point of argument was to do with the countermining radius of a charge. Some departments would disagree with the others and show their results with a different number, then the first department would defend their methodology, and so forth. It appears that many of the differences were down to environmental factors such as how wet the ground was, or even what type of soil or sand were used. It seems likely that as all mines would have been emplaced by hand, that there could be variance on the angle of the mine or how well the sand on top was replaced. A final matter arises in that any minor swells or bumps in the ground could provide a sheltering effect. All these elements likely contributed to the different claims.

In August 1942 Combined Operations HQ (COHQ) came up with the idea of using a Hedgehog launcher to clear mines during an amphibious assault. This idea was submitted to the Ordnance Board for review. During this review, the Ministry of Supply pointed out that the Hedgehog threw an elliptical pattern, and asked the question if this pattern could be changed to a much more useful line of bombs. Thus, the proposal was handed to the research establishment with the most experience in Hedgehogs, the DMWD. The project number allocated to Hedgerow was number 65, although the name would have come later. The name seems to be a wordplay indicating that it has a link to Hedgehog, but one that fires in a row. The DMWD formally started work in October 1942. The requirements issued to the DMWD asked for a cleared lane 120yd long and 8yd wide, with the start of the lane 100yd from the bow of the launching craft.

The DMWD's first attempt was a series of four I-beams, each one mounting six Hedgehog spigots at predetermined angles. These were fitted at the front of a Landing Craft Tank (LCT) Mk II, and were held in place by quick-release bolts. Thus, the LCT could beach itself, the Hedgerow could be fired, then the beams quickly removed to allow the tanks to disembark. The LCT chosen for this experiment was *LCT-162*. The firing circuit for the Hedgerow was fitted under the port wing deck, and it was exactly the same as the hand-cranked Hedgehog ripple switch connected to two 12v batteries. In January 1943 the first salvo was fired at Hayling Bay. However, the tides were misread and *LCT-162* grounded itself offshore. The salvo was still fired but landed in the water so no accurate results could be obtained. Following on from this it was decided to fit the Hedgerow to a smaller craft with a shallower draught.

A Landing Craft: Assault (LCA) was selected to carry the Hedgerow equipment. As the LCA was of lighter construction than the LCT the floor was strengthened by fitting an iron and teak bed, about 3in thick. The I-beams were bolted onto this, with two forward and two rear, which involved some

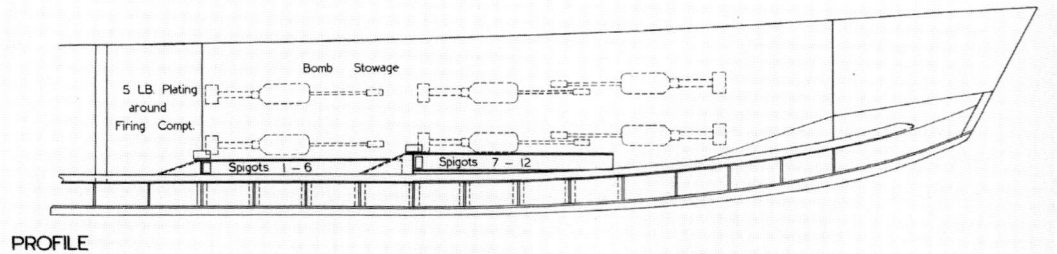

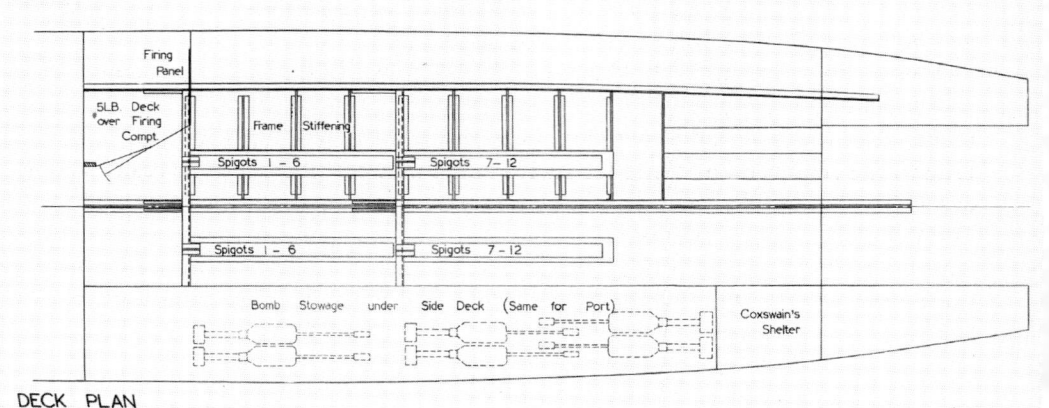

Plan of the LCR (HR).

alterations of the angles of the spigots. When this was fitted to *LCA-217* in early 1943 the firing gear, batteries and a safety system were all placed on the port side, and naturally formed a small compartment. Later a door was added to this compartment along with a speaking tube, to allow the gunner and coxswain to communicate. Full equipment trials were carried out on 22 March 1943, which the Hedgerow passed. The following day firing trials took place. Travelling from Portsmouth to Hayling Bay, *LCA-217* shipped a large volume of water, which got into the firing compartment and shorted out the electricals. After arriving at Hayling Bay the trials team set about replacing the batteries and drying all the wiring. When they were satisfied, they recommenced the firing trial. When the crank was turned the spigots started ripple firing. However, in the end, only fourteen of the twenty-four had fired. Inspection showed that the wiring had been crushed by the mounts which had flexed under the extensive recoil.

The design was reworked into a Hedgerow Mk II. This included much more stiffening to the floor, with another 350lb of materials. A new layout of wiring, including the use of a junction box to help with water logging issues. The biggest change was the addition of a ranging round. The first spigot on the port beam was wired up to a separate switch, which was placed in the coxswain's shelter. This enabled him to fire a ranging round to determine how the rest of the pattern would land. In addition to these mechanical changes to the Hedgerow, racks were fitted under the wing decks to carry another salvo of bombs. These alterations were all applied to the Hedgerow in *LCA-217*. A firing trial was held on 6 May 1943, in which all the modifications worked perfectly and the craft was undamaged. The following day a salvo was fired against a live minefield. Hedgerow performed almost perfectly, the only flaw was one round failed to detonate. The gap in the minefield was 9yd across and 130yd long.

This all came just in time. On the 17th an urgent operational requirement was issued, by the Commander in Chief of the Mediterranean. The requirement asked for five Hedgerow-equipped craft to be ready in just one month. Due to the requirement being for such a small number of craft to be ready so quickly it was decided that the simplest way to produce these was to put the DMWD in charge of the production. DMWD placed an order for the craft with Foster Wheeler Ltd of Egham for five Mk Is, as there was no time to tool up for the Mk IIs. The five craft were delivered with all trials complete on 9 June 1943. The crash course in trained crews held at HMS *Vernon* was completed on the 15th. The first-ever five LCA (HR) with numbers 550, 560, 626, 801 and 802 were handed over to Force J and Force V in June.

This photograph was taken from by the bow ramp of an LCA (HR). The coxswain's shelter is just visible on the left of the picture, and the door to the firing shelter is open at the stern of the craft. The firing shelter can just be made out. Each of the bombs is in place but has a safety cap over the fuse.

116 *Defeating the Panzer-Stuka Menace*

However, there was no attempt to keep the crews with their craft, thus the five craft arrived in Algiers with no crews and no instructions. The staff at the bases where the LCA (HR)s arrived had never heard of the Hedgerow, and so simply stripped out all the modifications to return the craft to LCA standard.

The urgent requirement had been issued for the craft to support the planned Operation Avalanche, the Allied invasion of Salerno. Obviously, someone in the chain of command realized that the newly ordered Hedgerow landing craft had gone missing, because on 15 August Sub Lieutenant A.P. Tod was ordered to train up two crews for Hedgerow duties. Two LCA, numbers 403 and 446, were supplied and the shipwrights at Algiers had just ten days to fit the Hedgerow equipment into the LCAs. This was made particularly difficult as there were no blueprints or any other paperwork to support the equipment. Literally, all the shipwrights had was the pile of parts that had been stripped out of the five original LCA (HR)s. It is also not recorded how much of the bracing and strengthening materials had been taken out of the original craft and retained. However, despite these problems two LCA (HR)s were completed, although they were described as very primitive examples. On the 25th the two LCA (HR)s were winched aboard an LCT by HMS *Howe*, and the LCT started for Djidjelli, arriving the following day. Here the Hedgerow detachment loaded all the available projectiles and fuses they could find. These were in bad condition, as they had been dispatched to North Africa onboard an LCT and due to miscommunication the stores had been loaded into the ship's well deck and this had become flooded with 5ft of water. This thorough soaking for the period of travel would cause severe problems later. The total ammunition that could be recovered was some 210 rounds. The LCT set sail for Bizerta, arriving on the 28th. There was some difficulty unloading the LCA (HR), due to the initial lack of suitable crane. Once a crane had been located and both craft unloaded the ammunition followed suit, only for Sub Lieutenant Tod to find that no provision to store the ammunition had been arranged, and it was just piled to one side. Sub Lieutenant Tod quickly commandeered a half-demolished villa as an ammunition store. The two LCA (HR)s were attached to provide support to the US Task Force COMLANCRABNAW. As there was a short lull at Bizerta, it was decided to hold a rehearsal in the bay. This would give the crews their first chance to fire a live Hedgerow salvo, something they had never experienced. During a force 8 gale, the two LCA (HR)s chugged out to sea and fired. Both craft launched a full salvo of twenty-four bombs. *LCA-446* started at the seams from the shock of firing, especially around the armoured bow door, and began to take on large volumes of water. Turning for shore, she settled lower and lower in the water until the large waves whipped up by the gale swamped the craft, and she sank in 15 fathoms of water. *LCA-403*, commanded by Sub Lieutenant Tod, suffered a similar fate, but just managed to

Another shot of the interior of the LCA (HR). On this particular vessel, the firing shelter door opens forward, and the bombs that have been racked appear to be either unfused or lack the extension tube, which might indicate an earlier version of the Hedgerow.

118 *Defeating the Panzer-Stuka Menace*

reach the shelter of the harbour, and safety. Sub Lieutenant Tod immediately ordered modifications to the craft. First, the armoured bow doors were removed, and the entire front sealed. The area in front of the coxswain's shelter was covered over to prevent water entry. It also gave a watertight space to store items for the crew such as rations, water and equipment, which would normally be kept under the wing decks but these locations held the spare projectiles.

From 1–4 September the stores were loaded onto the Navajo class tug the USS *Nauset (AT-89)*, followed by *LCA-403* being winched onto the deck on the 5th. Enroute to Salerno the crew of the USS *Nauset* provided invaluable assistance to the five-man Hedgerow detachment. In his report on the Hedgerow, Sub Lieutenant Tod had only the utmost praise for the US crew and pointed out they would never have been able to complete their mission without the support from the ship's company. The crew welded a smoke rack to the rear of *LCA-403*. They also repaired the bilge pump, a vital task as the LCA (HR) had an unidentified leak, and without the pump would have sunk. To give the pump a fighting chance the crew of the USS *Nauset* also coated the hull in red lead. In addition, assistance was provided to replace the batteries and fix other electrical wiring problems the little craft had. Finally, the crew of *LCA-403* were given a pair of Thompson sub-machine guns and a large stock of ammunition to supplement the two Lewis guns the boat carried.

While all this was going on, the crew of *LCA-403* was busy working with the ammunition for the Hedgerow. Of the ammunition loaded only three-quarters had passed checks as serviceable. However, upon closer inspection, it was found that water had entered the tails when it was submerged during shipping, and wrecked a large number of the primers. The same applied to the fuses. Eventually, after much work, four complete salvos were prepared and made ready. Two were to be loaded into *LCA-403* while the remainder would remain onboard the USS *Nauset*, allowing for a full reload should it be required. Of the total of 210, about 24 were jettisoned, around 50 had been found to be unserviceable and 24 were prepared for combat. One presumes the balance of rounds were kept on board the USS *Nauset*.

On the morning of 9 September, the USS *Nauset* was in her assigned column of craft approaching the beaches of Salerno. The plan called for the ships of the column to anchor some 350yd from the previous vessel. Then the support craft, of which *LCA-403* was one, would be launched. The craft would rendezvous at a vessel, which acted as a marker, which had the designation 'LOVE'. If all had gone to plan, *LCA-403* would have had to sail some 2 miles to point LOVE, with plenty of time to do it. However, the column took over an hour to get into position, and the USS *Nauset* was actually some 3.5 miles from LOVE. *LCA-403* arrived at 0304, with no sign of the other support craft, which were already heading inshore. The Hedgerow was to fire its first salvo at H-3, or in just 23 minutes, and they had another 3.5 miles to cover in that time. The cruising speed of an LCA, fully loaded, was just 6 knots, so to meet the target time a speed of nearly 8 knots would be required. Sub Lieutenant Tod, therefore, had to risk blowing up his engines and promptly ordered 4,000rpm.

At 0319 *LCA-403* pulled into its assigned station with the support wave, heading towards Red Beach, and the engines were able to be slowed. Almost instantly *LCA-403* had to pass forward of the support craft, as the plan required them to be at 50yd distance from the beach when the support craft were at 800yd so that all firing could be synchronized. *LCA-403* picked up speed again and headed into the beach. At 0330, H-hour and only 3 minutes late, the Hedgerow was fired. Immediately, both engines were thrown into full reverse, as the salvo had been fired at 40yd off the beach and there was a very real danger that *LCA-403* would run aground. The massive explosion from the Hedgerow salvo caused shrapnel to fall in the sea all about the LCA (HR), and even some lumps of metal to land inside the boat, however, all had gone according to plan.

At 0333, as the first assault wave landed, *LCA-403* turned northwards and took up a station about a mile off the flank of Red Beach to await developments. Here the Hedgerow was inspected. The force of firing had sheared the bolts holding the rearmost I-beams. These had then cut the wires to the front two girders. Equally the rear girders had shifted so that the spigots were about 2 degrees off. In the following 40 minutes, as the craft loitered, it came under light and sporadic shellfire. But ignoring this interruption, using a length of spare cable and insulating tape, all but two of the leads were re-joined with hasty repairs, and the second salvo was loaded. As this operation was finished Sub Lieutenant Tod had been listening to the wireless. The Beach Master on Green Beach was ordering that no further waves be landed, as the initial waves had been halted by a minefield. Sub Lieutenant Tod offered to blast an opening through the field, but after some deliberation this offer of help was refused due to the danger to troops already ashore.

As it seemed unlikely that the Hedgerow would be used at either Red or Green Beaches, due to the presence of friendly troops ashore, *LCA-403* was directed towards the main port of Salerno, to see if there was the possibility of opening that up to landings ahead of schedule. *LCA-403* chugged through the fading dawn, about 5 miles to the entrance to the port. As they closed the crew spotted that the machine guns covering the entrance had received direct hits from large high-explosive projectiles and were out of action. Sub Lieutenant Tod intended to tie up alongside the quay, where his Lewis guns had a good field of fire. When they reached the 80yd distance three rounds landed just in front of the LCA (HR). Not knowing where they were under fire from, or what sort of weapons were awaiting them inside the harbour, Sub Lieutenant Tod decided to fire the Hedgerow at the quay; if there were any enemy there it would certainly come as a surprise to them. If nothing else, it would provide cover for the craft to retreat. The damage to the Hedgerow, however, meant that the projectiles were scattered, some landing an alarming 30yd away from *LCA-403*, and six not even firing. Under the cover of this, *LCA-403* retreated from the harbour. By this point in the operation, the USS *Nauset* had been sunk, she had been set on fire and started listing by a near miss from a German dive bomber, then had drifted into a minefield and a mine had struck her bows sinking her. Thus, with an unserviceable weapon and no more ammunition available Hedgerow had completed its first operation. At 1030 on the 10th Sub Lieutenant Tod went ashore to view the results of his first salvo. A total of twenty-three bombs was found to have landed in a line, with the first round some 3yd from the water's edge, and the last about 90yd inland. The last six had landed in a German minefield and cleared a lane, however, the beach at that point was some 550yd wide.

The official history of the Hedgerow describes the entire sorry saga as 'pathetic', and, in truth, the Hedgerow lurched from one failure to another, nearly all of which were caused by the same faults that afflicted the introduction of Hedgehog. Namely, insufficient management and training. It is a testament to the can-do attitude of all involved, especially the crew of the USS *Nauset*, that there was even a single LCA (HR) to fire its salvo. The failures, especially the effect on the beach of that salvo, provided operational information that was fed back to the DMWD and other relevant organizations, and just in time as back in the UK the clock was rapidly ticking down to D-Day.

While the Hedgerow was undergoing its baptism of fire in the Mediterranean, back in the UK work was continuing on the Hedgerow Mk II. In June 1943 an order was placed with Thompson Brothers (Bilston) Ltd for twenty-five Hedgerow Mk IIs, the main difference being the addition of spreader bars between the I-beams. A handful of the Mk IIs was finished and fitted to the LCAs, however, the order was then halted. This was because the requirement for Hedgerow had altered. Hedgerow was originally designed to start clearing a path from the water's edge up the beach. However, reconnaissance had indicated that the Germans had laid most of their mines above the waterline. This information would subsequently be confirmed at Salerno. Thus, the pattern had to be pushed further inland to be of any use, which meant the requirement had a longer range. To achieve this a new round design was needed. The ammunition will be examined shortly, but to support the new ammunition and the longer range the angles of the spigots had to be altered. The new version of the Hedgerow became the Mk II* and forty-seven were manufactured. The existing Hedgerow Mk IIs were to be modified with a new set of sockets with the revised angles manufactured. These became the Mk II* (converted). Both were clearly marked as which version they were, and the beams on the Mk II* were 2in longer than the converted version.

The increased range necessitated a new projectile, originally Hedgerow used the standard Hedgehog projectiles filled with TNT. These were surplus to requirements when the Hedgehog ammunition was switched to Torpex filler, and so were readily available. A Mk I round was then designed specifically for Hedgerow. The round was to be fitted with a standoff probe, and trials were held to determine which length would be used, 20in or 40in. The longer version actually had to have two fuses, one on the tip of the probe in the usual place, and one halfway along the probe. The first fuse would detonate the second, which in turn would trigger the warhead. This chained fuse scheme proved unworkable, and the 40in probe made the bomb unstable in flight, so the 20in probe was selected for production. The standoff distance allowed for two advantages. First, the beach would not be cratered, and second, it would reduce the sheltering effect of any irregularities and bumps in the ground.

The actual fuse to be used was also trialled. A No. 152 and a No. 720 fuse were tested. It was found that the No. 720 would not arm due to the short acceleration period. Thus a No. 152 fuse, modified to have a weaker spring was selected. This became the 'Fuse Percussion No. 153 Mk I N'. It had a brass domed cap that would crumple on impact allowing the fuse to fire.

In March 1943 countermining trials with the TNT-filled rounds proved somewhat inconsistent in their effect. A new series of test-firing was added to the trial pattern which filled the warhead with a mix of 60 per cent RDX and 40 per cent TNT.

The increase in the range required the propellant charge be increased to 600 grains of FNH 025 powder. However, the standard Mk I tails would not be able to withstand those pressures. A new tail, which was manufactured by drop forging, was designed and tested, and likely became the Mk II round. The combination of the new spigot angles and the increased propellent gave Hedgerow Mk II* a range of 415yd.

For D-Day forty-five LCA (HR)s were to support the operation, in three flotillas. These consisted of twenty-five Mk II* (converted) and the remainder pure Mk II*. Once again bad luck was to dog the Hedgerows. The LCA (HR)s were to be towed across the Channel by larger landing ships. In the rough weather, many of the craft soon became swamped by the large waves. They would either be sunk at that point or be cast-off mid-Channel. LCAs were only for use inshore and were in no way suited to the storm-swept seas and the cast-off vessels would often be dragged out towards the Atlantic, then subsequently they would succumb to the waves.

122   *Defeating the Panzer-Stuka Menace*

Of the eighteen craft in Flotilla 591, nine were lost. Of the nine craft in Flotilla 592, eight were lost. Flotilla 590 also had eighteen craft, with three lost during passage and four arriving after the landings had taken place so could not fire. In total twenty LCA (HR)s fired on D-Day, with one later sinking.

Two samples of reports from LCA (HR) commanders have survived today. They come from Lieutenant R. Murray, commanding *LCA (HR) 712*, and Sub Lieutenant P.C. Lennard-Payne in charge of *LCA (HR) 1071*. Both officers were from the RNVR and both craft were part of Flotilla 590. The LCA (HR)s left Southampton on 5 June, *LCA-1071* at 0715, while *LCA-712* embarked 15 minutes later. *LCA-1071* was towed by a Landing Craft Gun, while *LCA-712* was towed, along with another LCA (HR), by a Landing Craft Flak, and both were heading for Juno Beach. For the next 18 hours both craft were battered by the sea and shipped large quantities of water, necessitating pumping out. *LCA-1071* was towed by a 3in wire and a 3in rope, both of which parted several hours apart forcing the LCA (HR) to follow the larger landing craft in, but *LCA-1071* made it to the beach. In contrast, the tow

A spectacular shot of a Hedgerow salvo mid-volley during trials.

ropes on *LCA-712* survived, however, as there were two craft to slip the tow upon arrival, it took considerably longer than planned. Both *LCA-1071* and *LCA-712* were to rendezvous up with Landing Craft Tanks carrying Churchill AVREs, but due to the delays *LCA-712* never made the meeting, but *LCA-1071* did. On the run-in *LCA-1071* stayed in the lee of her assigned LCT and at 100yd from the beach she overtook. As they ran in, Sub Lieutenant Lennard-Payne spotted his assigned target, it was a gap in the seawall filled with sandbags. Beyond there was a green-coloured house. When he was at a range of 250–300yd from the gap he fired his Hedgerow. The pattern straddled the target perfectly but raised so much smoke it was impossible to tell the effect of the bombs. The LCA (HR) had to swerve immediately to avoid hitting a beach obstacle, and as they did so small-arms fire erupted from the house, but luckily the Germans only managed to put a couple of bullets through the ensign.

On *LCA-712* things had gone a bit worse. Unable to link up with its LCT, it had proceeded directly to Nan Red Beach. *LCA-712* had to weave between German beach obstacles, known (confusingly) as 'Hedgehogs'. Lieutenant Murray reported that about a third of these had Teller mines or bottle-shaped objects on top, which were presumably explosive. At a distance of 80yd, a large shell landed just in front of the craft, badly damaging the front doors. When they were 10yd off the beach Lieutenant Murray gave the order to fire. The pattern landed astride the sea wall, just to the right of the church at Bernières-sur-Mer, and between two large, white-coloured houses. *LCA-712* then had to reverse hard to avoid beaching and as they extracted the Germans opened fire with small arms, but the fire fell short.

Both craft were recovered and winched aboard larger ships for return to the UK, although *LCA-712* was unable to reach the planned rendezvous point due to the damage caused by the shell and had to divert to a closer emergency recovery point.

After D-Day, reports filtered their way back to the UK and the DMWD. Brigadier Fergus Y. Carson Knox, of the 50th (Northumbrian) Infantry Division, stated that Hedgerows were invaluable in getting his men ashore. Flotilla 591 was described as doing 'magnificent work, far beyond expectations'. However, the biggest complaint came from the crews of the LCA (HR)s themselves. They were of the opinion that the LCA was a terrible platform as it was just so unseaworthy. This criticism was taken on board, and work began on the pinnacle of Hedgerow, the Mk III.

Work at the DMWD began almost immediately after D-Day, with proposals being submitted on 30 June, and design work beginning in July. This work incorporated all of the feedback from operational use. The LCAs were dropped as this type of craft was unsuitable. In the preceding two years at least

124   *Defeating the Panzer-Stuka Menace*

two out of fifty LCA (HR)s had managed to sink themselves. Thus, the decision was taken to fit Hedgerow Mk III to LCTs. Operationally the LCA (HR)s had been to support the LCTs carrying Churchill AVREs and other specialist armour, which were usually the first tanks to be landed in the primary assault waves. The thinking behind the Mk III Hedgerow being the LCT carrying the AVRE would beach itself as normal, then fire the Hedgerow. The tanks could then disembark directly onto the cleared lane, and go about their tasks. The decision to fit the Hedgerow Mk III to the wing decks of the LCTs only carrying the engineer tanks was confirmed. Only LCT IVs would be fitted, while it would be possible to fit to the Mk V versions it presented some difficulties, and the craft was unsuited. The decision was also taken to raise the sides of the LCT, which would provide protection to the bodies of the Hedgerow rounds, but not the fuses on their standoff probes. This was because by increasing the side height further the LCT was made much more susceptible to wind, and harder to control. During the same meeting it was revealed that there was a risk of firing so many projectiles, all in line with each other. If a tail burst upon firing, the projectile would not be launched sufficiently fast enough to clear the firing envelope of the next round, and the projectiles would collide. This could cause catastrophic damage to the LCT. However, the chances of this occurring were judged to be sufficiently low, just 1 in 150.

The starboard side of the Hedgerow Mk III. All bombs have been fitted, and the fuses have their safety caps on. Behind the bombs are the raised armoured flanks of the craft that provided shelter to the bombs.

The Hedgerow Mk III differed considerably to the previous versions. It consisted of twenty-eight I-beams, fourteen per side, in two rows. Each I-beam had six spigots. The entire mount had its spigots arranged to clear two lanes which converged about 400yd in front of the LCT. The lanes would be approximately 12yd wide. As the LCT would beach first there would be a short stretch of shallow water and therefore the Hedgerow had to work in up to 3ft of water. The landward end of the cleared lane would be marked by smoke rounds, while the seaward end would also need to be marked. With 168 spigots, and thus a similar number of electrical contacts, the Mk III mount also included the automatic ripple switch, as developed for the Hedgehog, but somewhat larger. It would take around 17 seconds for all the spigots to be fired by this switch.

The prototype Mk III was assembled and mounted on *LCT-684*. Thompson Brothers (Bilston) Ltd was the primary company involved in constructing it. Firing trials were conducted on 5, 6, 7 and 8 December 1944.

In January 1945 the future use of the Hedgerow was considered. It was obvious that the next major use would be in the planned invasion of Japan. The Royal Navy did have a dedicated LCT for service in the Far East under development, the LCT Mk 8. It was therefore decided that the Hedgerow Mk III would be fitted to the upper decks of the LCT Mk 8, and once again only those carrying AVREs. Thompson Brothers (Bilston) Ltd was to be awarded the contract for the production of thirty-nine Hedgerow Mk IIIs. To assist with manufacture all the existing Hedgerows were stripped out of their LCAs and returned to the company. The idea was to salvage and reuse what they could to save costs. In the end, the only parts that could be reused were the sockets and spigots. While box girders were seen as preferential, I-beams were readily available, so these were used. However, endplates were welded on as well as footer plates to improve stability and strength. Beams were arranged in two rows, and to achieve the desired pattern they were grouped together. Each beam had a letter designation to it. The groupings were beams ABCD in group one, EFGHIJ in group two and finally beams KLMN in group three. Ranging beams would be placed in front of beam A.

There were also some changes to the equipment to allow further tactical options. The ripple switch was to be modified, with the contract for thirty-six improved switches awarded to Ferranti Ltd . One of the changes was to allow skeleton firing. This was to enable partial firing of the loaded Hedgerow. Thus, you could fire some bombs on the run-in, then the remainder when beached, or whatever the mission required. Setting the new ripple switch to 'Skeleton X' would fire odd spigots in a group, while 'Y' would fire all the even numbered ones. A safety note suggested that you should not fire the spigots to the rear followed by groups to the front as inflight collisions could occur. The reason for the skeleton firing was to allow flexibility. For example,

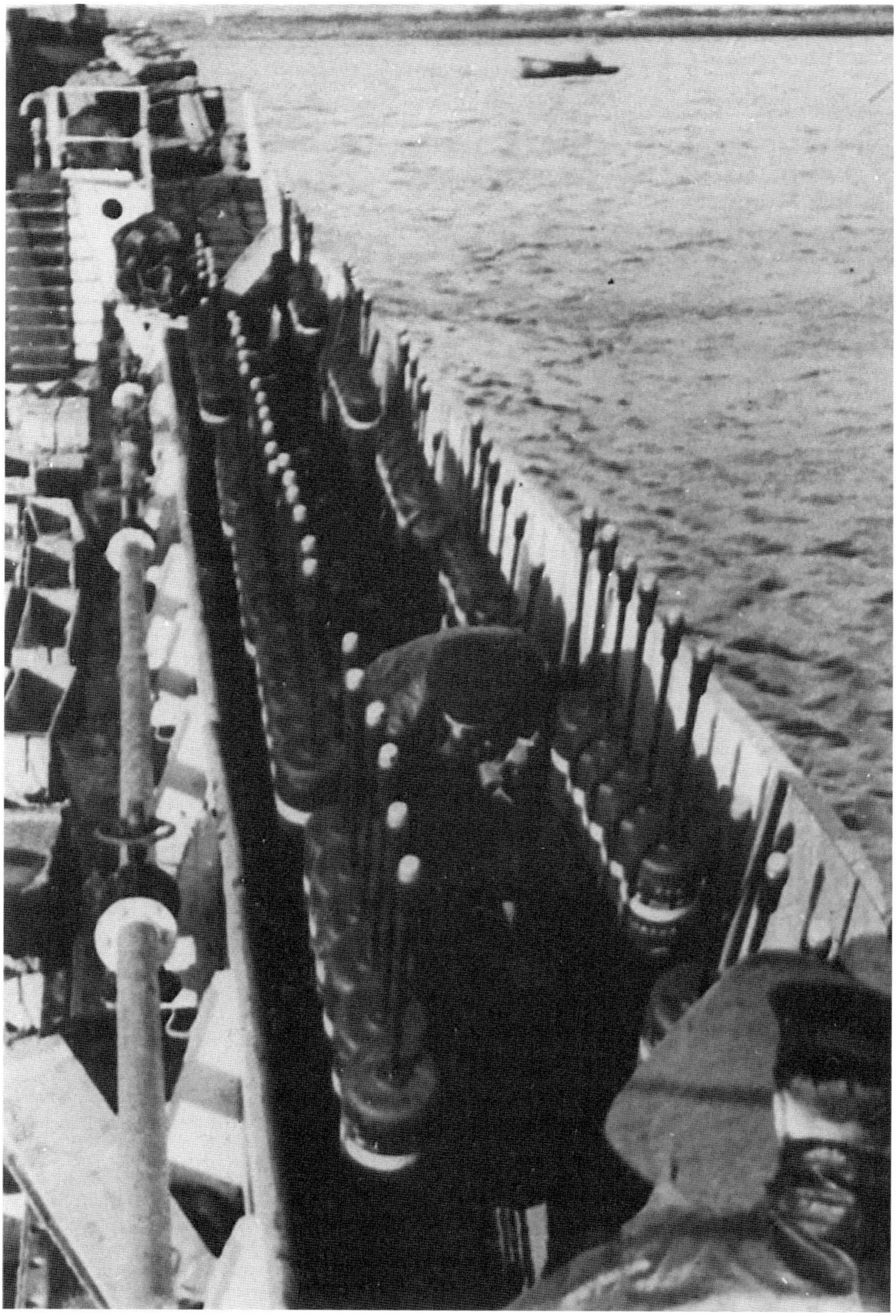

(*Opposite and Above*) Two images showing the reloading of a Hedgerow Mk III, onboard LCT 648. The sheer number of boxes visible here gives an idea of how laborious it must have been to prepare a salvo.

The Hedgerow Mk III salvo landing during the trials. The bombs are creeping across the beach in a rippling fashion.

in deeper water, the effect of the bombs is about three times the area of the same charge detonated in the air. This is due to the increased wave propagation and the ability for the waves to maintain their energy for longer. Thus, in skeleton mode, you could clear a lane theoretically twice as long. It was thought likely the most common use would be to fire groups two and three on the run-in as a ripple, then once beached group one.

To aid in firing on the approach to shore two ranging beams, each with six spigots, were fitted. These were fired separately from the main beams and could be used to check the range on the run-in. Although it was noted that changing the speed of the craft by 1 knot would alter the length of the pattern by a yard and that the ranging rounds would outdistance the normal projectiles by about 50yd.

The difference in flight distance between the ranging and normal projectiles was down to the filling. The ranging round would produce a bright flash, and to achieve this it was filled with a different warhead and weighed 10lb less than a normal round. To achieve the maximum range it was fired with a 600-grain charge. The main visual difference was there was a filling plug alongside the fuse hole. The projectile had not been finalized by the time the project was cancelled, so no formal markings were known.

The high-explosive projectiles came in four types. The only difference was in the propellant charge. Projectiles for beams A–D had 600 grains of powder, for E–G 523 grains, H–J 454 grains and K–N

The fall of shot from two patterns of the Hedgerow Mk III. Although at first glance there are gaps, keep in mind that the circle is only the 90 per cent zone, the charges would still cause mines to detonate outside of the circles, but at a reduced chance.

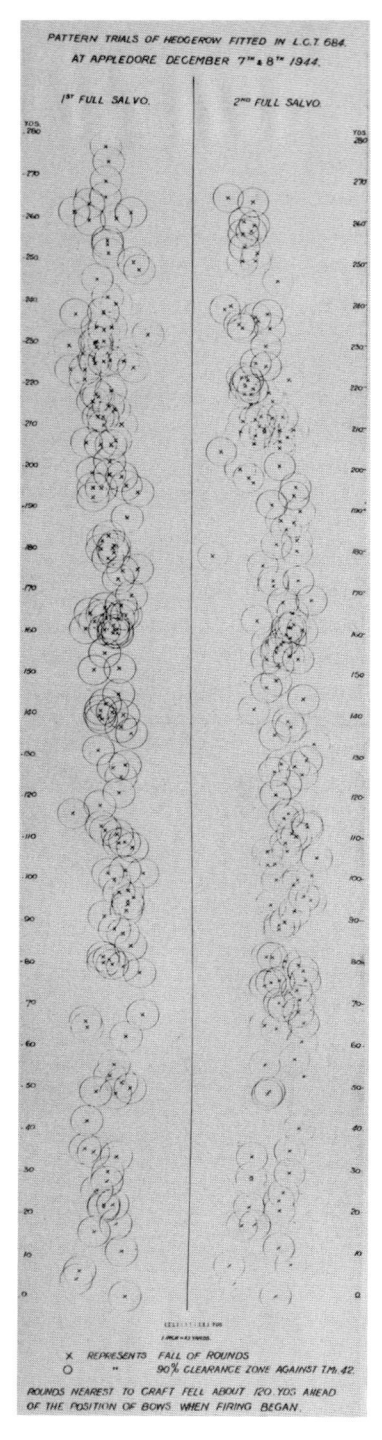

380 grains. Each projectile had a spring retained steel clip stamped with the charge weight. This clip was clamped to the tail tube upon the propellant being inserted at the factory. The tail drum was also stencilled with a beam identification letter that it could safely be fired from. That letter was also stamped on the shipping box. If a projectile with the wrong charge was fired from an incorrect beam then the trajectories of shots would cross, which could lead to collisions in mid-flight. Beams were not separated on deck but were clearly lettered. Due to this being visual identification, loading in darkness was not recommended.

Each explosive projectile was filled with 30.3lb of TNT. Torpex was seen to offer no advantage and would present additional challenges as it was not as easy to store in the heat and humidity of the Pacific. The explosive projectiles were painted green with a red band, and marked with the text '1 ¾" H.R. III TNT'. Projectiles filled with 600 grains were marked with the added text 'Long Range'. The fusing was a No. 153 fuse. A second domed brass cap was developed which enabled the No. 153 fuse to be used in water. The cap would take the impact on the water's surface, and cave-in, allowing the next impact to trigger the fuse as normal. Even with the cap, there were problems. It was considered likely that some rounds fired with 600 grains of propellent would detonate on impact with the water. Equally, the lowest charge bombs would likely lack sufficient velocity to be triggered on impact with even a shingle seabed. This would leave the bomb wedged upright and cause a significant hazard to the LCT or any follow-on craft. On 20 January 1945, it was suggested that a time-delay fuse which would activate on impact with the water surface and then 0.03 of a second later would detonate the warhead should be created. This was rejected because in water with a depth of under a foot the round would effectively air burst above the water surface. This would result in a sharply decreased counter mining radius. A drill round was also created, differentiated by a yellow band.

The landward marker projectile was only to be fired from the forward most spigot on beam A. It would emit smoke for approximately 4 minutes, and weighed the same as the normal high-explosive projectile. The filling was SR 585 (Red Cascade), which was contained inside a tin canister situated within the body of a normal Hedgehog round. The fuse would rupture the canister on triggering. There were some minor visual differences from the standard round such as the short fuse holder, held onto its cover plate by six hex nuts, and four 1in openings cut into the conical base of the warhead and covered by tin.

The Sea Marker rounds were filled with calcium phosphide, in a similar tin canister within the body of the round. When ruptured the chemicals would form a patch of fire on the surface of the sea which would last for about

Sea Marker bombs under trial. In the first picture, the Sea Marker is just entering the water, while in the second picture the effect of the marker is visible.

5 minutes. There was a long-range version to replace the land markers if the entirety of the pattern was to land in the water. The Sea Marker carried the text '1 ¾" H.R.I. Sea Marker, Cal.Phosphide'.

Up to about August 1945 twelve Mk III sets had been manufactured, and some 329 high-explosive rounds had been fired from the prototype. However, the design of the land marker had lagged behind, as had the work on the LCT Mk 8, with the first vessel only being completed the previous month. With the surrender of Japan and the end of the war, the need for amphibious operations against a defended beach had disappeared. Thus, the entire project was cancelled.

There is, however, one final part to the Hedgerow story, which occurred a few months earlier. In January 1945 COHQ were beginning to plan Operation Plunder, the amphibious crossing of the Rhine. They made enquiries into the possibility of fitting a Hedgerow to a LVT and creating a sledge with a Hedgerow on it. Work began on 9 February 1945, when three complete sets of Hedgerows were removed from their LCAs and sent to E.38, No. 7 Central Workshop at the Woolwich Arsenal. By 26 February, the equipment had been fitted and trials carried out. The sledge was obtained from MD1. During the trials, it vibrated, and thus the pattern had breaks in it with some degree of clumping. In addition, getting the sledge into position was difficult. While a truck could carry it, a crane would be required to unload, and as it was very tall it would take considerable work to emplace.

The LVT fared much better initially. When a salvo was fired from her sitting on dry ground the LVT suffered no adverse effects and was able to drive cross-country immediately afterwards. The problems came in the water. In the first trial, the ripple took 5 seconds to launch, and the current of the river had swung the nose of the LVT during firing. This led to a sporadic pattern with large gaps in the cleared lane, which was of no use. The LVT was modified again. This time a sight was added for the gunner, who was sitting next to the driver, as well as an intercom. The ripple order was changed. In a subsequent test, a clear lane was created but it was curved. It was suggested that a straight lane could be created by angling the LVT against the current, but this would result in a lane running at an angle from the water's edge. By early March COHQ had decided against the use of the Hedgerow LVT, because of the curved lane, and it would mean sacrificing valuable lift capability.

The first two marks of Hedgerow always seemed somewhat underdeveloped and flawed. On the Mk I the lack of range was its critical technical failure, along with the same problems that plagued the introduction of the

The Hedgerow fitted to the Porpoise sledge supplied by MD1.

The Hedgerow as fitted to the LVT. Below is a close-up of the junction box.

Hedgehog. The Mk II*, and its sub-mark, were more bedevilled by its deployment platform being inadequate, although it still gave some sterling service on D-Day. The Mk III promised to be the most effective service equipment but was let down by the lack of an operation to be used in. During the Second World War, work was being carried out on line charges, explosive-filled hosepipes launched into position then detonated. These had significant advantages over the Hedgerow, but it would take several years after the end of the Second World War to perfect them, at which point the Hedgerow really was surplus to requirements.

PART FIVE

THE PIAT
BABY BOMBARD, JEFFERIS GUN AND PIAT

Chapter Twelve

From Parthian to Production

The biggest problem in looking back at the history of the PIAT is where it all started. Invariably the early stages of the weapon's conceptualization are badly recorded and leaves a lot to guesswork. There is also a modern trend to attribute the design of the weapon to either Jefferis or Blacker, when, as will be shown, neither was wholly responsible.

In September 1940 Blacker was in London and working on the early stages of the Bombard. Blacker's fertile mind was also considering new weapons and new means of warfare. One already encountered has been described, the AA Bombard, but he also had other ideas. On the 30th he submitted a very short paper outlining his new ideas for warfare, and thesey were based around a new class of solider.

He named these revolutionary troops 'Parthians Divisions', alluding to Alexander the Great's use of Parthian horse archers. In this analogy, the armoured force became the Phalanx. Blacker proposed that the soldiers of his Parthian Division be mounted not on horses, but on small, simply constructed one-man helicopters. The machines were to be so simple they would not have any instruments, and Blacker really did perceive these to be like Dragoons but using the third dimension to leapfrog defences. These would fly at a low level and enable a mass of troops to be deposited wherever they were needed. Blacker suggested their use to harry the flanks and cut off lines of retreat. He also said they could be used to strike at strongpoints on the French coast. A swarm of these machines would descend, depositing their fighting men, who would launch an infantry attack on the fortification, then withdraw, re-mount and fly off. Blacker had even identified suitable engines for the craft, such as the Gypsy Six. He predicted that the machines would need to be constructed in the USA and if this was possible there was a type of Continental engine that would be suitable.

With the suggestion of the helicopter, at such an early stage of its development, it is possible, if not likely, that Blacker was the first proponent of helicopter-borne troops which would quickly become such a vital part of the modern army after the Second World War.

In his proposal Blacker had spotted that the Parthian Division would lack the heavy support weapons of a normal infantry force, indeed, he even fought against such equipment stating:

> The success of rotaplane troops depends on arming them with a personal weapon of outstanding performance. This is in contradiction to the present system of loading a battalion up with a great multiplicity of arms, each of which is only suitable for one particular target. An outstanding weapon exists in the shape of the hand 'Bombard' which is now nearly ready to be put into production.

Blacker's concept was simple, the entire division would be armed with these weapons, which would provide anti-tank firepower and the abilities of a grenade launcher and light mortar all rolled into one. This would give the firepower needed to perform the duties he had in mind and remove the requirement for the heavy weapons. While the British Army was in favour of the idea, or so Blacker stated in a letter in January 1941, the Air Ministry resisted. After that, the idea of helicopter-borne infantry disappeared until helicopters had undergone significant development. However, the 'Hand Bombard' would frequently be linked to paratroops and air landing formations.

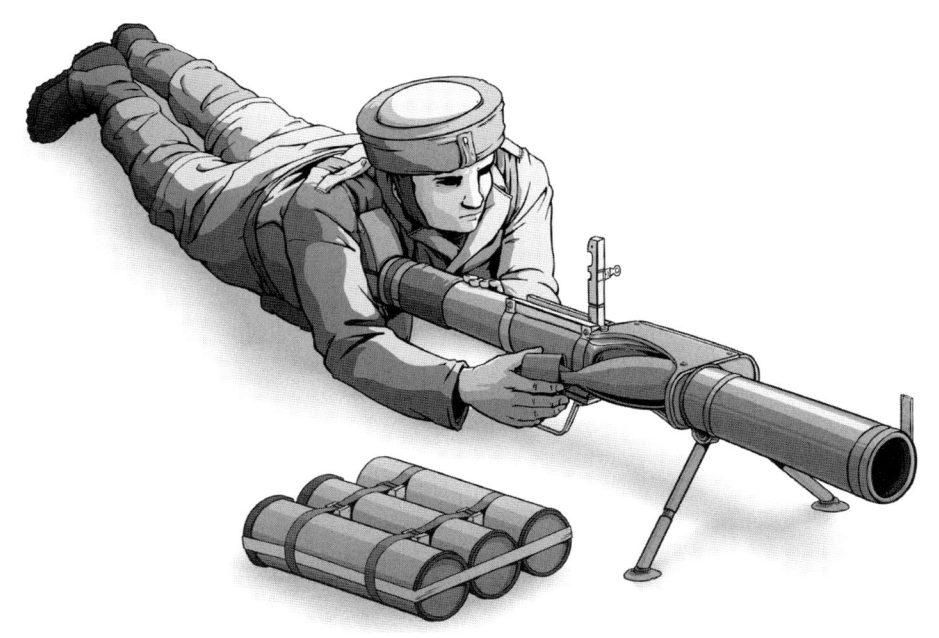

An artist's impression of a Parthian Division soldier armed with a Baby Bombard. The Bombard is based upon the description given in the documentation.

The Hand Bombard seems to have been called a great many names by different individuals. Hand Bombard, Shoulder Bombard, Baby Bombard and 1940 Pattern Bombard have all been documented. The most common seems to be the 'Baby Bombard'. Unfortunately, no surviving picture or plan has been found detailing it, but there is a description of the weapon.

The Baby Bombard was a recoiling spigot design. The total weight of the weapon was 21.5lb, slightly less than an unloaded Bren gun. The Baby Bombard seems to have been tube-shaped, much like the later PIAT. Where it differed from its illustrious descendant was in its loading mechanism. The projectile was loaded from the side via a loading opening described as similar to a Martini-Henry rifle. It was also described as semi-automatic. This description has caused some confusion among researchers, as it implies the weapon was self-loading. Blacker owned a patent submitted in May 1939 for a magazine-feed system for a spigot weapon, however, it appears the other features of the Baby Bombard do not align with this patent, as it needed to be a top feed, whereas the Baby Bombard is a side-feeding weapon. Many people have tried to work out a semi-automatic arrangement for the weapon, however, it always comes up with a horribly unwieldy design. Therefore, it is likely that the term semi-automatic actually refers to the breech type and is a description taken from artillery pieces, where a semi-automatic breech will close automatically after a shell is inserted. This would follow as Blacker's background was in artillery. The vague word description also seems to imply that there was a lever of some sort which would cock the mechanism, again drawing parallels with the Martini-Henry.

The Baby Bombard fired a 3in HESH projectile weighing at 2lb, 6oz at a muzzle velocity of 225fps. The propellant charge was 28 grains of cordite. As one would suspect, it was filled with Nobels 808. Penetration wise it would make a 2.5in hole in 1in plate, but as it was a HESH round it would likely scab on a much thicker surface.

With the failure of the Parthian Division concept, Blacker adapted his views so that the Baby Bombard would replace both the anti-tank rifle and the 2in mortar, and for it to be issued as a section level weapon. Blacker also saw it as a means to obtain an improved version of the Bombard, suggesting once the development work was done on the Baby Bombard it could be scaled up and a simple tripod attached to create a lighter version of the full-sized weapon.

At this point in the war, 1941, the Boys Anti-Tank Rifle was looking on decidedly shaky ground and in dire need of replacement, especially for airborne troops. An airborne unit would only have access to Boys Rifles, Sticky and No. 68 grenades to defend itself against any armoured attack. The situation for paratroopers became so bad that any device for anti-tank work was seized upon, such as the Projector, AT Portable, No. 1, Mk 1. This was an

140   *Defeating the Panzer-Stuka Menace*

11-litre tank filled with 9 litres of hydrogen cyanide (HCN), a poison gas more infamously known by its German name of *Zyklon B*. At the base of the tank was an aluminium foil disk which contained the HCN inside the tank and stopped it flowing out of the pipe and nozzle that ran from the tank. The operator would aim the nozzle, then close a switch which connected the battery in the nozzle to a small cordite charge inside the tank. This would detonate, filling the tank with pressurized gas. The aluminium foil would rupture and the entire 9 litres of HCN would be squirted out the nozzle dousing the target tank with the deadly gas. The concept was simply if you cannot go through the armour, then go around it. The projector was developed towards the end of 1941, underwent some testing, including issue to air landing infantry units for troop trials, then the first fifty were stored against further need and the project ceased. The reason for this cancellation was, as well as the fear of initiating gas warfare, was that other work had been carried out on hollow charge warheads.

The idea of replacing the Boys Rifle with a hollow charge warhead had come about sometime in 1941. Work had begun on a projector to fire the No. 68 grenade. The reason for a separate projector was that the No. 68 when fired from a cup discharger had a very violent recoil that required the rifle to be braced against a solid object as firing from the shoulder would result in an injury to the gunner. Once work was underway it quickly became apparent that limitations would be placed upon the design due to the strength of the human body. Simply put, the designers calculated the force of recoil that would break an average human's shoulder, and lowered the amount of recoil force produced by the weapon to just below that level. The design work concluded that a dynamic spigot would help with the recoil forces. The No. 68 Projector was fired at Bisley on 18 December 1941.

Trials on hollow charge warheads had shown that better performance could be achieved by using a larger diameter warhead, and it was well known that the performance of the No. 68 grenade was inferior, only providing around double the penetration of a Boys Rifle, which would soon be inadequate for defeating armour. It was estimated that a 3.5in warhead would have around about 500 per cent more penetration than the Boys. Work on such a warhead produced a 3lb projectile containing 1lb of explosive that should have met the requirements laid out by the General Staff. As this was a new design of projectile a new weapon was needed. Such a gun could be designed from scratch to be a dynamic spigot weapon, so the No. 68 grenade projector was dropped. It is almost certain that Jefferis began working on the design at about this time, although he (and MD1) could have been involved from the start. This weapon would, in time, be called the Jefferis Gun.

The Jefferis Gun was again tube-like and had a cocking wire with a loop on the end. The operator's foot was placed in this loop and used to draw the cocking mechanism. The wire was attached to a lug, which was drawn down a slot in the side of the gun. When not in use the wire was secured to the body of the gun by a clip. The weapon was muzzle-loaded, and the round fitted onto the spigot. The weapon weighed 28lb. The projectile, now called the MD1 round, had altered a bit in its design. Documents seem to imply it originally contained a base fuse. Testing at the Armaments Research Department at Woolwich had shown the importance of standoff and how it needed to be related to the diameter of the warhead. Thus, the projectile had been redesigned to include 3.5in of separation between the nose fuse and the main warhead. This, in turn, had required research work at ICI on initiating trains of Cordtex from the fuse to the warhead. The finalized round was 2lb 13oz and was fired at a velocity of 270fps from the Jefferis Gun by 52 grains of cordite. The bomb was stabilized by a twisted tail-fin arrangement, which more than likely rotated the projectile in flight, and consequently lowered its penetration performance.

The Jefferis Gun was fired at a demonstration at Bisley on 11 February 1942. It seems that Blacker was invited to the demonstration and arrived with his Baby Bombard which he exhibited to the people in attendance. There are conflicting documents that say the Baby Bombard was fired on that day, however, there is only one set of trial results, and those are for the Jefferis Gun. Thus, it is likely that it was not fired and its presence came as a surprise to MD1, and became a bit of an ad hoc show-and-tell by Blacker. The Jefferis Gun fired several bombs, in multiple trials. A maximum rate of fire of six rounds in 45 seconds was recorded, although due to the suspect quality of ammunition the loader was stationed much further back than he would have been in service use. This was a safety precaution in case the bomb detonated on, or near, the spigot, but did mean he had to run several feet before commencing loading, then retire the same distance before the gun could be fired.

The velocity of the bomb was about 250fps, which achieved an accuracy of a 3.5ft group with five rounds at 100yd, and three bombs into a 4ft group at 150yd. The MD1 bomb's performance was also tested against a variety of thickness of armour at various inclinations. The first target was a 60mm plate at 30 degrees. The MD1 hollow charge warhead put a 0.75in hole through that. The jet of molten metal, with the spall from the armour, then struck the witness plate creating a hole 5in by 4in, and marking the plate with considerable splash. The second target was a plate at 40 degrees, against which the round appears to have failed to function. Target three was a 75mm plate at 30 degrees, which the bomb put a 0.625 hole through. The same-sized hole was punched through target four which was 115mm thick at 0 degrees. The ground behind all the targets was scoured to a distance of 3ft.

Three days later, on Valentine's Day 1942, a meeting was held at the Ministry of Supply. At the meeting were Major General Clarke, Blacker,

The Jefferis Gun (top) and the same weapon being ready to be fired (bottom). These pictures were likely taken around the time of the Bisley demonstration, which Blacker and his Baby Bombard upstaged. Of note is both the shape of the MD1 bomb and the ammunition carriers for it, worn as part of the webbing. (*Lord Cherwell collection, G.272/22, Nuffield College Library, Oxford*)

Jefferis and the representative of ICI, Mr F.E. Smith, as well as a few other related departments and interested parties such as the Ordnance Board. The aim of the meeting was to discuss the next steps for the project and decide whose projector would be taken forward to production and service. The MD1 projectile came under scrutiny first. Concerns were expressed about the safety of the fuse and waterproofing of the bomb, Jefferis agreeing to look into these flaws. Additionally, when Major General Clarke asked about an alternative filling to Nobels 808, Jefferis agreed to research other explosives. As can be seen, the MD1 hollow charge bomb was seen as the desired round, which would mean that the Baby Bombard would need to be scaled up slightly if it was to fire the same round. Equally, the Jefferis Gun would need redesigning for production as the cocking slot down the side of the tube was not seen as a viable production proposition.

At this point Mr Smith asked if the responsibility for the weapon would be placed with ICI, which was agreed, and Mr Smith was asked to design a new weapon, with the best features from both the Baby Bombard and the Jefferis Gun incorporated. Three of these prototypes would be built. The priority was quick and easy production of the weapon, as the General Staff wanted the process to start by August. There were also the requirements for the weapon to be under 28lb and use a Bren Mk II Bipod. There was a brief discussion on the safety of the fuse. If the body of the weapon was to be lengthened, so that the bomb's projecting fuse was inside the weapon and protected from impacts, it would involve a considerable increase in weight. It was decided that this question would be dealt with at a later time, as it would be relatively simple to extend the body to provide protection. Another feature that those at the Valentine's Day meeting asked for was a method of cocking, achieved by a movable butt plate that was connected to the mechanism and a sight similar to the No. 4 rifle's sight, with ranges set to 75 and 125yd.

Later, on the 17th, Blacker amended a set of minutes with some comments that were untouched upon. He first pointed out that he had rather a lot of experience in the field of spigot weapons, and based upon that knowledge he suggested some items that would contribute to the success of the weapon. The most critical of which was using a drum tail, over the fins currently on the bomb. It was Blacker's opinion that the fins would be sufficient in still air or against headwinds, but against a quartering wind the drum tail would provide better stability in flight, and thus consistent shooting. He also named a company, I.A. Hodgson & Co. of Newcastle, that had solved the difficulties in mass production of drum tails. Finally, he suggested a small gun shield was essential. The drum tail had originally been suggested at the Valentine's Day meeting by an Ordnance Board representative, Colonel Saunders-Knox-Gore.

144   *Defeating the Panzer-Stuka Menace*

It can now be seen that the constant argument over who designed the PIAT, Jefferis or Blacker, is actually the wrong question. Both contributed parts of the design which were merged by Mr Smith. However, there is one more invention to come from Blacker, the vital retaining clip.

Once again, there is little information about this, indeed in this particular case, even less than usual. One flaw of a spigot weapon is that if the spigot is pointed downwards, the weight of the projectile will overcome friction and the projectile will slide off. This was not a problem with the Bombard, as the spigot on that only ever pointed level or upwards, and was practically impossible to point downwards to any degree. But with a handheld infantry weapon, there were multiple occasions when aiming downwards would occur, and potentially leave the gunner severely inconvenienced, and somewhat embarrassed, as the bomb slid out of the gun.

On 27 February 1942 Blacker submitted a patent for a retaining clip that would prevent such occurrences. At the base of each projectile's tail tube there was a flanged collar around the edge of the tail tube, this was called the guide ring. This ridge was slotted behind a raised lip of metal on the projector housing, known as the retaining clip, and would securely hold the bomb in place. When the projector was fired the bomb would remain in place until the guide ring failed which would allow the projectile to be launched. How the guide ring was attached to the tail tube is not entirely clear, as Blacker in

A diagram of the PIAT practice round. This was a simple steel tube that could be reloaded with a new cartridge and guide ring, the latter is shown clearly on the left of the diagram (marked 'loading clip' here). The practice round was to give the gunner a sense of what it would be like to fire the PIAT, although it had a slightly different trajectory to a live round.

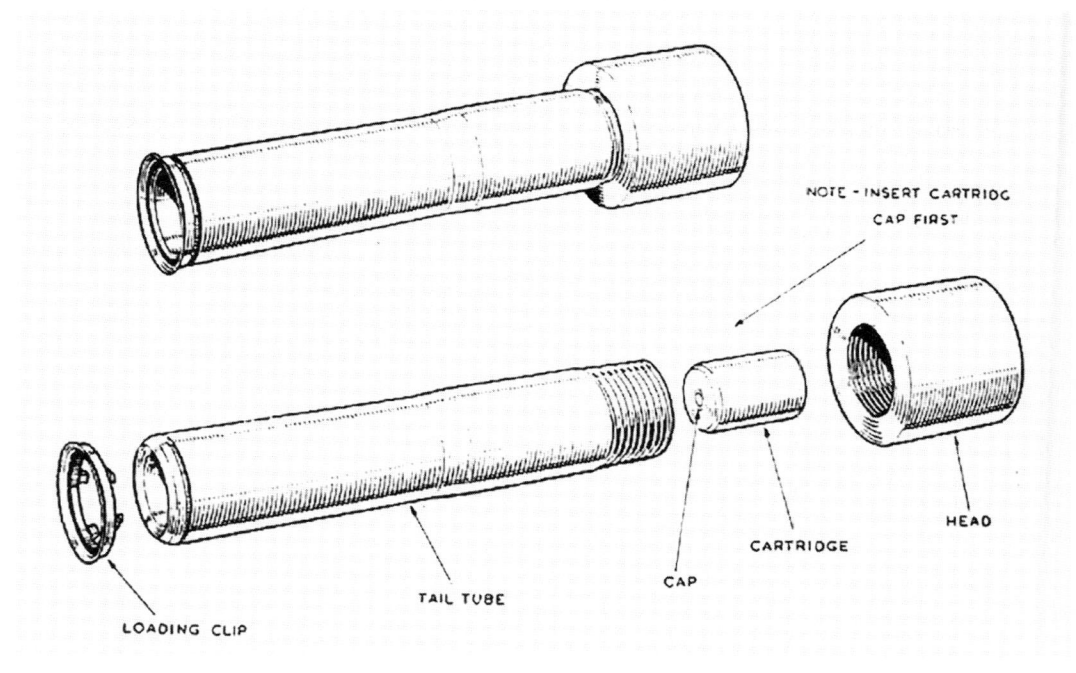

his patent suggested several means of achieving the desired effect, such as welding, soldering, shear pins or rivets to hold the guide ring in place. Other authors have suggested it was held in place by spring tension. Either way, the guide ring would separate from the tail tube, when sufficient pressure had built between the spigot and the bomb. The guide ring would be left behind, and then would drop out the bottom of the retaining clip, either through gravity or the process of loading the next round pushing it downwards. There was a large hole at the base of the loading tray to allow the guide ring to fall away from the weapon. In Blacker's patent, he also covered the idea that the guide ring would remain attached to the tail tube and deform, achieving an almost identical effect. Whichever method was chosen did mean that there was a noticeable lag between pulling the trigger and the round being fired. When the PIAT entered service with this clip the delay between pulling the trigger and the projectile firing often caused the inexperienced gunner to relax. This would result in a much more severe recoil blow when the gun did fire. The period of relaxation could also cause inaccuracy as not only would relaxing shift the aim point, but the mass of the spigot and bolt sleeve slamming forward would also cause the centre of balance to move forward.

Blacker had designed an infantry projector, which looked close to a PIAT but did not have the distinctive loading trough. It relied entirely on this clip to hold the bomb in place, it was called the Stewblac Platoon Projector. At least one prototype was built as the mechanism survives. Where or how this projector was involved is difficult to say, but the Valentine's Day meeting notes do include a note that 'some sort of shute or trough is desirable to assist rapid loading'. This may well be a direct reference to the Stewblac Projector, which lacked such a feature. However, against such a theory is the request that the spigot was not fully retracted during loading so that the bomb was at least partially loaded onto the spigot. Doing so seems utterly impossible while using the bomb retention clip. At this time there is not sufficient information to say if the Stewblac Projector was an attempt at a later weapon by Blacker, or something that ran parallel with the Baby Bombard. All that can be said is that Blacker's retaining clip was incorporated into the final design.

On 17 March, the Ordnance Board held a series of tests of the MD1 round at Shoeburyness, where it penetrated a 100mm plate angled at 30 degrees.

Between the Valentine's Day meeting and late June ICI were working on the design of the new weapon. During this period there were a number of changes to the design, mostly centred around the bomb. The most significant alteration was to the weight and size of the bomb. It was reduced to 2.5lb and 3.25in in order to lessen the recoil of the weapon and make designing the projector easier, and the final design a bit lighter. To give you an idea of how much trouble the recoil was giving designers, later on in the PIAT's life ICI were asked how much extra recoil could be sustained by the human shoulder

STEWBLAC PLATOON PROJECTOR ½ FULL SIZE

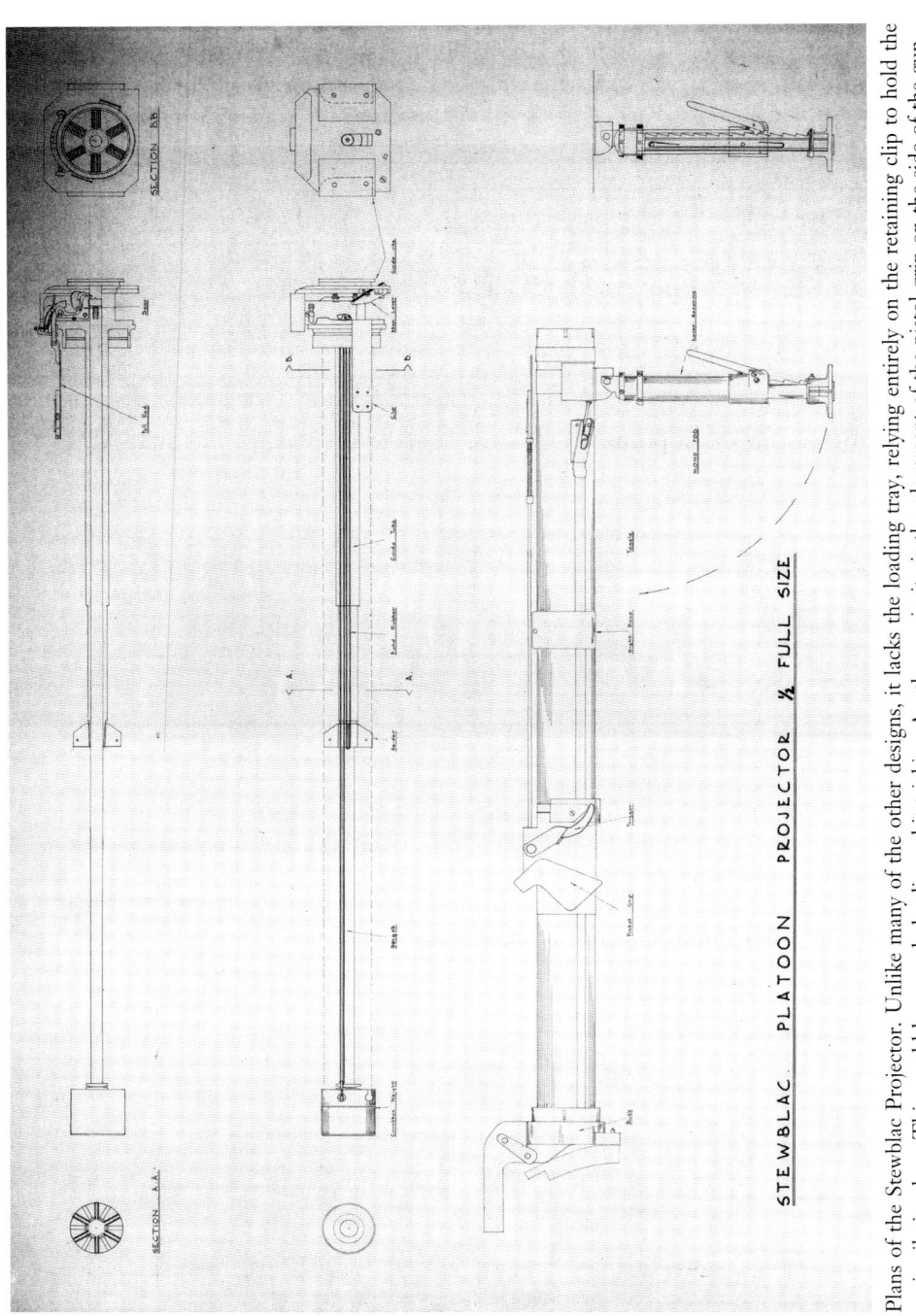

Plans of the Stewblac Projector. Unlike many of the other designs, it lacks the loading tray, relying entirely on the retaining clip to hold the projectile in place. This would have made loading a bit trickier. Another curiosity is the placement of the pistol grip on the side of the gun.

before injuries occurred. The aim of this enquiry was to increase the accuracy and range by raising the muzzle velocity, which would also increase the recoil. ICI considered there was only about a 5 per cent increase available before injuries were caused.

Other changes included switching the way the two halves of the bomb were joined from a lug to a thread and screw. There were a number of changes made to the explosives of the warhead. In most warheads of the period, there were two types of explosive, a primary and a secondary explosive. The primary was normally present in tiny amounts and was very sensitive. The fuse would act upon the primary explosive triggering it. The detonation of this primary explosive then triggered the more inert, but more powerful, secondary explosive, such as TNT or RDX, which made up the majority of the warhead and provided all the warhead's force. In the case of the MD1 bomb, the fuse was linked by Cordtex to a primary explosive pellet at the base of the metal cone in the hollow charge warhead. The majority of the secondary explosive was behind this pellet. It was decided that better results could be achieved by moving the primary explosive to the rear of the main charge. To do so, however, would mean the Cordtex running through the Nobels 808 acting as the secondary explosive. To prevent the chance of premature detonation the Cordtex was given an insulating sleeve of TNT. The original MD1 bomb had been created using pre-formed explosives. This was dropped as it would remove a step in the manufacturing process, and make the bombs quicker to produce. Finally, a cambric washer was added. Cambric was a densely woven cotton cloth and could come in a primed form that was impregnated by gunpowder, although no details mentioned which type was used in the PIAT round. It was used to prevent the plastic Nobels 808 leaking out of the top of the bomb when the cone was pressed into the plastic explosive while the bomb was being filled. This new bomb was tested on 28 June 1942 and successfully holed 100mm at 30 degrees again. With this success, the new bomb became the Mk I bomb and the designs were sealed.

The exact date of the order for the PIAT is not recorded, however, it is known that 100,000 PIATs, 10 million rounds of live, 1 million each of practice live and inert and 300,000 rounds of drill ammunition were ordered. In December 1942 it was reported that ICI was anticipating producing 10,000 PIATs, each with fifty rounds of ammunition, by the start of January 1943. Part of the production battle was how to fill the bombs. As the War Office had given the PIAT project the highest priority they were expecting production of 400,000 bombs per month. After reviewing their facilities ICI concluded that to meet the army's demand they would need significantly to expand their facilities, and thus entered into negotiations with the Treasury for additional funds. ICI estimated that approximately £19,200 would be required to modify and extend existing buildings, about £41,810 for new and

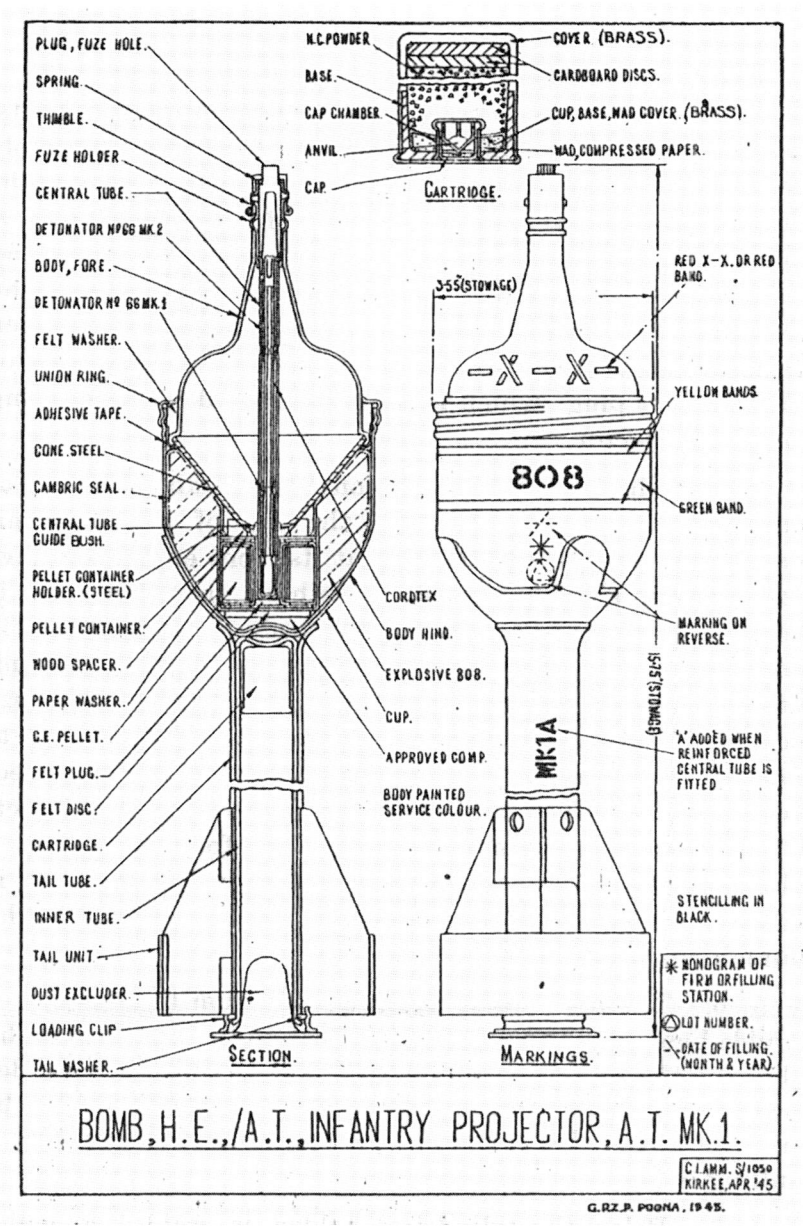

A sectioned view of the Mk I PIAT round, showing all the salient parts and how the round was constructed. The right-hand diagram shows some of the markings on the early rounds. The colouration of projectiles was green for live and black for drill and inert bombs. The live bomb had a ring of red crosses around it, while the drill was marked with the word 'drill' in white letters and had its tail tube plugged. The inert bomb had a yellow ring around it and marked as inert. The bomb carriers were also marked with the corresponding markings, red crosses for live, yellow band for inert and white band for drill.

modified plant equipment, as well as some £21,000 for other costs, such as £2,000 spent on architects, giving a total cost of £82,610 for expansion of their Featherstone filling factory. In May the Treasury approved up to £200,000 for provision of ammunition and a further £81,500 for setting up projector production. The total spend would spiral upwards in due course with an extra £33,000 having been spent by March 1943, and the total estimated cost having risen to £358,000. This included repurposing machinery from Bombard ammunition production, and even then they only achieved a rate of 200,000 PIAT bombs per month. The cancellation of the last part of the Bombard ammunition production also allowed the freeing up of supplies of explosives which could be used in filling the PIAT bombs. The Treasury

The first of two two pictures from the MD1 demonstration. This first image shows the impact point of the pelleted bomb when it hit the turret of the Churchill Tank and filled the interior with smoke.

The second image shows the side of the Churchill with three impacts from pelleted bombs, each marked by a white cross.

was keen to recoup costs by cancelling the outstanding Boys Rifle ammunition production. At the time the stocks of .55 Boys amounted to some 10 million rounds, and production was running at 15 million per year. It was only in the second quarter of 1943 that the authorization for a reduction in the production was given to the Treasury.

Whenever production did start a few projectors and specially prepared ammunition were available in November 1942. On the 2nd, MD1 put on a demonstration of several of their new weapons at Princes Risborough. The first demonstration was range. First, a ranging shot was fired, then two salvos of three rounds. The ranging shot went 450yd, and the two groups of three rounds were 15yd out, one over and one under, but still on the correct

From Parthian to Production 151

One of a series of pictures from the test on a static Churchill hulk with live ammunition. The side has taken three hits, two penetrated but one failed.

A close-up of a further hit from a live round, this time to the turret.

Before the test was carried out wooden silhouettes of crew were installed in the appropriate seats. Here are the remains of those wooden crew. Several have been decapitated, others would have taken shrapnel damage.

line. Demonstration two was for PIAT smoke rounds, which will be covered later. The last demonstration involved three PIATs firing rounds with the secondary explosive removed. The three guns engaged a manoeuvring A.22 Churchill Tank at 100yd. Five hits were caused within 20 seconds. The commander of the vehicle reported that the primary explosive charges detonating caused his tank to become filled with smoke and prevented him from bringing his gun to bear on the infantry. All was in place for the PIAT to enter service.

Chapter Thirteen

Defeating the Panzer Menace

From the outset there were questions about how the PIAT would be deployed, such as which formations would be armed with the weapon, would the RAF or Home Guard be armed with it? Which theatres would have priority? Where in the unit organization would the weapon go? Even as late as October 1942, how effective would the weapon be? The last question was answered in a set of notes on the PIAT sent to Major General Hastings Ismay at the end of October from Lord Melchett, which read:

> The German land striking force is largely concentrated around the use of tanks, and all their outstanding successes have been as a result of the use of tanks. Therefore a blow to their tank force will do more than merely stop their tanks, but must have a widespread undermining effect, not only on their troops, but on their staff.
> [...]
> The British Infantryman has one marked superiority over all other armies, his traditional capacity for obeying the order 'wait till you see the whites of their eyes', and therefore a short range weapon in his hands would be more effective than a short range weapon in the hands of any other troops. From this point of view a short range weapon is taking the greatest advantage of the superiority of which we possess over other armies.

While the implication of the short range of a PIAT being a good thing is rather dubious, it does show how the PIAT was viewed by the British higher-archy, such as the General Staff and the Cabinet, during the war. Defeat the panzer, and you will defeat the German. To that end, the idea was to give the traditionally stubborn British infantryman a weapon that could destroy a German tank, then no matter where the panzer went it would meet stiff opposition. Because of this, the initial production of PIATs was to be issued only in theatres where heavier armour was most likely to be encountered. To give the infantry enough firepower, it was decided to issue three PIATs to every company. These could then be sited where and when needed, but the most likely deployment by the company commander would be to give each platoon a single projector. In January 1943 it was suggested to send 200 projectors along with 100 rounds per gun for trials in North Africa.

Within the week this was significantly increased to equipping the entirety of the 1st Army with PIATs and having a reserve of 400 weapons. Along with this one officer and six NCOs were sent to train instructors on the weapon. The latter would in turn set up local training schools and then the crews for the weapon could be trained on a two-day course.

The weapon demonstrated at the training schools would have been utterly unlike any weapon the soldiers would have seen before. The PIAT was 39in long, weighed 34.5lb and was made entirely of metal tubes. The fore-end was a loading tray, made from an open-topped tube. When uncocked the spigot protruded about two-thirds of the length of the loading trough. On at least two prototype versions the sides of the loading tray extended upwards to be in line with the top of the PIAT's body, however, these were likely dropped for ease of production. The spigot was connected to the sleeve bolt, which made up the recoiling mass inside the main body. The cocking rod ran through the sleeve bolt's centre, and the rear was connected to the stock. Around the outside of the sleeve bolt was the mainspring. This was the sum of the working parts. When assembled the components fitted into the tube-like outer casing, with the spigot protruding through a hole into the loading tray. The rear of the outer casing was closed by an end cap which screwed into position and was also held by a spring catch, the stock protruding beyond the

A combat shot of a PIAT, from the hedgerows of Normandy or maybe Italy. It seems impossible to identify the AFV that has just hoved into view down the road before being killed by the PIAT.

end cap. On the left-hand side of the body were the sights, which could be folded down for storage and to avoid damage. The rear sight had two apertures, the top one was for 100yd, while the lower was for 70yd. At the bottom of the outer casing was the trigger mechanism which also had a simple safety catch. Close to the point where the loading tray merged with the body was a monopod. This could be extended by releasing a simple spring catch on the front. When the monopod was fully extended, and the buttstock rotated through 90 degrees to be parallel to the ground, the PIAT could be used as a light mortar for 'house busting', to quote the instruction manual. When in this configuration, the maximum range was about 350yd, and there was a white stripe down the top of the body to use as an aiming mark. There was also a bubble sight fitted.

On the first 800 or so guns the monopod was a fixed unit. On 22 December 1942, a trial was held to see if the PIAT could replace the 2-inch mortar. The concept was to have an adaptor similar to the training adaptor which would allow the weapon to fire 2-inch mortar style bombs. The Ordnance Board that oversaw the trials asked that the adaptor plate be fixed permanently to the weapon but would have some form of mechanism to allow the PIAT to be switched from anti-tank to 2-inch mortar bombs at need. The trials also included new modified monopod that could be adjusted for height. After the trials were completed it was recommended the new design of monopod should be accepted for production forthwith. The idea of using the PIAT to replace the 2-inch mortar was dropped. This report also recommended the switch from a concave buttstock to the more familiar straight one. The Ordnance Board rejected this advice, but referred it to the D of A for review. Interestingly, there is no mention of a change of mark for these modifications, and in the usual course of things the changes would have resulted in a Mk II or Mk IA. The requirement to fire the modified 2-inch HE bombs was dropped by the General Staff by the end of January 1943, however, the adjustable monopod and new sights remained. This allowed the PIAT to be used as a much more accurate, if slower, firing mortar to provide additional flexibility to the infantry platoon's firepower.

Attached to the side of the loading trough, just forward of the monopod, was a chain with a cork on it. This fitting was to protect the spigot against dirt and dampness. When there was a chance of combat the PIAT could be carried cocked quite safely for extended periods. The cork was then used to plug the opening the spigot would slide through in the body. With this in place, it kept the internals free of dirt and maintaining the PIAT cocked for a long period did not harm the spring. Upon sighting an enemy tank, or other suitable targets, the cork was pulled out, and the bomb placed into the tray. The guide ring was pushed firmly into the retaining clip, by pressing the flat of the hand

Defeating the Panzer Menace 157

down on the top of the drum tail, and the PIAT was ready to fire. The entire process of inserting a bomb, pressing the guide ring home then clearing the gunner's line of sight leaving the PIAT ready to fire took about 2–3 seconds.

The main causes of misfires were a loose or bent guide ring, failure to push the guide ring home fully or if the spigot was contaminated by dirt. To unload a misfire from the PIAT a bayonet was placed between the body of the gun and the drum tail and used to lever the bomb forward until it was halfway along the loading tray, at which point the bomb could be drawn out forwards. This was done as most of the ways the weapon could misfire were due to something stopping the spigot from striking the cartridge case. Should this blockage suddenly clear, then the spigot would slam home, and if the bomb was still in position it would fire. With the bomb tail levered halfway along the loading tray then the spigot was too short to reach the cartridge, and the weapon was safe, even if the spigot cleared the blockage. One other fault experienced with the PIAT was the failure of it to re-cock itself. The most common reason for this was the gunner not bracing the weapon tightly enough with his body. The simple fix was to re-cock the weapon and continue firing.

Cocking could be done by placing your feet on the buttstock, grasping the pistol grip and using the force in your body by simply straightening up. This could be done standing or lying on your back. Like the Bombard, a PIAT should never be fired when it was unloaded as it could cause significant damage to the weapon. This was down to the energy in the spring having to be transmitted somewhere, and normally that is into the projectile. Thus, to uncock the process of cocking was reversed. You stood on the buttstock, drew the weapon out to the fully cocked position, which was easy to do as there

A PIAT team on exercise. After the bomb is inserted into the tray the guide ring will be resting on the top of the retaining clip. The loader will then press down firmly with the flat of his hand on the top of the drum tail and the guide ring will slide into position and be seated aligning the tail tube with the spigot.

would be no resistance. Then while holding firmly onto the gun, by the pistol grip you would pull the trigger, and ease the weapon back to its resting position.

For training, there was a special adaptor plate that could be inserted into the loading tray. This plate clipped on at the front of the weapon, and then a pivoting thumb screw could be latched into place and hand tightened to hold the loading plate in place. It produced a raised channel in the loading tray, in line with the spigot. Onto this plate, a practice round could be loaded, which was made out of a steel tube with a weighted head. The head unscrewed and a standard PIAT propellant cartridge was loaded. The base of the tube also had the ability to mount guide rings. As the practice round was only intended to simulate the loading and firing process, it only had the same weight as a live bomb. The trajectory on the practice shot was flatter than a live bomb, so any targets to be fired at needed to be offset to achieve the same results. When using the 70yd aperture on the sights the target needed to be at 77yd, and for the 100yd aperture 113yd.

The accuracy of a PIAT was subject to investigation with a series of trials against a Covenanter being driven at 10mph. The bombs fired were mostly inert, although a few were fired with fuses to test reliability. At first glance the results were not promising for the PIAT, with the final report suggesting that somewhere between seven and twenty-three bombs would be needed to achieve a 'virtual certainty' of a kill on a panzer, all depending on the behind armour effect of the bomb, a factor that the trials team could not calculate. Overall the accuracy was given as 57 per cent and was judged to be of above-average shooting standards. However, these figures were an average, for example, the number of bombs needed included all factors involved in the attack, such as accuracy against crossing targets and fuse reliability.

The trials were of three target classes classified by how the target tank was moving in relation to the gunner. These were closing, receding and crossing. There were no shoots carried out against stationary targets. All the trials used 110yd as the upper limit for shots. The crossing course had a variable range of the target, but the closest was 70yd. On the closing trials firing stopped at 65yd. On the receding target, the shooting started at 35yd and extended to the maximum. Curiously, it was deemed that the closing target was actually the hardest, due to the urgency of a tank driving at you. On approaching targets the chance of hits was 35 per cent, crossing, however, was 60 per cent and receding the highest at 72 per cent. The trials also looked at ranges and the idea of holding fire until a closer target. It was found that there was a difference in the chance of a hit at ranges under 85yd, which the report estimated as about 33 per cent. The report cautioned against the concept that withholding fire would result in a certain hit.

Another training exercise. Originally this was captioned in the *War Illustrated* as being a combat shot, however, the lack of any indicators of combat make this unlikely.

The fuse for the anti-tank bomb was originally a percussion graze fuse designated as No. 425. From the outset it caused problems. In March 1942 the MD1 bomb was suffering a high number of failures to detonate. These fuses were redesigned, however, even by November fuse production was lagging seriously behind. At a time when 800 guns had passed proof and there were 50 rounds of ammunition per gun, the lack of fuses was hampering deployment. ICI stated the lack of production of the small springs in the fuse was causing the delay. By the end of December, the fuse issue was so critical a series of trials on the weapon had to be suspended as there were just no fuses to be found. However, just nineteen days later the supply of small springs had arrived, and production was assured. ICI was able to report confidently that the situation was resolved. In the accuracy trials against the moving Covenanter, the No. 425 fuse would only detonate in about 75 per cent of strikes, which accounted for a good part of the high number of rounds needed for a certain kill. From about December 1943, a new improved fuse was issued. This was, unsurprisingly, called No. 426, and acted in both a direct action and a percussion manner. It was much more reliable for detonating. The main visual difference between the two is that the No. 425 had a flat nose, while No. 426 had a domed one. The No. 426 was also slightly longer, which meant that the bomb carriers had to be resized to accommodate them. However, very rough handling trials showed that the shorter bomb carriers could be partially closed with a No. 426 fuse fitted, and that no damage was sustained, thus in the short term the older service carriers could be used with the new fuse until longer models became available. About 45,000 No. 426 fuses were rushed by air to North Africa for immediate use. There were a number of different marks of PIAT bombs, of which only the first three (Mk I, Mk IA and Mk II) were fitted to take the No. 425 fuse, and would later have an adapter to alter them to take the improved fuse. The No. 426 fuse proved entirely safe. There is one account of a soldier hurrying forwards responding to the report of tanks. As he crossed a ploughed field, he tripped and fell face forwards. His PIAT, which was loaded with a bomb, planted into the earth with the standoff probe and fuse acting like a bayonet, and stuck upright in the furrowed ground. The soldier hauled himself upright, yanked his PIAT out of the ground, and continued forward. When he reached the panzer he fired at it with the mud-coated bomb, which seems to have detonated, as the German tank promptly surrendered.

When the Mk I bomb entered production two problems became apparent. The first was that a high number of bombs failed to detonate, despite the fuse having triggered. This was traced to the flange holding the Cordtex train in place. The simple addition of a second flange and a washer overcame this issue. This design became the Mk IA bomb, but was otherwise identical to the Mk I.

The other problem arose after about six months of production. At the time ICI was producing some 80,000 bombs per week. Large numbers of bombs were failing the penetration proof tests, which in turn meant that bombs cleared for service were beginning to run low. The initial fix was to drop the proof requirement from penetrating 100mm at normal to 91mm. This solved the supply problem while investigations were carried out. It was found that the act of fixing the hand-pleated cambric seal was pulling the explosive filler away from the metal cone that was so important to a hollow charge's function. Trials were carried out, and it was found that the use of pre-formed explosive fillers and cambric seals would restore the penetration to its previous value. The introduction of this change became the Mk II bomb. The Mk II bomb also coincided with the introduction of the No. 426 fuse and the new holder for it.

From the end of 1943, RDX/TNT filling was used, and this became the Mk III bomb. This was poured into the upright PIAT body, then the cone front part of the warhead, along with the detonating assembly, were pushed

Defeating the Panzer Menace

MD1 Bomb

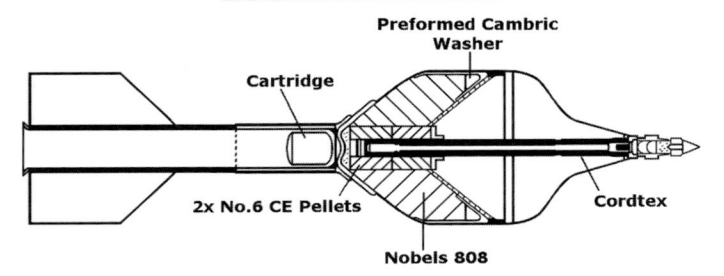

- Preformed Cambric Washer
- Cartridge
- 2x No.6 CE Pellets
- Nobels 808
- Cordtex

PIAT Bomb Mk.I

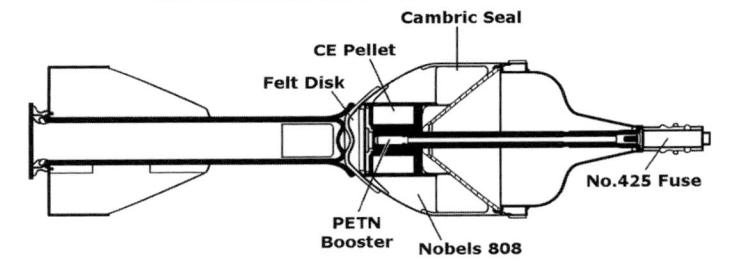

- Cambric Seal
- CE Pellet
- Felt Disk
- PETN Booster
- Nobels 808
- No.425 Fuse

PIAT Bomb Mk.III

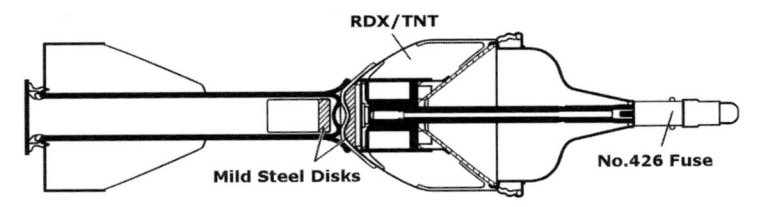

- RDX/TNT
- Mild Steel Disks
- No.426 Fuse

PIAT Bomb Mk.V
(Proposed)

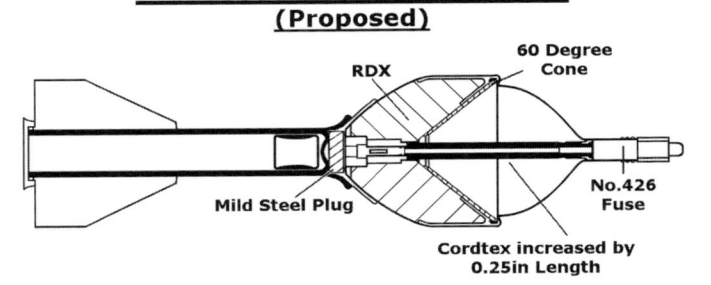

- RDX
- 60 Degree Cone
- Mild Steel Plug
- No.426 Fuse
- Cordtex increased by 0.25in Length

Evolution of the PIAT bomb.

into the liquid explosive. After this was done, the case was upended and the RDX/TNT mixture allowed to set. Inverting the body of the bomb meant that the explosive settled into contact with the cone, and thus maintained performance. There was some concern that upending the bomb during drying would mean the explosive solidified away from the primary explosive. However, as the primary explosive was quite large and designed for Nobels 808 there were no failures to detonate reported.

After a year of action in North Africa and Italy, some accidents with the PIAT were reported and this resulted in the Mk IV bomb. Upon detonating the explosive warhead was causing shrapnel to be fired back up the tail tube. The shrapnel consisted of any leftover pieces of the cartridge, and the small part of the warhead case that was within the diameter of the tail tube, which acted as a gun barrel. These were found to be moving at some 3,000fps. Due to the angle of impact of the bomb the tail tube was usually pointing upwards, and the shrapnel would fly high over the gunner's head. However, in a small number of cases the bomb would wobble during flight, and the tail tube would end up pointing back towards the firing position. The simple fix, which entered service in July 1944 with the Mk IV bomb, was the addition of two mild steel disks to reinforce the base of the body of the bomb.

At the end of 1943 work began on a bomb that would have taken the Mk V designation. This was a wholesale refinement of the weapon, using a new understanding of the principles of the hollow charge warhead. As well as superior penetration, the bomb also included improvements in the ballistics. When this bomb was tested in January 1944 it penetrated 100mm sloped at 30 degrees. An order for 2,000 bombs was produced and these were to be used in development work. However, no bombs were built and the order was cancelled in May 1945.

There were other experimental bombs. The first appears to be an attempt at a HE bomb using a Pentolite explosive filling. At the Valentine's Day meeting in 1942, an investigation into using this explosive filling had been requested. This was done to save nitroglycerine, as Nobels 808 would not need to be used. There is no evidence that this was successful, and the only documents about a Pentolite filling date from January 1944 and mention measuring fragment velocities and sizes, which would indicate there was an attempt to develop an anti-personnel round. It seems the concept of a dedicated HE round was never taken up. One wonders if this was down to the hollow-charge round producing fragmentation from its case, or if it was a worry about ammunition that a PIAT team could carry, and diluting the primary role. If a PIAT team was only able to carry six rounds, switching even one to a HE round was of limited use in combat, but would significantly deplete the number of rounds for anti-tank use. On the question of the inherent fragmentation of the anti-tank bomb, there is a note in a US manual

Defeating the Panzer Menace 163

from 1945 reviewing street-fighting techniques. One of the weapons assessed is the PIAT and its effect on brick walls. The jet generally would penetrate a wall, however, the majority of incapacitating damage on witness boards was within 18in of the path of the hollow-charge jet. An earlier test held in 1942 by the British had splinters and fragments being found some 25ft behind the wall, with extensive blast in the direction of the jet. Other trials also found the standard hollow-charge bomb produced splinters out to a radius of 15ft and had a considerable blast effect. The US manual goes on to discuss the best role for the PIAT, 'A much more effective use of this round is to fire it through windows and thus to utilise its anti-personnel effect', which would indicate a

This brick wall was fired upon as part of the MD1 demonstration on 2 November 1942 at Princes Risborough. There were several hits from PIATs in the same general location to cause this much damage.

normal anti-tank bomb causes fragmentation. The report notes that if a heavy wire is placed to protect the window, all that does is cause the PIAT to detonate at the window, and blast fragments of wire inside the room. Interestingly, the same report talks briefly of an experimental white phosphorus bomb that had been developed for the PIAT, although very few details are given.

The other experimental round, which there are some records for, was a smoke projectile. The idea first came about in October 1942, when COHQ realized that assault troops would often come across enemy positions such as bunkers that they had no way of destroying. The simplest and most practicable answer was simply to neutralize the position by the use of smoke. The 2-inch mortar smoke round was judged to emit too little smoke, to be of use. Therefore, new options were being sought. The COHQ requirement was for the weapon to have a range of 500yd. There were three options being studied, a modified 2-inch rocket with a 9lb warhead, a disposable single-shot mortar that fired a No. 18 smoke generator and finally a smoke round fired from a PIAT. MD1 designed a round that was based upon the 2-inch smoke round. The PIAT smoke bomb was filled with the same composition as the 2-inch bomb. Nine rounds were fired in trials in March 1943, the round weighing some 2lb 9oz, and achieving a maximum range of 558yd, although most rounds fell close to the 505yd mark. The bomb would start to emit smoke as it reached the top of its curve, and would keep emitting for about 2 minutes. This was considered a satisfactory performance, and a development order of 200 was requested, and a review of the problems linked to the use of coloured smoke compounds. It is not known if this order was placed, but there certainly seems to have been no service ammunition of this type ever issued.

Leafing through accounts from soldiers, it is evident that a large number of men were sent for training on the weapon but who never carried it in action. The next most common use of the weapon was as a mortar, or to attack non-tank targets, such as boats, or in one case a safe at a factory in Germany. In the latter case, the safe-crackers barricaded the door to give themselves cover, but left a small opening to fire the PIAT through, the single round 'peeled' the safe open. The flexibility of the PIAT meant it found use on all fronts and theatres Commonwealth troops were fighting in. Around 1,000 PIATs and 100,000 rounds of ammunition were sent to Russia as part of Lend-Lease aid, however, they appear to have been disposed of by the Russians without any attempt to issue them to front-line units.

There are a number of short descriptions of the PIAT's use, such as the occasion when a Panzer IV blundered into a British position at point 239 near Ortona in Italy. This occurred at dawn and surprised the defenders. The PIAT crew managed to get their PIAT cocked and loaded but had no time to raise the sights. The crew also only had one fused bomb. Using his common sense, the PIAT gunner used the top of the bomb and the white stripe as an aiming point and fired. The bomb had a No. 425 fuse in it and ricocheted off the Panzer IV without exploding. The PIAT crew managed to get another bomb fused and loaded, and by now the Panzer IV was only 20yd away. This time the bomb hit squarely and stopped the tank and two panzer crew bailed out. One was captured and one killed. The halted panzer was then set on fire by a nearby Sherman. However, this sort of incident seem quite sparse and ill-reported, but to illustrate the PIAT in use two accounts with sufficient detail have been located.

The first comes from the fighting in Normandy. The Battle of Lingèvres is most famously known for the actions of the 4/7th Dragoon Guards' Firefly commanded by Sergeant Harris. After the British forces captured the village, Sergeant Harris' Firefly destroyed a Panther. Then, as the 9th Durham Light Infantry advanced through the settlement Sergeant Harris moved his Firefly up to provide covering fire, and not a moment too soon. Charging down the road towards the village was another Panther, and Sergeant Harris ordered his gunner, Trooper Mackillop, to deal with the tank. The round struck the tracks of the Panther, which skidded off the road and out of sight of the Firefly. Sergeant Harris' Firefly remained in roughly the same position for the rest of the day and accounted for a further three Panthers that blindly rushed down the road. However, the first Panther was still operational, and although it could not move, its firepower was undiminished. Step forward Major John Mogg, who was acting in command of the battalion after its commander had been killed when his Universal Carrier had been hit by a *Nebelwerfer* earlier in the day. Major Mogg led a two-man tank-hunting party from D Company. When, after sneaking close to the Panther and into a position Major Mogg was happy with, about 15yd from the tank and behind a bank which the PIAT was resting on, Major Mogg gave the signal for the private with the PIAT to fire. The private looked aghast and said, 'But I don't know how to fire the bloody thing, sir!' When Major Mogg asked the other man in the tank-hunting team, he too admitted he had no clue on how to fire the weapon. Luckily, the extreme simplicity of the PIAT allowed Major Mogg to figure out how to work it, and at 15yd it was all but impossible to miss. The bomb smacked into the Panther causing a sheet of flame to rip out of the hatches. Two Germans scrambled out of the tank and set off at a run. Reeling from the recoil, Major Mogg grabbed his pistol and opened fire. All this achieved was to encourage the Germans to run faster.

The second account of the PIAT in action comes from Holland during Operation Market Garden. On 22 September 1944 the 5th Duke of Cornwall's Light Infantry (DCLI) was ordered to pass through the Guards Armoured and move up to the banks of the Rhine, and to try and make contact with the Polish Paratroopers on the other side of the river. Supported by the 4/7th Dragoon Guards, the infantry loaded as many men as they could onto

(*This page and opposite*) A curious experiment by the men of the 16th Field Company, Royal Canadian Engineers in November and December 1944. In the War Diary it was referred to as the 'Mobile Battery'. In November the division the engineering unit belonged to was asked to devise a harassing weapon to make the Germans' life difficult. The first design comprised eighteen PIATs mounted in three rows on the back of a Ford 60cwt truck, several salvos were fired with no felt recoil. Reloading trials were even carried out, taking 1 minute, 20 seconds to reload all the PIATS. Due to the lack of recoil in the truck mount the Carrier mount pictured here was constructed, this time containing only fifteen PIATs. The Carrier mount was also fired, and there was no felt recoil. However, even with a following wind, the best range achieved was just 410yd, with the normal range about 300yd. The range was too short to be effective or even to reach the German lines from the Allied ones, and the entire idea seems to have been dropped shortly after these pictures were taken.

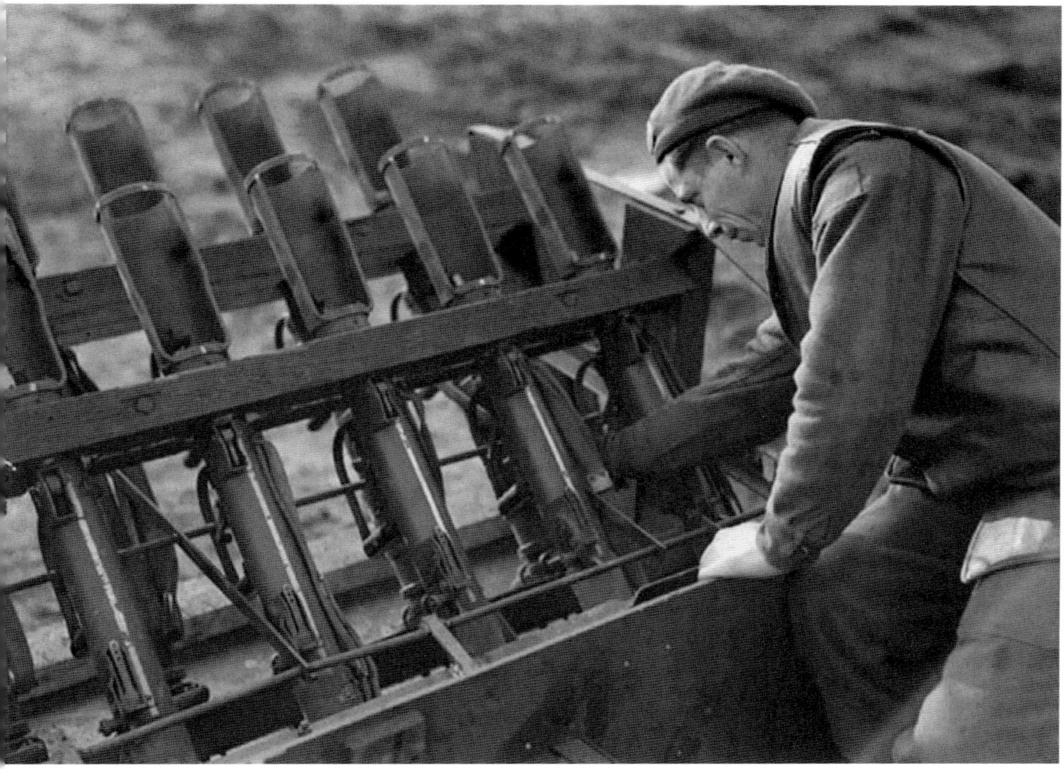

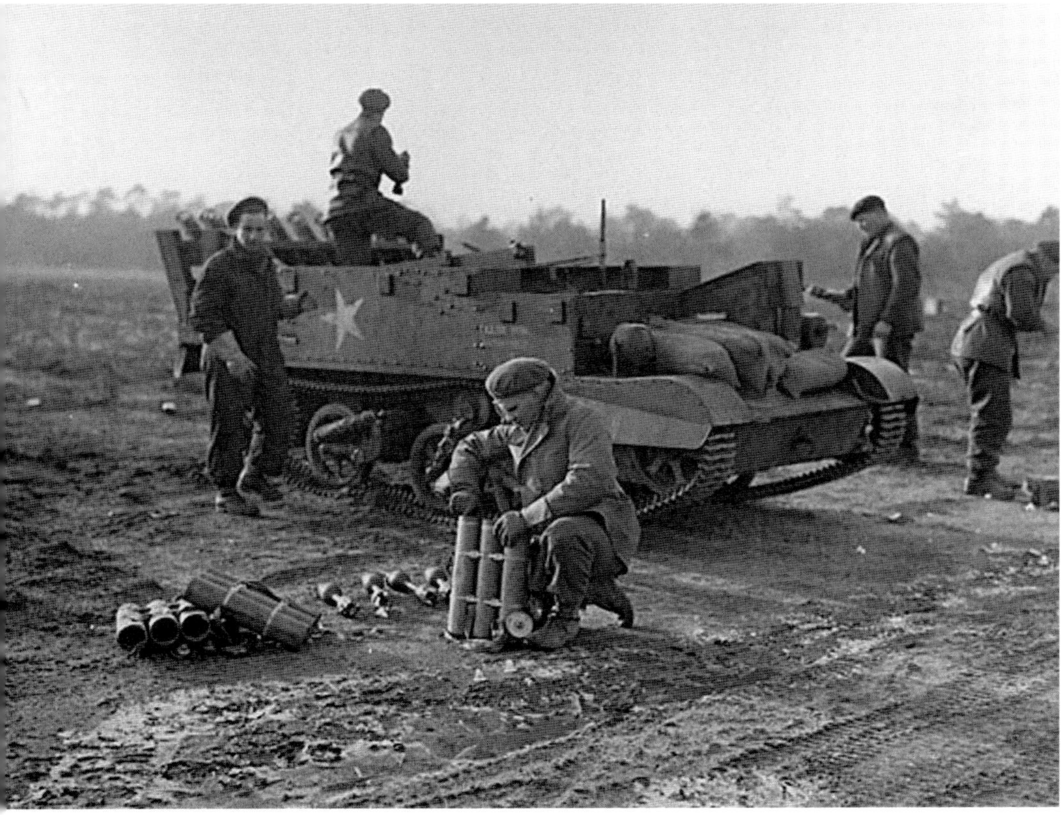

Three soldiers equipped with Stens during house-to-house fighting in Geilenkirchen, December 1944. Of note is the PIAT gunner also carrying a Sten and none of the soldiers seem to be carrying tubes of bombs. It is possible from the fact that the soldiers are carrying a little more kit than they usually would for combat that this picture is close to but not actually at the front lines.

their carrier platoon, then the rest clung onto the tanks. Two DUKWs brought up the rear, loaded with stores. The road the flying column needed to take was a series of road junctions, first a right, then a short while later a left turn. The leading part of the column completed this manoeuvre, however, a German counter-attack from five Tigers cut off the column. The DCLI's A Company laid an anti-armour ambush. During the night the five Tigers approached, launching flares to illuminate their surroundings. The lead tank ran into a mine placed to block the road and lost its tracks. At this signal, the infantry laid out along the length of the killing zone opened fire to keep the Tigers suppressed. The PIAT gunners immediately killed the first tank with a salvo of bombs, and seconds later they destroyed the second in line. By now the rearmost Tigers were frantically reversing, unable to spot the deadly British weapon. The third Tiger in line reversed over a mine that had been pulled into the road, and suffered the same fate as the lead Tiger, with its track blown off and then smashed by the rapid-firing PIATs. The last two tanks in their haste managed to reverse off the road and immobilize themselves.

There are many stories of the PIAT in action, and indeed an entire book could be filled detailing them all. But here are some hints for further research.

About five VCs were won by PIAT-wielding Commonwealth soldiers and the first Panzer destroyed by ground fire in North-West Europe fell to a PIAT at Pegasus Bridge.

Up until now, only the PIAT Mk I has been discussed. Indeed, it seems odd to refer to the PIAT as a 'Mk I' as this appears to have been the only version. However, there was a PIAT Mk II and it was a completely different weapon. It is not known exactly when Blacker began work on the Mk II, but it is clear when his plans were completed. All the plans of the weapon are dated about 5 March 1943. Blacker named this weapon gun No. 100, but seems to have used this interchangeably with 'PIAT Mk II'. From what little is known it seems the weapon was an attempt to make a lighter PIAT for airborne troops. Counterintuitively, the body of the Mk II was longer than the Mk I. However, Blacker had designed the weapon to be semi-collapsible. The handguard around the trigger and the pistol grip could be folded flat and locked against the buttstock. In addition, the loading tray was much smaller and could be pivoted through 180 degrees to lie flat against the body of the weapon. In doing so the tray had to pass through the spigot. Thus, the weapon had to be stored cocked, which raised some eyebrows at the trials. Two Mk IIs were

The two surviving PIAT Mk II prototypes (centre and bottom), with what appears to be an early prototype of the PIAT (top). When compared with the photograph of the Mk II it can be seen that the loading tray is very different.

The only known photograph of the PIAT Mk II. At the rear is the standard PIAT, and it is instantly clear that the Mk II is longer but uses the same bomb.

sent to the Small Arms School at Hythe for trials. On reception, one of the weapons was uncocked, stripped, reassembled, cocked and placed back in its transport case. Two days later the weapon was prepared for its trials. It was found to be inoperable on two points, first, a small screw on the trigger had sheared. The trigger had not been disassembled in the initial strip. Second, the clip holding the monopod had broken. Indeed, the means of attaching the monopod to the gun came in for quite a lot of criticism. It should be noted that there appear to be several modifications of the PIAT Mk II, so it is likely that Blacker tinkered with the design at some point. One variant had a much more substantial loading tray. The other is reported as having a monopod attached to the trigger guard. There is a single picture of a Mk II with the larger loading tray and a monopod in its traditional place. There are two surviving Mk II's with the reduced loading tray, and an identical monopod placement to the one in the picture. There is one reference to the monopod attached to the trigger guard as 'Experimental Delta', although there is no mention of what this means, but could it be the fourth gun made?

In the trials, using normal PIAT ammunition, the Mk II fired five rounds without fault, then on the sixth, and once again on the eighth, the recoil caused the loading tray to jump up slightly. It was judged the spring-loaded clip holding the tray was insufficiently strong. The Mk II proved to be more accurate than the service weapon at 70yd, and about the same at 100yd. This was despite having slightly less muzzle velocity, 255fps against the service weapon's 262fps. Despite this, it was decided not to continue with the development of the Mk II, with the decision to cancel being taken on 4 January 1944, and confirmed by the Ordnance Board on the 26th of the same month.

The PIAT had several advantages, and few disadvantages when compared to the platoon level infantry anti-tank weapons of the other nations, such as the US Bazooka or the German *Panzerfaust*. In the case of the Bazooka, the first hint of the weapon was when a memo was sent to Winston Churchill from the Military Mission in the USA in July 1942. It talked of a new anti-tank rifle that fired rockets, and stated one was en route to the UK. The weapon had arrived and was demonstrated on 15 August. The results were very disappointing, to say the least. During the demonstration, the T1 Bazooka had proved woefully inaccurate being unable to hit the target plate set up for it. It was judged impossible to fire safely from the prone position due to the backblast. Safety reared its head again when the loading drill was reviewed. It was judged that the weapon had a very high risk of prematures. Finally, the entire contraption was seen as weak, fragile and of a rather poor ability to stand up to robust field conditions.

When compared with platoon level anti-tank weapons used by other nations, the PIAT seems to be largely superior (see Table 6).

Table 6. Comparison of Platoon Level Anti-tank Weapons

	PIAT	Bazooka (M1 and M6A1 rocket)	*Panzerfaust* 60
Weight Launcher	32lb	18lb	13lb
Weight Projectile	2.25lb	3.5lb	
Length	39in	54in	41in
Calibre	3.25in	2.36in	5.86in
Danger Area	None	49.21ft	15ft
Penetration	Mks I and IA: over 91mm Later Mks: over 100mm	76mm (later over 100mm)	200mm
Muzzle Velocity	262fps	265fps	148fps
Range			
Effective	115yd	100–150yd	40yd
Max.	350yd	400yd	60yd
Accuracy at 100yd (*Panzerfaust* 60 at 60yd)			
m.d. Height	14.8 mins	11.4 mins	27.8 mins
m.d. Line	8 mins	11.4 mins	13.5 mins

A PIAT crew in Tunisia, 1943. The team appears to be rather well-armed, with the loader carrying both a 1928 Thompson SMG and a revolver.

Oddly, exact figures for the penetration of the PIAT or Bazooka are not available, although records show armour values that they beat, but not what the maximum figure is. The issue arises as many documents do not detail what particular mark or model of the round they are firing. There was a trial in the first half of 1943, most likely involving the Mk I or Mk IA bomb and so suffering from reduced penetration performance, which gives us an idea of the effect of the PIAT. First a Panzer Mk III was used as a target, and unsurprisingly the bomb penetrated both the front and side armour. The behind-armour effect was considerable, with the walls on all sides of the fighting compartment being flayed with splinters and shrapnel, as well as the inside of the cupola. Next, a Tiger tank was used as a target. The trials held no surprises, with the PIAT being effective against all but frontal shots. This at first glance seems to raise a contradiction, with the tests in the UK showing penetrations higher than the front hull plate on a Tiger. However, if it is considered that the first bombs had reduced effectiveness due to manufacturing defects, then it all becomes clearer. A Mk I or Mk IA only had a 91mm proof requirement, due to the mistakes in the manufacturing process, and later these were fixed and the proof went back up to 100mm. The advice for the tactical employment of the PIAT likely came to some degree from these tests, and so has become part of the myth surrounding the weapon.

On a point of interest, these tests also included trials of the No. 74 Sticky Bomb against a Tiger, which was found to be highly effective.

It should also be noted while looking at Table 6 above, that the Bazooka incorporated some data from later models of the M6 rocket, and the *Panzerfaust* 60 is from later in the war than the other two. Matters were not going to improve for the Germans either, with the *Panzerfaust* 100 having an accuracy with a mean deviation in height of 40.6 mins and line of 16.5 mins at 100yd. To give you an idea of what this means, a minute of angle equates to about 1in or 2.5cm at 100yd.

One cannot help but think the PIAT was, instead of a comedy weapon as portrayed by a great many commentators, actually the best platoon level anti-tank weapon of the Second World War, either matching or beating the Bazooka, and certainly being more robust and having a dual purpose round. The *Panzerfaust* 60, a weapon designed a year or two after the PIAT, is not even in the same league, being inferior in almost every way. The other weapons also lacked the anti-personnel effect and the rate of fire. This might account for the PIAT's success after the war, which will be discussed in a later chapter.

PART SIX

ENGINEERING SPIGOTS
PETARD, DENNY GUN AND BUFFALO

Chapter Fourteen

The Stolen Tank of Victory

At just after 0530 on 19 August 1942, between 5 and 10 minutes late, the tank landing craft's bow doors crashed down onto the chert beaches of Dieppe. With their way clear, the Churchill Tanks of the Calgary Tank Regiment lurched forward onto Red and White Beaches. What happened over the next few hours is well documented, with innumerable books and webpages providing minute detail for the historian to pore over. The vast majority of the actions on that day are outside the scope of this work, however, some parts are the start of our next story.

One of the soldiers scrabbling through the gunfire that day was Lieutenant Colonel George Clive Reeves. From March 1942 he was the assistant director of the Special Devices Branch, a department within the Department for Tank Design (DTD). He was at Dieppe as an observer, especially of the engineering solutions used in the operation. One such solution was a type of rolled mat to help vehicles cross the chert beach, but these were laid by hand. To get across the sea wall there was a plan to build a ramp from wooden beams unloaded from a landing craft, and, finally, for low walls there was a device not too dissimilar to the Bobbin from later in the war. However, in the operation, the engineers were mown down by German gunfire from bunkers, and the return fire from the Churchills was unable to dent the German positions. Not one of the timbers was unloaded for the ramp over the sea wall.

On his return, Lieutenant Colonel Reeves summoned his department to a meeting, where he outlined the problems he had witnessed and asked for thoughts and ideas to overcome the German beach defences. One of the people at the meeting was the Canadian Lieutenant John James Denovan. Lieutenant Denovan became quite obsessed with the idea of an engineer tank and proceeded to work on it with some ferocity. By August 1942 he had drawn up some plans, and with Lieutenant Colonel Reeves' permission he submitted the paper to the War Office on the 27th. It was just three pages long and entitled 'The Engineer Tank'. A meeting with the authorities and Lieutenant Denovan was duly scheduled. Lieutenant Colonel Reeves accompanied the young officer, to give him some backing and support. The War Office agreed that there was a case for an engineering vehicle, however, they indicated the usual process would be followed for new equipment. They stated the Special Devices Branch was an advisory group to the departments,

Abandoned tanks litter the chert beach at Dieppe, while a landing craft burns in the background. Both Churchills appear to have thrown their tracks, likely caused by the terrain.

and thus work would be carried out elsewhere, and Lieutenant Denovan was to return to his usual duties. Understandably, Lieutenant Denovan was rather upset at this turn of events. Lieutenant Colonel Reeves apologized to Lieutenant Denovan, but agreed he had to follow orders. Lieutenant Colonel Reeves did say that Lieutenant Denovan could use the facilities of the Special Devices Branch outside of office hours to work on the project. That is why, towards the end of 1942, the UK had two armoured engineering vehicle projects underway, the official one and Lieutenant Denovan's highly unofficial one.

Lieutenant Denovan calculated that by removing the turret basket on a Churchill Tank, along with its ammunition racks, 144 cubic feet of space would be freed up. Into this space, Lieutenant Denovan determined you could fit a crew of five men and up to 500lb of engineering stores. His concept, at this time, seems to have been that the tank is landed and goes about its engineering tasks to allow conventional forces to get off the beach. Then it heads towards the nearest ammunition supply point, loads up on main gun ammunition and acts as a slightly inferior gun tank. The engineering tasks that Lieutenant Denovan had in mind were mostly demolition related. He seems to have concluded that it would be difficult to build a ramp over the sea wall or other obstacles, and so simply demolishing the structure was the way to go.

This new design had a pair of petrol-driven jackhammers that could be operated from inside the tank through an opening in the side, and used to create holes in the concrete. Then a series of folding armoured doors could be extended from the side of the tank to create a safe space for the engineers to work installing the explosives. During this activity the tank would be parallel to the surface the engineers were working on. A later iteration of the design did away with the armoured screen and the tank would use its bulk to provide shelter, as the driver would place the corner of the tracks against the wall, leaving a space behind the angled hull that was sheltered from enemy fire. Towards the end of September, Lieutenant Denovan had decided he had gone as far as he could on paper. What he needed now was a Churchill Tank to modify into a prototype. Obviously, he could not obtain one officially as he was not meant to be working on the subject.

Then one day, in the second half of September, a brand-new Churchill Tank arrived at a Canadian Engineers workshop commanded by Captain S.W. Schortinghuis, who was Lieutenant Denovan's partner in crime, quite literally as it turns out. The tank had been stolen. Lieutenant Denovan was, at the time, seeing a young lady who worked for the tank department of the Ministry of Supply. The office she worked in controlled all movements of tanks and routing of the finished vehicles to units. The unnamed lady simply shuffled some papers around, altered a form or two and a tank was rerouted from its intended destination and into Lieutenant Denovan's clutches. It is a curious twist of fate that the Churchill is likely the one tank that this could happen to, or at least was most susceptible. Even today we do not know exactly how many Churchills were produced, simply because there were so many sub-contractors, and Vauxhall used a card-index system that was often corrected and modified, leaving a confusing mess behind. The stolen Churchill was placed at the back of the workshops and Lieutenant Denovan was able to work on it in his own time. By 6 October, he had completed some considerable work and had even removed the gun. It is highly likely that the workshop unit lent him unofficial help beyond just giving him a place to store his project.

On 1 October 1942, the now promoted Colonel Reeves travelled to Farnborough to view the official engineering tank project. Only it was not a tank, but a wheeled vehicle, and in fact it was actually two lightly armoured trucks. Neither had been put through any trials at the time of Colonel Reeves' visit, so he was only able to give a few details of the project, but even these did not seem promising. The vehicles were designed to operate in pairs, with a demolition and a compressor version to make up the pair. Both appeared to be unique in shape, and readily identifiable even at 2,000yd and so would attract fire. Each vehicle was only protected by 14mm of armour, but even that was straining the limits of the short wheelbase. New front springs had been installed to compensate for the overloaded weight, but it was expected that all the other parts of the running gear would fail and require stronger versions to be fitted. Neither vehicle was armed with anything more than personnel weapons. The demolition vehicle carried a driver and four others, with 5cwt (about 560lb) of explosives in the boot of the vehicle. The compressor vehicle has a single crewman as the driver but carried a TS20 compressor manufactured by Air Pumps Ltd. This was driven by a power take-off from the engine. The truck also carried the usual assortment of tools one would expect to find with such a compressor. The engines on both vehicles gave 78bhp and were four-wheel drive. If either vehicle was knocked out the remaining one became all but useless. Colonel Reeves closed off his report emphasizing the importance of an engineer tank. Unsurprisingly, the two-engineer vehicle solution was deemed unworkable and disappeared from the records shortly after this. However, there was another official project. On 29 September 1942, Lieutenant Colonel W.J. Cardale put forward the idea of an engineering tank based upon a Churchill. The Director of Special Devices agreed to produce some drawings to illustrate the rough idea of what was needed in such an engineer tank. On 22 October it was decided to create a prototype of this vehicle, and one Churchill in good working order, albeit no requirement for it to be brand new, was requested to be delivered to a Canadian workshop company. Both prototypes seem to have been given official sanction by 14 January 1943. Lieutenant Denovan's unofficial project also explains why at the Hankley Common demonstration on 25 February 1943 there were two tanks showcasing their engineering abilities, one armed with the Petard, the other without.

The range of dates and events for these vehicles is quite diverse, and this is because of the source documents. Most of the material is based on eyewitness accounts, which are always unreliable, particularly given that they were produced about eight years after the events. It is notable that no mention is made of spigot weapons, and this is because the involvement of these weapons in the project was just as convoluted and confusing and some documents are even contradictory. Therefore, it is at first helpful to have an outline of the development of the engineering tank.

When Lieutenant Denovan had written his first paper, in August 1942, he had already been experimenting with a Bombard. The idea was to mount the Bombard's spigot directly onto the turret front, with a vane sight on the roof. Reloading would have been impossible, so Lieutenant Denovan's plan was to carry several pre-loaded spigots on the tank, with the main gun still in place. The role of this spigot launcher was to replace explosive devices such as the Onion or Carrot, which required a tank to drive up to the appropriate location with the explosive charge on the front of the tank, drop the charge and then reverse to a safe distance before detonating. Lieutenant

Denovan recognized that it was much easier simply to fire the explosives as a projectile.

Lieutenant Denovan found his spigot arrangement did not work as the spigots bent as they absorbed all the recoil, and equally the welds that held the spigots to the turret cracked. This implies that Lieutenant Denovan had some form of testing apparatus and a firing range on which to test from the start of his project.

In September Lieutenant Denovan, as part of his duties, visited a demonstration of demolition weapons in Sussex. It appears this work would result in the famous Flying Dustbin projectile, although at this time there was no gun to fire it and no official requirement for the weapon. One of the people at the demonstration was Jim Lorren from ICI. Lieutenant Denovan must have confided in him to some extent about his tank because that evening Mr Lorren took the young Canadian officer for a short drive to a large stately home. Wondering what was going on, Lieutenant Denovan was greeted by none other than the now retired Stewart Blacker. There is no record of that meeting, but one can make a good guess how Mr Blacker reacted to Lieutenant Denovan's story of bureaucracy and officialdom. More than likely, the maverick act of stealing a tank, if this tale were told, would have appealed to Blacker. Lieutenant Denovan outlined what he wanted. Ideally a large, scaled up PIAT, capable of firing a projectile weighing up to 50lb. As Blacker Developments Ltd had recently finished work on the PIAT, Blacker was only too happy to help, immediately grabbing pencil and notebook and scribbling down ideas. Over the next couple of months, Lieutenant Denovan stayed in contact with one of the engineers from Blacker Developments Ltd, a Mr Farrow, and designs began to come together. However, the trigger mechanism was causing problems and delays. This situation caused Lieutenant Denovan considerable frustration, so he went ahead and designed and built his spigot mortar along the lines of what he wanted, which he called the 'Denny Gun'. By the end of November and early December Blacker Developments Ltd had overcome the difficulties with the firing mechanism and the work had speeded up. There were firing trials between the prototype Petard, as the Blacker weapon became known, and the Denny Gun. In this test the weapons were likely fired from ground mounts, the Petard performing perfectly, but the Denny Gun suffering a defective firing pin. Due to this and the Petard nearing completion, the Denny Gun was scrapped. Lieutenant Denovan carried on working with Mr Farrow to design the mountings for the weapon. There would need to be two types of mounting, one for a Churchill turret that mounted the 2-pounder and one for the 6-pounder mounting. Three 2-pounder versions were built and fired from the tanks. The ammunition design was also complete at about this time. Following the Hankley Common demonstration, the decision had been taken to create engineer tanks, now termed Assault Vehicle, Royal Engineers (AVRE), on 6-pounder tanks only.

The accurate range of the Petard was 150yd, although there was a significant amount of holdover needed to achieve that range, so much so the gunsight was only 1.9 magnification to allow the reticule to fit in the picture.

The loading sequence of the Petard was rather unique. The vast majority of tank guns are breech-loaded of one sort or another. Thus, the gun can be loaded from inside the tank turret. As spigots are, to all intents and purposes, loaded from the muzzle this created certain difficulties. Especially in the case of the AVRE, as the tank would most likely be under intense enemy fire during its deployment, and thus the chances of survival for anyone clambering around on the outside of the tank would be rather limited. The solution was a tilting loading tray. With the spigot in the cocked position, and thus retracted, the loading tray would pivot through 90 degrees so that it was pointing directly upwards. This would be swung over the co-driver's roof hatch, which was replaced by a sliding plate. The loader could then simply

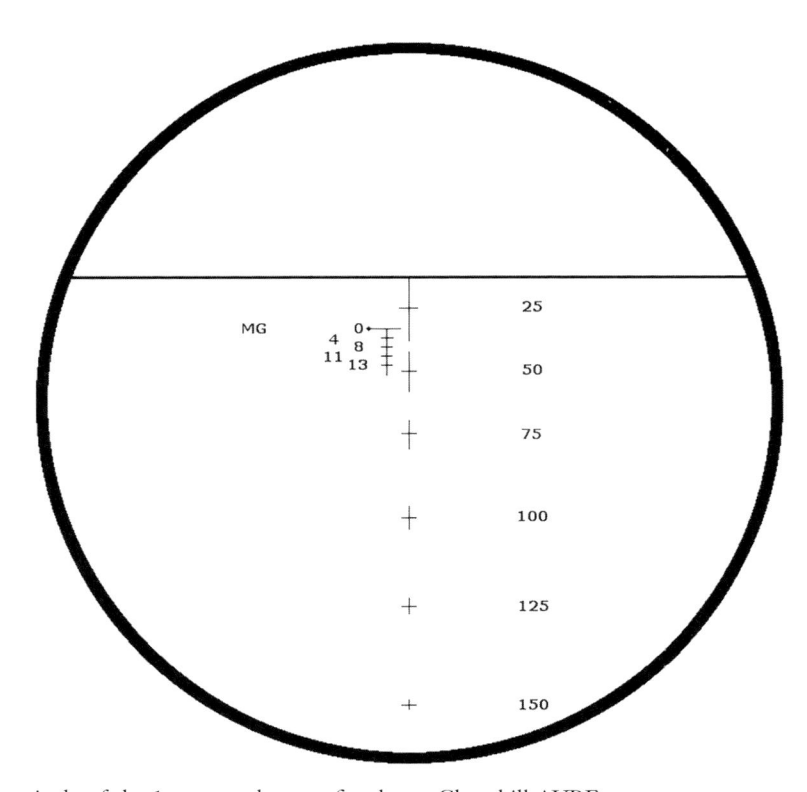

The reticule of the 1× gun telescope fitted to a Churchill AVRE.

shove the projectile, known as the Bomb, Demolition, No. 1, 40lb, but more commonly called a 'Flying Dustbin' by the crews, into the loading tray where a spring clip would hold it in position, at which point the tray would be locked back in its firing position. The projectile came with a very similar loading clip to the PIAT, almost identical in design and shape, just larger, so the Petard could be quite freely depressed with no risk of the Dustbin falling out. This ingenious design of the loading tray was created by James Williamson & Son Ltd in December 1943.

To cock the weapon there were two means available, either a manual winch, which took longer, or a pressure system. The latter was fed by a revolving cylinder with six cartridges. When one of these was fired the burning cordite would be vented into the combustion chamber. From here the gas pressure would re-cock the spigot.

The Flying Dustbin, as the official name would suggest, was a 40lb projectile with a base fuse. The filling was a combination of Nobels 808 explosive in the forepart and a Pentolite charge at the base around the fuse. There is

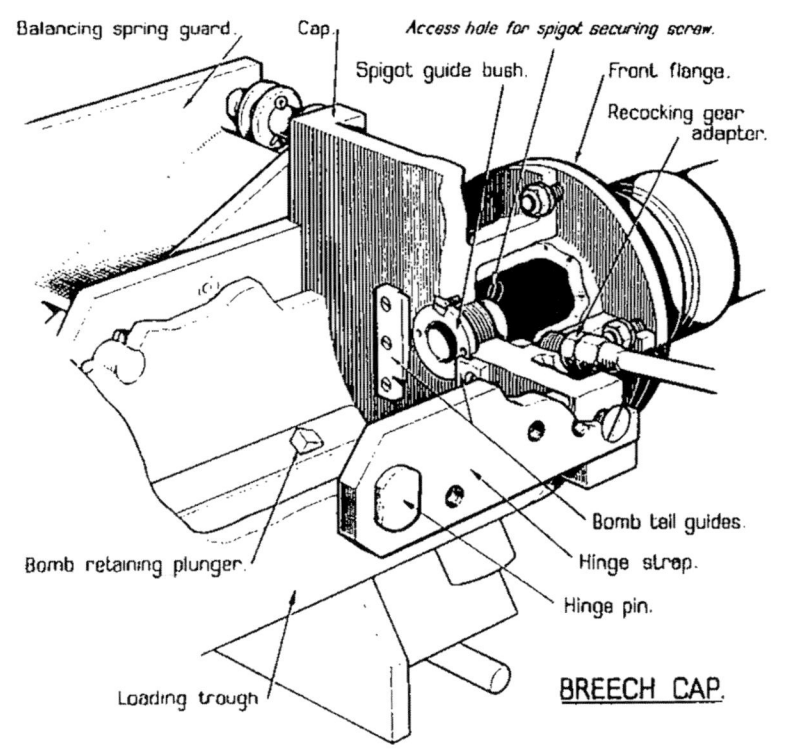

A diagram of the Petard's loading tray. The part marked 'bomb tail guides' functioned in the same way as a retaining clip on a PIAT.

speculation that this was used so the plastic nature of the Nobels 808 filling spread out but the blast was reinforced by the Pentolite disk sitting on top of the wad of plastic smeared over the target. The Dustbin, like the smaller Bombard projectile, was a HESH round. This was due to the capabilities of HESH, which was very good at destroying concrete obstacles and fortifications. As with all HESH rounds, it retained its anti-armour functionality, as would be shown on 17 July 1944 at Tilly-sur-Seulles, when an AVRE fired at a Panther that blundered out in front of the Churchill at just 50yd. By sheer chance, the round hit a telegraph pole in between the Panther and the

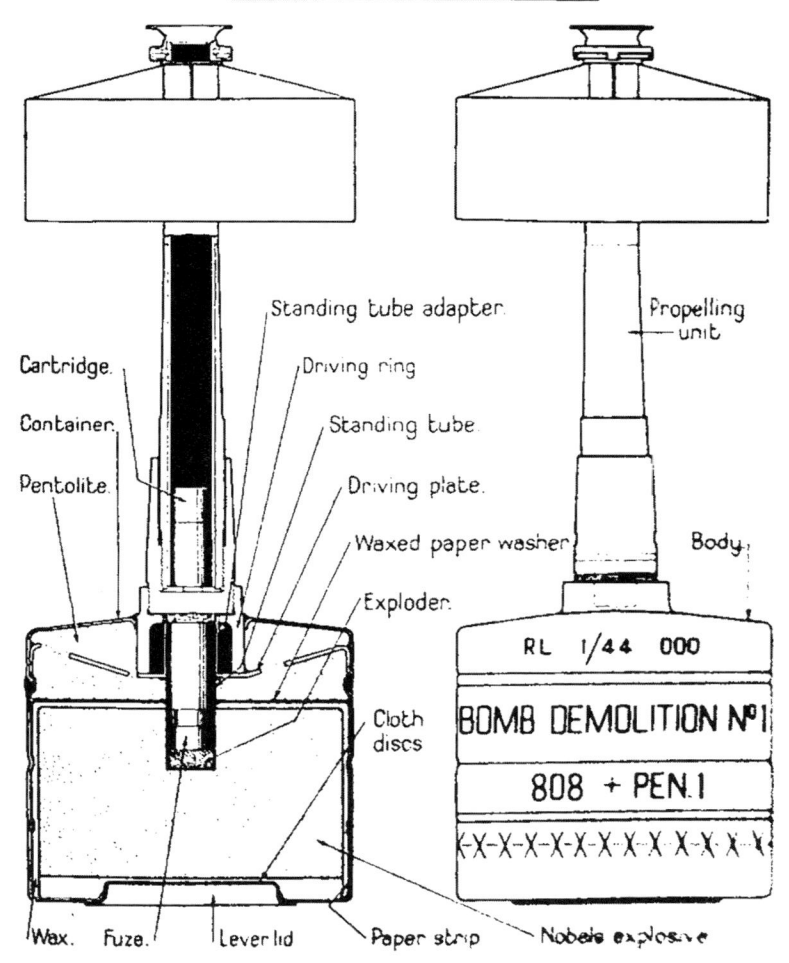

A cutaway of the No. 1 Demolition Bomb, and its markings.

AVRE, but even then the blast was sufficient to immobilize the Panther. If the round had hit, the 25.99lb of explosive filling would certainly have obliterated the German tank. The Petard bomb could also be fused to detonate about 6ft above the ground. The blast from this would clear a circle of about 12–15ft diameter of mines.

One curiosity with the Petard is the nomenclature. Modern works all describe it as '290mm'. This appears to be false, with the diameter of the bomb being 229mm, or 9in, which would have been the measurement used at the time. There appears to be no record of when, or why, the 290mm measurement arrived in the historical record.

An AVRE crewman of the 5th Assault Regiment screws the tail of a Petard round into its warhead. A second warhead awaits its turn. This picture was taken on 29 April 1944 so these bombs are likely being prepared for D-Day.

186 *Defeating the Panzer-Stuka Menace*

The original plan was for the AVRE to be converted in unit workshops, much like Lieutenant Denovan had done. However, there is a curious lull in paperwork relating to the AVRE and the Petard between the Hankley Common demonstration in late February 1943 and the next firm date of early September 1943. There is no accounting for these lost six months, and one can only guess that the exact roles of the tank and devices to be attached were being developed. On 6 September 1943, there was a meeting held to discuss the AVRE. There were several amendments and additions tabled, and it was decided that the new tank would be based upon the Churchill and that it should be capable of mounting a winch for bridge laying, have the ability to carry and release a fascine and the internal storage arrangements needed to be revised with the addition of protected ammunition bins. This work was judged to be beyond the capabilities of the unit workshops, and so it was requested that a manufacturing company be brought in to convert the tanks. The 79th Armoured Division, which was to be the main operator of the tank, felt this was a criticism of their abilities, and continued with their plans to convert some 108 tanks. However, as time went on it became clear the required modifications really were beyond their expertise and Cocksedge & Co. were brought in to help. Even then the workload kept on expanding, so MG (the car manufacturer) was also drafted in to assist with the work.

By October 1943 Denovan had been promoted to captain and he put forward an alternative idea to replace the Petard, which was called the Churchill Buffalo. This involved the use of a fixed spigot, instead of a recoiling spigot. It was vastly simpler than the Petard and even cheaper than one might expect as it used parts from a Bombard. The fixed spigot was mounted directly onto an interrupted screw thread, which passed through a matching tube in the mount. At the opposite end of the interrupted screw to the spigot was a handle. By turning the handle by 45 degrees the screw thread was disengaged, and the spigot could be pulled backwards. This allowed a new bomb to be loaded, in a manner identical to the Petard. Once the loading tray was back in position the spigot was pushed forwards into the tail tube, and the handle turned to re-engage the screw thread. It appears that the weapon was not adopted due to concerns about the range.

The finalized AVRE entered production in very late 1943, just a handful of months before her greatest show. About 475 AVREs would be converted throughout the last two years of the war. The cost of these conversions was £88,000. In total there were 164,000 Flying Dustbins produced, setting the Treasury back some £704,000.

On D-Day, the AVREs blasted, bridged and bobbined their way through the Atlantic Wall, launching the Allied troops into Europe. The specialist engineering tanks, including the AVREs, of the 79th Armoured Division, were in the first waves and their presence made the Commonwealth landings

A Churchill AVRE fitted with a Bobbin carpet-layer. These would be unrolled as the tank advanced across the beach, serving to both flatten any wire encountered and to enable other vehicles to cross the beach without becoming bogged down in the sand.

vastly easier and cheaper than the US assaults. From that initial success, the AVREs were present at many assaults, helping to reduce fortresses such as the radar station at Douvres, and the fortification at Le Harve.

At the later battle, the Commonwealth forces faced possibly one of their tougher challenges. The city was surrounded to the east, south and west by water, so the only overland route was to the north. The Germans, of course, were well aware of this and had crammed every single defensive measure they could into the area. There were dense minefields, with an anti-tank ditch, both covered by concrete bunkers bristling with weapons. Behind were artillery pieces and other support weapons, all pre-registered on targets and

188 *Defeating the Panzer-Stuka Menace*

aiming points. The Commonwealth forces had to charge straight into this killing field swept with fire. The main instrument of breaching these defences was the AVREs.

On the evening of 10 September, the assault began. The late start was to ensure there was enough light for the engineering tanks to breach the lines but that the infantry would have the cover of darkness to close with the enemy. Some light was provided by searchlights shone into the air over the city, and this added diffuse illumination and gave the attackers a way of orientating themselves in the confusion of a night battle. It was known as 'Monty's Moonlight'.

The AVREs advanced and behind them they were towing 'Snakes'. These were very long Bangalore torpedos, made from 3in pipe filled with explosives, and could be up to 400ft in length. As the AVREs reached the first defensive layer, the anti-tank ditch, the engineers opened the hatch in the centre of the AVRE's floor. From there they could access the Snake and push it forward into position. When the Snake was located correctly, the wire linked to the detonator was fixed in place. With the wire still inside the tank, the AVRE backed off a short distance and the line charge was blown. This would clear a small lane in the minefield beyond the anti-tank ditch.

Then more AVREs advanced, carrying Small Box Girder Bridges which were laid over the ditch, so that the far end of the bridge was in the start of the lane cleared by the Snakes. Then the Flail tanks were sent over to clear the lane properly and widen it. All the time German fire was rattling off the AVREs'

As the sun sets on the horizon a Churchill AVRE advances on Le Harve, 10 September 1944.

thick armour. Foot engineers in such a situation trying to perform these tasks would have had an impossibly short life expectancy. Once the lane was clear, infantry and the AVREs moved forward. The AVREs used their Petards to silence any troublesome pillboxes. AVREs, Crocodile flame-throwing tanks and Flails formed small task forces that supported the infantry pushing forwards. Before dawn on the 11th, a group of these tanks found themselves near the harbour. They waited until daylight and approached one of the main German fortresses within the town under a flag of truce. The negotiators offered surrender to the Germans, which was rejected. Upon returning to the lines a Crocodile was ordered forward, it blasted a jet of flame into the wall of the fortress, as a fearsome promise of what would happen next. The Germans promptly surrendered. In total, some 11,300 Germans surrendered in Le Havre, although some die-hards kept fighting until the following day. The AVREs had been instrumental in reducing the fortress, and without them the cost to just get into the outer layer of defences would have been staggering. As it was, about twenty-nine Sherman flail tanks were damaged, along with six AVREs.

The Churchill AVRE would serve as the only British armoured engineering tank until 1948 when it was supplemented by the FV3903, based on a Churchill Mk VII armed with a 6.5in demolition gun; see the author's title *The Dark Age of Tanks*. Both tanks would serve side by side until the early 1960s. The Petard-armed AVREs were retired in 1962, as the Centurion AVRE came into service. The FV3903 was retired a couple of years later. The Petard was the last spigot weapon in service with the British armed forces and had proved its worth. The fact that it remained in service for about twenty years when a more conventional weapon had been developed hints at its utility.

PART SEVEN

THE MATILDA HEDGEHOG

by Thomas Anderson

Chapter Fifteen

Spigots in the South-West Pacific

In the latter half of the Second World War Australia found itself committed to a conflict that was radically different to the war that was experienced by many of its Commonwealth allies, and indeed a radical departure from the war Australia had anticipated fighting. Naturally, it follows that the employment of spigot weapons by Australian forces was both unorthodox and innovative in the context of the South-West Pacific.

When war was declared against Germany on 3 September 1939, the structure of the Australian armed forces was relatively unchanged from what had been established at the end of the First World War in 1918. Small-scale experimentation and refinement had been conducted in the interwar period, however, overall a lack of funds and prevailing political circumstances had precluded any major deviations from the established orthodoxy or the ability to maintain a supply of up-to-date armaments. The limited funding available was wisely directed towards establishing a local production capacity to support existing types of conventional armaments as well as the more up-to-date models that were anticipated to enter service soon. Hence in the initial phase of the war, Australian industrial and military priorities were focused on directing this carefully hoarded industrial capacity to supply the latest models of standard British armaments, such as 25-pounder field guns and Bren light machine guns. Furthermore, the prevailing opinion within the armed forces was that the Australian Army would function as an auxiliary force to the larger British Army, relying on them for logistical support and more specialized equipment that could not be produced locally. Therefore, development of armaments adapted to the needs and climate of the Australian continent was disregarded in favour of maintaining consistency with British armaments and organization. The Australian General Staff predominantly focused on structuring the 2nd Australian Imperial Force (AIF) for manoeuvre warfare, in emulation of existing British forces deployed to Europe and North Africa. Particular attention was paid to the development of mobile arms such as motorized artillery, anti-tank guns and fighting vehicles, such as Bren carriers and even tanks. Indeed, it was with great ambition that the Australian General Staff intended to raise no less than three full armoured divisions, with the first to be equipped and ready by the end of 1941. In hindsight we know that none of the Australian Armoured Divisions would ever see action overseas at full

Troopers Hoskin, Lear and Elton sitting on the cupola turret of tank 10194, Australia, 1946. The markings of 4th Armoured Brigade Group and the 2/4 Armoured Regiment can be seen on the front of the vehicle. The angled side plates of the production projectors and the mesh anti-bomb screens fitted to the top of the projector and engine decks are visible.

scale, and indeed none of them would ever reach their full complement of men and equipment before being disbanded in late 1943. Nonetheless, in 1941, the state of affairs in North Africa and the presumed eventual progression to combat on the European mainland made such dreams of large-scale manoeuvre warfare seem more pragmatic. With the bombing of Pearl Harbor and the subsequent declaration of war against Japan in December 1941, Australia was forced to weigh up the division of its military force between the Middle East and the Pacific. Subsequently, the Australian 8th Division, which had been preparing for deployment to the Middle East, was hastily equipped and split into four forces stationed at Malaya, Rabaul, Ambon and Timor. Matters continued to escalate with the fall of Singapore and the decimation of the 8th Division as Japanese forces swept through East Asia and the South Pacific in early 1942. Furthermore, the Japanese occupation of Papua New Guinea in early to mid-1942 gave the impression that a Japanese invasion of the Australian mainland was a very real and imminent threat (although, unbeknown to the Allies, the Japanese had swiftly abandoned any plans to invade Australia as logistically impossible). The general organization and armoured divisions established for war in the Middle East were therefore retained under the logic of maintaining a large mobile force for defence of the Australian mainland against a Japanese landing. After the Allied counter-push into the Pacific in the later part of 1942, the need for a mobile anti-invasion force decreased while the challenging circumstances of jungle fighting in the South-West Pacific became increasingly apparent. In early 1943, to meet the new requirements of the harsh jungle environment, the standard infantry division was reformed into a new 'Jungle Division' structure, which had a greatly reduced complement of heavy equipment such as vehicles, heavy machine guns and artillery. The three armoured divisions were gradually disbanded and reorganized as either part of defensive forces stationed in North-Western Australia or integrated into the new 4th Armoured Brigade Group. The 4th Armoured Brigade Group consisted of several armoured regiments transferred from the disbanded armoured divisions and reorganized on a 'tropical scale' for deployment in jungle conditions. The units of 4th Armoured Brigade Group were not intended for massed armoured actions, but rather to allow small units of tanks to be parcelled out independently, on a squadron or troop basis, to support infantry forces at various locations throughout the South-West Pacific Theatre.

Beginning in 1942, as Australian forces battled against the Japanese through Papua New Guinea and the South-West Pacific, it became apparent that there was an increasing need for offensive armaments capable of demolishing Japanese defensive positions. The typical Japanese bunker encountered was a fighting pit, reinforced by interlocked palm logs and roofed with either timber or sheet metal, on top of which a layer of earth approximately 18in thick was placed on the roof and sides of the bunker. Its low profile made it incredibly difficult to identify in a jungle environment and the nature of its construction made it very resistant to light weapons fire, particularly weapons with impact or graze fuses where the explosive force was absorbed by the earth layer. Australian forces encountered great difficulty when faced with these defences, as the resilient structure meant that even if the firing port was destroyed the soldiers inside were often unharmed, which resulted in attacking Allied soldiers bypassing the presumably destroyed bunker only to be assaulted from behind by the emerging Japanese defenders.

The initial tool for dealing with these defences was the 'blast bomb', otherwise known as the 'Grenade Initiated Ammonal Charge', a field expedient constructed by attaching a standard infantry grenade to a tin full of ammonal explosive. While this may seem to be a crude solution, a standardized design was developed that was both simple and effective. The primary charge consisted of a tin 4in in diameter and 4.5in deep containing 2lb of loose ammonal explosive. The baseplate of a rifle grenade (7-second fuse type) was placed inside the tin with a small hole cut in the side of the tin allowing the baseplate threading to extend outside. A length of primacord was also threaded through the hole with a section remaining outside the tin. A No. 36 infantry grenade formed the primary fuse of the weapon, attaching to the tin of explosives by being screwed onto the exposed threading of the rifle-grenade base. The exposed end of the primacord was then looped around the grenade and secured in place with adhesive tape. In action the weapon functioned identically to a regular grenade, albeit producing a far greater blast, with the pin being removed and the trigger released to activate a 4-second fuse. By late March 1944 it was recommended that a refined 'Blast Bomb Mk II', which substituted the ammonal charge for 1 ¾ lb of TNT, be adopted and issued at a rate of 1,000 bombs per division. Although effective enough to be adopted for standardization as a production armament and recommended for further refinement, the blast bomb still had limitations. Primarily the blast effect of the weapon was only enough to destroy a Japanese bunker if detonated inside the structure, and external detonation would only result in superficial damage. Furthermore, as an infantry grenade it required soldiers to approach the target close enough that the bomb could be reliably thrown through the firing slit into the interior of the bunker. A variation of combining the 2lb ammonal charge with a No. 68 rifle grenade was considered to allow for greater range, however, static testing showed that external detonation of the charge resulted in little effect and the rifle grenade was deemed unable to project the bomb through the firing slit reliably. A 25-pounder cartridge case filled with gelignite was also considered but found to be too bulky for easy manipulation by infantry, while a charge of TNT detonated by a Murphey Switch was deemed too complicated for infantry without specialist training.

In January/February 1943 a series of firing trials was conducted against various simulated bunker targets at the School of Armour, located at Puckapunyal, Victoria, to assess the effectiveness of various tank and infantry weapons against Japanese bunkers. Testing revealed that the low-calibre weapons such as the 2-pounder and 37mm guns were ineffective against bunkers with either High Explosive (HE) or Armour Piercing (AP) ammunition. Larger calibre weapons such as the 6-pounder or 25-pounder were considered effective when firing HE. However, these were not practical solutions as Australia did not possess any self-propelled mountings for the larger guns and moving towed models of the 6-pounder and 25-pounder was extremely difficult in the conditions of the South-West Pacific.

The Australian Army and Ministry of Munitions had been broadly aware of the Blacker Bombard by mid-1941. Several reports received from Australia House in London suggested that adoption of the Bombard as a standard weapon of the British Army was imminent, however the Australian General Staff advised that no action be taken and to maintain the policy of focusing on proven armaments currently in production. Additionally, Mr L.J. Hartnett, the Director of the Ordnance Production Directorate (OPD), had received further information regarding the Bombard from an unexpected quarter via Mr Rowland Morris, Managing Director of the Morris & Walker packing company. Mr Morris had been corresponding with Mr Arthur Stevenson of the Hugh Stevenson & Sons company of Manchester. According to Mr Stevenson, his company had been involved in production of certain elements of the Blacker Bombard, namely the packing tube/stand assembly for the bombs. Stevenson directed Morris and the OPD to contact a Captain Hayton Cowap at the Kynochs Works of Imperial Chemical Industries (ICI), in Birmingham. Morris made several impressive claims (although of a somewhat dubious nature), notably that the Bombard had previously been delayed due to incompetence on the part of the Ministry of Supply, and furthermore that the weapon had been provided to the Russians where it had proved a great success. Nonetheless, the army was to take no further interest in the Bombard for some time. Discussion of the Bombard would be revived in mid-1943 following a memo from Captain Buckler of A-Branch, Advanced Land Headquarters, suggesting it as a potential anti-bunker weapon. Some knowledge of the weapon had been obtained by Australian officers who had served in the Middle East, particularly at Tel el Eisa where Bombards had been issued to Australian forces but not used due to 2-pounder anti-tank guns proving better suited to the open range. The large explosive charge of the Bombard was considered ideal for the task of destroying Japanese defences. A proposal was formulated for the Bombard to be issued at a scale of two per Anti-Tank Platoon, in addition to the existing four 2-pounder guns of the platoon.* The rationale was that the Bombard would provide a weapon that could be man-packed into positions inaccessible to the platoon's 2-pounders, and that the flatter trajectory and greater blast effect would provide better performance than the 3-inch mortar. This proposal was met with resistance from the Quartermasters branch, which presented the argument that the weapon should only be adopted if all other standard weapons proved unsuitable, and this reasoning was not without precedence. At El Alamein in 1942 the infantry battalions of the 9th Division had in general 19 standardized weapons in inventory (in addition to standard rifles and bayonets), with quantities as high as 171 items of a single type held by each infantry battalion. By comparison at El Alamein only two Bombards were available in the entirety of the 9th Division, both being issued to one infantry battalion. It was further

---

* During the war the Australian military adopted the terminology of 'Tank Attack' in place of 'Anti-Tank', believing the former conveyed a more aggressive intent. The term was used for both weapons and units, hence Tank Attack Gun/Rifle and Tank Attack Regiment are commonly encountered terms in Australian documentation. Considering, however, that some units retained their designation as 'Anti-Tank Regiments' during the transitional period and bowing to more widely held convention, the term Anti-Tank is used for much of this chapter.

198   *Defeating the Panzer-Stuka Menace*

argued that as each Jungle Division only had a single anti-tank platoon per infantry battalion (with nine battalions per division, a total sum of eighteen Bombards per division) the limited scale of issue and intended implementation as an auxiliary weapon ran the risk that the Bombards would not be readily available to front-line units when and where they were needed during operations. Lastly, it was considered that the issue of the weapon as an auxiliary armament would impose an increased maintenance burden on the anti-tank platoon, while supply and transport of the relatively heavy bombs under jungle conditions would cause disproportionate difficulty for relatively few Bombards. By July 1943 it was decided that no further action would be taken to adopt the Bombard for use in the South-West Pacific, but it was noted that the new PIAT spigot weapon might be a superior alternative to the Bombard.

Subsequently, in late 1943, the PIAT (termed PITA in Australian service) was trialled for its suitability as a bunker busting weapon.* In July 1943, the weapon was tested at Redbank rifle range alongside the standard infantry No. 68 anti-tank rifle grenade and the Boys Anti-Tank Rifle. The target was a 0.375in plate of submarine steel, separated by a 10in gap from a backing plate of 0.25in mild steel. The No. 68 grenade and Boys Anti-Tank Rifle both showed similar success in perforating the plate, with the results described as 'clean cut with little evidence of blast effect'. The PIAT showed even more impressive results against the target, with both shots creating a 2in hole on the submarine steel followed by a 3in hole in the mild steel. It was also noted that 'on both plates the blast effect was very pronounced, the edges of the holes showed that the metal had been in a molten state due to the passage of the explosives and splinters of metal were blown back towards the firing point'. However, against bunkers the PIAT met with far less success. The fuse was shown to be unreliable, requiring a direct hit at 90 degrees to successfully arm, and those hits that did properly detonate showed that the blast effect was insufficient to substantially damage a bunker. Although praised as an anti-tank weapon, the PIAT was not considered suitable for the purposes of destroying a Japanese bunker. By early 1944 enough PIATs had been obtained to allow user trials under non-combat conditions in Papua New Guinea. For testing, PIATs were issued to the New Guinea Force (NGF) Training School, several units of the 7th Division and three brigades from 2nd Australian Corps. Although each testing group used slightly different methods and targets, the aggregate results were consistent and far from encouraging. First, the fuses of the PIAT were a recurring problem, with

---

*Owing to the Australian difference in terminology, the PIAT was given a slightly modified designation of PITA, or Projector, Infantry, Tank Attack. The original British designation was used in the early days before the weapon became more established within the Australian Army, and post-war was reverted to PIAT.

Private A.C. Kotz and Private W. Spence of 2/10 Battalion, Australian 7th Division, take cover behind a tree in the Balikpapan town area with their PIAT during Operation Oboe 2, 3 July 1945. The weapon has been painted with a jungle camouflage pattern.

many bombs either not detonating when the striker pin had hit the target, or simply burying into soft targets with the striker pin unfired. The fuses suffered from a generally high level of unreliability with the trial units reporting a fuse failure rate of 30–50 per cent per test. Second, while the penetration capabilities of the bombs were praised, the lack of fragmentation from the bomb itself was found to be insufficient to do anything more than cosmetic damage. Bombs detonated statically inside the test targets only created small craters without inflicting any significant structural damage. Additionally, the weight of the weapon and ammunition was criticized as unsuitable for a single man to carry over more than very short distances, while the comparatively loud sound of discharge and physical difficulty involved in re-cocking the weapon raised concerns about concealability of the operator in combat. On the positive side, the consensus was that the PIAT was an eminently suitable weapon for use against AFVs, and that the weapon should be issued to ordnance depots on a reserve capacity as insurance against encountering higher concentrations of Japanese armour. The report from 2nd Australian Corps further recommended that the PIAT be issued to training schools to provide a pool of experienced instructors, which would allow units to be trained quickly in the use of the weapon should its issue become necessary.

The conclusions of the report from the NGF Training school provided some sage advice:

> It is considered undesirable for [the PIAT] to be issued to infantry or other arms with the information that the weapon will 'smash' a bunker as the soldiers would soon lose confidence in the weapon and discard it, thus ruining the confidence of the troops in a first class weapon for use against targets for which it has been designed.

As a result, in January 1944, it was recommended by the Advance Land Headquarters that the PIAT not replace the Boys Anti-Tank Rifle as the standard man-portable anti-tank weapon. However, as enough stocks (305 PIATs with 28,000 rounds of ammunition) had arrived by this time it was deemed that the weapon would be kept stored in ordnance depots in theatre, as insurance against the possibility that more heavily armoured Japanese tanks would appear. If the need arose it was determined that the scale of issue should be one PIAT per company (as opposed to the British issue of three per company). It was decided that 100 PIATs and 10,000 rounds of ammunition would be retained in Papua New Guinea, while the remaining 205 weapons and 18,000 rounds would be returned to mainland Australia. In March 1944, it was decided that fifty PIATs would be issued per division for training, in order to familiarize soldiers with its operation and build confidence in the weapon. It is important to note that this was not a formal adoption of the weapon, and it was specifically outlined that once the new No. 426 graze fuse became available in July 1944 the PIAT would be tested further to determine if it was suitable to replace the Boys Anti-Tank Rifle. Nonetheless, army documentation detailing the rifle-platoon structure of 1944 specifies a single PIAT per platoon. Ultimately, the value of the PIAT in the South-West Pacific was uncertain and how much use it saw in theatre is unclear, but photographic evidence shows that the weapon was at least issued to combat theatres such as Operation Oboe 2 on Balikpapan, as well as to the Australian element of the British Commonwealth Occupation Force in Japan. The PIAT would be retained in the Australian inventory after the Second World War until 1957 when, with the adoption of the L1 Self-Loading Rifle and Energa Anti-Tank Rifle Grenade, it was declared obsolete and scheduled for disposal.

Australia's most extensive and arguably most successful foray into spigot weapons was the Hedgehog projector and its adaption for use as a land-based weapon under the designation of 'Projector, Hedgehog, (Aust), No. 1, Mk 1'. Originally a naval store, the Hedgehog was also used on vessels of the Royal Australian Navy, however, in this capacity they did not differ from the application of the British Royal Navy and as such will not be dealt with here. In early 1944 a series of requirements was issued by Brigadier Denzel McArthur-Onslow, the commander of the Australian 4th Armoured Brigade Group,

Private R.O. Smith carries out maintenance on one of 3rd Battalion, The Royal Australian Regiment's (3RAR) PIAT guns after it had been in the open all night for defence exercises with the British Commonwealth Occupation Force (BCOF), Haramura, Japan, 10 August 1950.

to develop a series of specialized armoured vehicles for use in the South-West Pacific. Included among these requirements was an AFV-mounted weapon capable of 'destroying completely' a Japanese bunker. For this purpose, the Hedgehog was selected as a readily available weapon with a large explosive payload, and subsequently developed for mounting on the A.12 Matilda infantry tank. A functioning mock-up was manufactured by the 4th Armoured Brigade Group Workshop and subjected to initial trials in August 1944. For the test vehicle, six Hedgehog spigots were mounted in line along a 5in-diameter Vibrok steel shaft set between a pair of rotary bearings. The bearings were in turn mounted to a pair of short girders which were welded to the rear track guards of the tank. Each spigot was enclosed in a sheet-steel cylinder to provide protection and support for the Hedgehog bombs. The cylinders were arranged to bed down on the engine louvres when not in the firing position. The spigots were rotated into the firing position via a hydraulic ram actuated by a hand pump located in the turret. Firing was controlled by an electrical switchboard inside the tank, with elevation interlocks preventing the weapon from firing if the turret would obstruct the path of the projectile or if the spigots were elevated to greater than 75 degrees. The original Hedgehog fuse, being designed for use underwater, was not suitable for the intended use against terrestrial hard targets. Therefore, it was replaced with the No. 152 direct action fuse taken from the 3-inch mortar. This was fitted using an adaptor which screwed into the bomb above a stacked detonation charge. The charge stack consisted of a 1.75in by 1.7in CE pellet, followed by a 1.25in CE pellet. The pre-existing 12-dram CE pellet and 1.25in TNT pellet were retained below the modified fuse and charge stack. For the tests twelve inert bombs were fired from a single spigot at an angle of 45 degrees, resulting in a range of 200yd with a longitudinal variation of 5yd and a line dispersion of 1yd. A further three salvos of six inert bombs were fired yielding a range of 200yd with a longitudinal variation of 5yd and a line dispersion of 1.5yd. Reduction of elevation to 35 degrees resulted in a decrease of impact to 190yd, although it was noted that inert bombs gave on average 10yd less range than filled bombs. Firing live bombs resulted in blast craters 2ft deep and 7ft across, vegetation was cleared completely in a radius of 6ft from the blast, while concertina wire was cleared in a radius of 4ft. A salvo of six bombs completely cleared thick vegetation and concertina wire from an area of 35yd by 14yd. A mock-up bunker was constructed from two layers of 15in logs covered with sandbags and earth to a depth of 2ft. The whole target measured 10ft by 8ft. Out of seven bombs fired, three direct hits were obtained; the first hit cleared most of the earth while the remaining two blew away the logs and exposed the interior of the bunker. It was noted that the flash and blast of the bomb was impressive, however, the fragmentation effect was considered unsatisfactory beyond 10yd.

 The results of the 1944 tests were enough to justify further development of the weapon, and the refined design was subjected to more rigorous testing in March/April 1945. In December 1944 it was also suggested that the Hedgehog could be satisfactorily mounted on the rear deck of an M3 medium tank, but this option was ultimately not pursued. In addition to the test vehicle another five tanks would be fitted with Hedgehog projectors, for a total of six vehicles, with the fabrication and fitting work being conducted throughout 1945 by the engineering firm of A. & P. Uscinski, based at Corparoo, Queensland. The refined weapon retained the same support cylinders and transverse axle mounting, but increased the number of spigots to seven, now protected within a box of locally produced 11mm weldable Australian Bullet Proof Plate No. 3 (ABP3). An additional armoured plate at the front of the mounting covered up the bombs when the weapon was fully depressed, protecting them from damage due to shrapnel or enemy fire. The production examples of the weapon would also feature additional angled plates of 11mm ABP3 on the sides and front of the projector, as well as mesh anti-bomb screens on the top of the projector and the engine deck of the vehicle. A series of paired struts which slotted into the cylinders when the weapon was closed were added to support the bombs and prevent the fuses from being damaged in transit. The spigots could be elevated and depressed via a hydraulic controller and solenoid switch located on the left-hand side of the driver's position. The controller and hydraulic pump itself were a repurposed 'Logan' Gerotor type from an M3 medium tank, driving a pair of hydraulic rams repurposed from aircraft landing gear. The pump, motor, and oil reservoir were contained in the left-hand chain locker on the front of the tank, and power was supplied via the tank's main batteries. A simple blade sight was

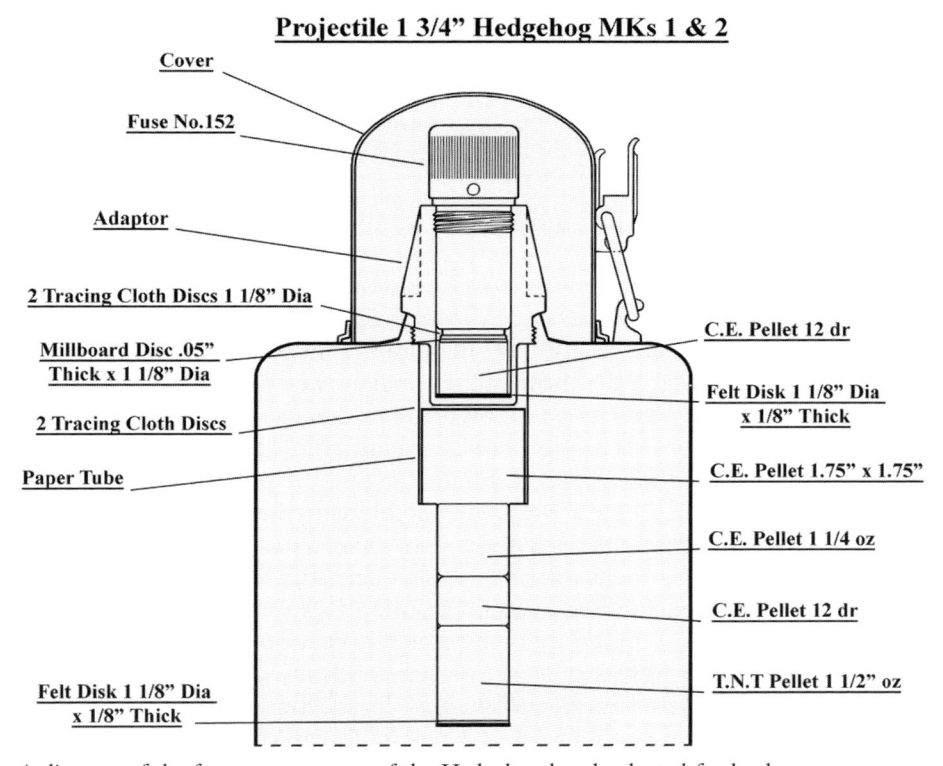

A diagram of the fuse arrangements of the Hedgehog bomb adapted for land use.

Men of 2/5 Armoured Regiment, 4th Armoured Brigade Group, in the process of loading the 1944 trials projector. The six spigots and protective cylinders that support the bombs are considerably more exposed than on later versions of the design.

attached to the turret at the 12 o'clock position to allow the commander to provide a rough lay of the weapon on target. Ranging and aiming was controlled entirely from the elevation of the spigots and the direction the vehicle was facing. The driver had a mechanical elevation indicator mounted on the right side of the driver's position. This was driven by a chain sprocket attached to the spigot shaft and a piano-wire linkage. Issues with deviation of line due to tilt of the tank led to a simple hanging tilt indicator being added to production vehicles. Firing was controlled by an electrical switchboard in the tank turret, located to the left of the gunner's position. When conducting the firing process, the operator inserted the firing lead into the socket of the corresponding spigot and then pressed the firing switch to close the electrical circuit. Bombs could be fired individually, or if required the operator could hold down the firing switch as he switched between sockets to fire the bombs in a 'ripple' salvo. Using the latter method, it was determined that the projector could fire seven bombs with 0.33 second intervals and all seven bombs could be in flight at one time. A set of electrical interlocks were included to prevent the bombs from firing when the spigots were elevated below the level of the tank turret, or to an angle greater than 70 degrees. Additionally, in order to prevent potential damage to the tank's wireless aerials an extra interlock was installed on the fifth spigot circuit. This prevented the bomb from firing unless the tank turret was turned to the 2 o'clock position. An additional offset sighting vane was provided to allow for aiming the fifth spigot when the turret was rotated.

A stereoscopic rangefinder for the Hedgehog was developed by Major Alan Milner, head of the 4th Armoured Brigade Group's mechanical workshop, and in January 1945 the design was submitted to the Australian Solar Observatory at Mount Stromlo for manufacture. The design was derived from a Barr & Stroud stereoscopic rangefinder and operated under a fixed coincidence principle where a prism within the sight would align the two eyepiece images into a single coherent image when the correct range had been achieved. The design was set to a fixed range of 200yd but, based on army projections that the range of the Hedgehog may be increased up to 500yd, it was intended that the central prism be removable to allow for an increased range scale (this was later reduced to 330yd). A prototype was produced and

The rear view of the 1945 trials projector. The spigots have been raised to full elevation and the mounting girders welded to the rear track guards are clearly visible.

Looking from the turret into the cylinders of the 1945 trials projector.

tested in a limited capacity alongside the tests of the production Hedgehog in March/June 1945. The rangefinder worked satisfactorily against distinct targets (a 6in-wide pole) in open ground, giving coincidence at 200yd with an approximately 5yd deviation (inexperienced operators increased this deviation by an extra 10yd or so). When trialled against obscured targets in heavily wooded terrain results were less satisfactory, as the overlap of dense vegetation prevented the operator from clearly distinguishing the transition to image coincidence of the target. The trials report concluded that the rangefinder was not an army requirement, however, technical report No. 16 from October 1945 states that a coincidence rangefinder would be supplied for tanks fitted with Hedgehog projectors, although it is unclear if any other examples were produced, other than the trial prototype, before work on the Hedgehog was discontinued.

The 1945 tests yielded very similar results to the prior 1944 tests, with good performance noted in several areas. First, the large blast produced by the bomb was effective at removing foliage from an area, with a noted tendency for the blast to 'flatten' foliage within its radius. This task had previously been achieved by using the tank's coaxial BESA machine gun to 'strip' foliage from a target area, which while effective had been recognized as an inefficient expenditure of ammunition. A salvo of seven Hedgehog bombs, with enough accuracy, could clear jungle foliage in a strip with an estimated area of 135yd by 27yd. Second, the bombs were recognized for their potential utility in mine clearing. Testing revealed that given enough accuracy from the tank crew a corridor 72yd by 6yd could be cleared through an anti-personnel minefield. Conversely, it was recognized that the utility of the Hedgehog would be greatly reduced against anti-tank mines due to the much higher tolerance to blast effect in these types of mines, and it was further noted that scarce data was available about Japanese anti-tank mines. Lastly, it was considered that such a large blast effect, combined with the fact that the firing vehicle outwardly appeared identical to a regular gun tank, would have a significant morale effect upon enemy infantry. Regarding the weapon's main objective, the destruction of Japanese bunkers, results were less satisfactory. The major problem identified was that the impact fuse meant that the bombs detonated before achieving enough penetration to demolish the target. Attempts to delay detonation by firing with the fuse cap in place resulted in bombs burying into the ground without detonation, and it was identified that a delayed action fuse would be needed to provide suitable results. The 1945 report does not specify if a delayed fuse was obtained during the trials, however, the provisional tactical notes from March 1945 suggest a penetration value of 4ft of earth with a delayed action fuse, although it is unclear if this is a confirmed value or an estimate. Furthermore, concerns were raised regarding the accuracy of the weapon. With only seven bombs available it was considered impractical for ranging shots to be made, and without a suitable

Tank number 35357 'Bull Pup' fitted with the 1945 trials model of the Hedgehog projector. Note the vertical sides and exposed mounting girders that would be covered by additional armoured plates in the production model.

rangefinder available during trials it was found to be difficult to accurately judge the distance to the target to achieve a first-round hit. In addition to this the bombs were observed to wobble in flight which led to inconsistency in accuracy between individual shots. The blunt nose and cylinder type tail vanes of the bomb were judged to be the main cause of this issue, and it was recommended that a more aerodynamic nose cone and larger fin-type vane on the bomb would reduce this. However, there is no evidence that either modification entered production, and they are not mentioned in any subsequent documentation. Aside from the standing requirement for a delayed action fuse to be obtained at the nearest opportunity, the major conclusions to the accuracy issues primarily focused on emphasizing crew training and proper ranging of the weapon, with the accuracy being otherwise regarded as 'serviceable'.

A series of survivability trials were also conducted to assess the vulnerability of the weapon as well as the outcome of a possible detonation of one or more bombs on the tank. For this purpose, a mock-up bomb rack was produced from armoured plate and attached to the rear of a spare Matilda tank. Multiple weapons were fired against the mock-up projector assembly, including .30 calibre rifle ammunition, rifle grenades, 20mm AP shells, 37mm AP shells, 75mm HE shells and a simulated Type 99 magnetic mine. Against

An area of Lantana scrub prior to test firing of the Hedgehog projector. This level of foliage was analogous to that encountered in the jungles of the South-West Pacific. The standing soldier would be difficult to spot, a low-profile bunker almost impossible.

The same area of Lantana scrub post firing of the Hedgehog projector. What was once dense foliage has now been stripped away, exposing any concealed obstacles or defensive positions.

.30 calibre ball and AP ammunition the projector was deemed completely immune while closed, and only vulnerable at the opening of the cylinders when open. The bombs showed a favourably low volatility, with a tendency to burn rather than explode when hit. Direct hits from the 75mm HE and Type 99 charge resulted in the bomb rack being blown off the back of the tank, while the bombs remained safely undetonated. The M9A1 rifle grenade and 37mm AP round both penetrated the armour of the projector but again the bombs burned rather than detonating. When a simulated rack of seven bombs was detonated the turret of the tank was lifted and turned, however, readings of blast pressure showed that, discounting mechanical injury to the crew, there was a greater than 50 per cent chance of a crewman surviving the blast effect of the detonation of the bomb payload.

Further testing was conducted in mid-1945 to determine if alternative propellants could be used to increase the range of the Hedgehog reliably. Information from the UK had indicated that a charge of FNH025 propellant could increase the range of the Hedgehog bomb by an additional 100yd without risk of bursting the bomb tails. FNH025 was not available in Australia, hence approval was given by the Director of Armaments for testing to be conducted using NH025 propellant instead. The tests revealed that a propellant charge of 500 grains NH025 cordite would provide an increase in accurate range to approximately 330yd vs the 200yd range of the standard charge of 260 grains HSCT. Inspection of the projector and hydraulic systems showed that the weapon could handle the increased force from the new propellant, and it was noted that the vehicle moved off under its own power in good order after the test firing was completed. However, the increased pressure gradient of the new propellant resulted in potential damage to the electrical contacts in the spigot, with the spring being compressed out of alignment such that the contacts would not reliably fire subsequent bombs. Hence it was recommended that if NH025 propellant was to be adopted, the cartridge case in the bomb should be modified to alleviate undue pressure on the electrical contacts, although this was noted as difficult due to the bombs not being in production locally.

The exact outcome of the Hedgehog trials is something of a confusing matter, and this is not helped by a confounding quirk of documentation. Memorandum No. 49 of the Operational Research Section reported rather favourably on the Hedgehog, however, in memorandum No. 50 the opinion appears reversed and several criticisms were raised. First, the accuracy of the weapon was called into question, with an estimated hit probability of only one bomb in five to six being deemed inefficient for a weapon with only seven shots, something that would be further exacerbated by the uncertainties of a combat situation. Second, the lack of penetration and poor fragmentation of the bomb was noted as insufficient for anti-bunker or anti-infantry work, although it was noted that the bombs could be suitable for delivering white phosphorus as an anti-infantry incendiary weapon. Third, the vulnerability of the weapon was questioned, and while noted as being largely resistant to detonation from rifle fire, it was noted that the weapon was still vulnerable to anti-tank grenades and other armour piercing weapons and that in the raised position would likely draw significant enemy fire. Finally, it was considered that seven bombs with ammunition cases, at a total weight of 490lb, would present a logistical difficulty to supply as well as adding an increased physical burden on the crew when loading the weapon. As a final postscript to the memorandum the Director of Mechanical Vehicles appended the following comment:

> It is considered that the 'Hedgehog' equipment is NOT suitable for mounting on a tank unless designed so as to provide arrangements for traversing the equipment independent of the tank.
>
> However this would require considerable design and from the report on the potentialities of this weapon, it requires thorough investigation before being accepted as an Army requirement.

To clarify matters it is worth noting that Memorandum No. 50 was published in March 1945 and its criticisms are in reference to the 1944 trials, while memorandum No. 49 was published in June 1945 and refers directly to the 1945 trials. The overall conclusion that can be drawn is that despite its recognized faults, the tank mounting of the Hedgehog projector was deemed acceptably useful for further experimentation and adoption by the army.

By March 1945 it had been decided that the six Hedgehog tanks scheduled for production would be issued to the 2/9th Armoured Regiment to develop doctrine for use of the weapon in cooperative actions between armour and infantry. The provisional doctrine for the Hedgehog outlines the weapon as such. 'A Matilda tank equipped with a Hedgehog retains all the armament and characteristics of the regular Matilda tank and is primarily used as such. The fighting qualities are unimpaired. The addition of the Hedgehog gives it extra armament – "Something for nothing".' Tactically the Hedgehog was considered a specialist weapon which would operate in a standard troop of three Hedgehog-equipped tanks. They could, if needed, be attached to infantry

Tank number 35357 'Bull Pup' fitted with the 1945 production model of the Hedgehog projector and mesh anti-bomb screens. A member of 4th Armoured Brigade Group is demonstrating the loading of a Hedgehog bomb into the third spigot cylinder.

Tank number 35357 'Bull Pup' fitted with the 1945 production model of the Hedgehog projector with the spigots raised, showing the attachment of the mesh anti-bomb screens. A Hedgehog bomb with the modified No. 152 fuse is visible on the ground behind the tank.

forces or integrated within a tank troop on a singular basis, but it was considered that deployment as a unified troop would be normal. When operating in conjunction with other armoured units the Hedgehog tanks would deploy and operate in the same way as an ordinary tank, with the Hedgehog projector being employed when suitable targets of opportunity were presented. Crews were encouraged to consider the weapon in the same way as a mortar, but with the added advantage of mobility and a greater blast effect, and the disadvantage of limited shots. Hedgehog tanks could be assigned to engage specific targets if prior reconnaissance had identified a need for such action, however it was specified that the tanks were to remain *in situ* and fight as standard gun tanks once their payload of bombs had been expended.

Suitable targets were identified as:

- Enemy troops in the open defiladed from direct fire.
- Enemy troops in foxholes.
- Suspected anti-tank weapons and machine-gun positions.
- Neutralization of enemy defensive areas including bunkers.
- Clearance of scrub around restricted enemy locations.
- Clearance of enemy wire and anti-tank obstacles.

When operating in direct support of attacking infantry it was advised that the tank crew be assigned a specific and direct task for their Hedgehog to engage, and that the main tank armament should be treated as secondary armament until this task was accomplished. Considering the limited ammunition supply, crew commanders were instructed to conduct thorough reconnaissance to select suitable firing locations and avoid overhead obstructions which would block the flight path of the bombs. It was further noted that arrangements should be made prior to battle to allow the tanks to withdraw and replenish their bomb loads, unless it was intended for them to remain in the role of standard gun tanks. The close-support radius of the weapon was specified as a 100yd safe area from the point of impact, and it was noted that the Hedgehogs should be incorporated into mortar/artillery fire plans, with pre-arranged fire being coordinated through the tank-troop commander. Close communication between the commander of the Hedgehog troop and infantry commanders was identified as crucial, either via wireless or through the external telephone mounted on the rear of the tanks.

Testing of the Hedgehog would continue throughout 1945 until the end of the war, and although the exact date that work on the weapon was discontinued is unclear, the available documentation ends in about September or October 1945. Some published sources claim that the six Matilda Hedgehog tanks were sent to Bougainville for field trials in mid-1945. However, considering that archival evidence shows that only three tanks had been delivered by July 1945 and that the six tanks produced were held by 4th Armoured Brigade Group pending instructions for disposal in September of 1945, it is clear the vehicles never left Australia. Of the six vehicles produced only one surviving example, tank No. 35357, remains at the Australian Army Tank Museum, Puckapunyal, Victoria.

PART EIGHT

THE WORLD'S SPIGOTS

TREE SPIGOT, GROUND SPIGOT, PLATE SPIGOT GUN, BIGOT, *LEICHTER LADUNGSWERFER* AND TYPE 98 320MM

Chapter Sixteen

The Other Spigots

Every spigot that has been examined here has been from, for the want of a better description, the Blacker family tree. They all used the radially expanding cartridge that Blacker had designed and made spigot weapons viable. There was another group of spigots that did not use the radially expanding cartridge and evolved during the war. As this second family was developed under the auspices of the Special Operations Executive (SOE), this involves delving into the murky realms of clandestine operations. Because of this, there are precious few documents available to piece together the story. The weapons were designed by the brilliant Cecil Vandepeer Clarke.

The main difference between the two weapons was the means of propulsion. In the Blacker weapons the radially expanding cartridge made sure of a tight gas seal and was blown out of the back of the tail tube. In the Clarke weapons, a blank 12-gauge shotgun cartridge was used. When this was triggered it would act in a similar manner to the Blacker cartridge until the bomb had been propelled off the spigot. Then a brass washer, and sealing wad, on the base of the tail tube would stop the spent shotgun cartridge, and effectively form a tight seal. In the Blacker weapons, there was no flash, only the report of firing the gun. In the Clarke spigots, the bang was also muffled, effectively making a silenced spigot. Reports suggest that an observer at 600yd might only hear a clicking like the working of a rifle bolt and the whistling noise as the projectile flies through the air. As the lip on the end of the tail tube was welded in place it would sometimes fail, but this would not have hugely affected the trajectory of the projectile as it would have been in flight. In one trial on eleven of ninety bombs the sealing washer failed.

Clarke had been a junior officer with the infantry in the First World War and later transferred to a sapper unit, where he was involved in the digging of tunnels and mining and would go on to earn himself a Military Cross. In between the wars, he did work within the automotive field, and then set up an engineering firm. Clarke constructed a novel new type of very large double-decker caravan with excellent suspension, and even gimbal-mounted toilets so the caravan could be occupied while being towed. These caravans caught the attention of *Caravan & Trailer* magazine's editor Stuart Macrae. Macrae visited Clarke and was impressed by his engineering skills. Later, when Macrae was brought into the field of weapons research to help on the

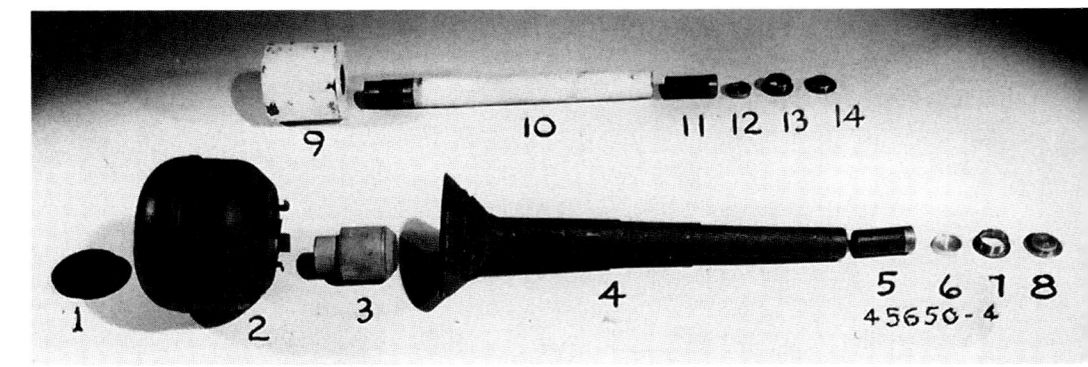

The components of a Clarke Spigot Bomb and its practice round. These are: 1. Cap for bomb head; 2. Bomb head; 3. Fuse; 4. Tail; 5. Cartridge; 6. Wad; 7. Stop ring; 8. Stop-ring protector; 9. Practice bomb head; 10. Practice bomb tail; 11. Cartridge; 12. Wad; 13. Stop ring; 14. Stop-ring protector.

limpet-mine problem, Macrae enlisted the help of Clarke. The limpet mine's final design was more or less entirely down to Clarke's work. After this project, Clarke then went on to work on the Infamous Cultivator No. 6, nicknamed 'Nellie'. This was an attempt to make a trench-digging tank to enable it to cross no man's land safe underground, and deliver infantry right into the enemy front lines unmolested by enemy fire. This project was cancelled after the fall of France.

At this time Clarke was tasked to join SOE which had some technical troubles with the limpet mine that needed fixing. Once these had been completed Clarke remained with SOE turning his inventive mind to the assorted problems that the SOE needed solving. It is during this period that Clarke designed his spigot weapons. The exact date, impetus for the weapons design and the development of the Tree Spigot remain a mystery. This spigot first surfaces in official documents in May 1943, when several US officers paid a visit to Experimental Station 6 at Knebworth for a demonstration of it. Their report gives a hint of the role of the weapon, stating the guns 'were designed to provide lightweight close range firepower for diversified application'.

The Tree Spigot was 15in long in total, most of the length made up by the spigot, and weighed just 4.75lb. The spigot was mounted on a gimbal in the base. Opposite the spigot was a large screw. Sticking out from opposite sides of the base were two rods to be used as handles. To set up the weapon, first, the bark had to be removed from the tree. To this end, one of the handles on the base was formed into a chisel to aid with the task. The screw was then drilled into the wooden item, such as the stripped patch of the tree or a handy telegraph pole. Complete setting up would take between 3 and 4 minutes. Should the screw need more force to seat it than could be provided by the two handles, a bomb would fit over one of the handles for added leverage. An optical sight was then placed over the spigot, which turned the sight picture through 90 degrees. This allowed the operator to stand beside the tree with the gun in place and adjust the gimbal and aim the weapon at a particular spot, such as a set point on a road. Once aimed, and the gimbal was locked in place, the sight would be removed and a bomb placed on the spigot. The Tree Spigot had a muzzle velocity of about 200fps and a maximum range of 200yd.

A firing mechanism was provided that could be triggered by a lanyard, tripwire or even timer. The bomb was a 5in warhead filled with 3lb of Nobels 808, and its total weight was 5.75lb. The bomb could put a hole through a 50mm plate or 25mm at up to 60 degrees. As the projectile was a HESH warhead, it would be able to cause damage against thicker armour, although that exact thickness is not recorded. The weapon also proved perfectly capable of smashing concrete walls as well.

The same bomb was fired from the other two examples of the Clarke family of weapons. The next simplest was called the Plate Spigot Gun. This, as the name would suggest, was a spigot, identical to the Tree Spigot Gun but instead of being mounted to a gimbal and the base, it was attached to a small steel plate that was 0.18in thick. The weapon had a rudimentary sight and a pair of handles. The plate was not bulletproof, although it did provide limited protection against shrapnel. The plate also provided a morale boost to the gunner. The idea behind the Plate Spigot Gun was it enabled teams to go hunting armoured vehicles, using a common type of ammunition. Maximum range was 150yd, while accurate range, against a moving target, was 100yd. When tank hunting a two-man team would carry four bombs each, and the weapon was considered extremely concealable. Like all the Clarke family, it had no flash or report. Two complete Plate Spigot Guns, broken down along with sixteen bombs, could be packaged into a standard airdrop container. The gun could be unpacked from the container, assembled and in action in about 53 seconds.

The final of Clarke's spigots was the Ground Spigot Gun. This consisted of a $2ft^2$ metal plate, with a pair of legs sticking out the back acting as trails. Each leg was 40in long. Between the two legs was a cloth sling that the gunner could rest his elbows on. The gun could traverse through 60 degrees and elevate up to 30 degrees. In total it weighed 50lb.

There appear to be no reports on the use of the weapon, if any were indeed employed. It does seem likely that the Tree Spigot was put to some use operationally, although details are not available. It is known that one was supplied, along with a single bomb, to Jozef Gabčík and Jan Kubiš for Operation Anthropoid, the assassination of Reinhard Heydrich, although the weapon was not used in that mission. This shows that the Tree Spigot was at least in the armoury of SOE and considered operational.

Curiously, towards the end of the war, the USA began to show an interest in the Tree Spigot Gun and arranged for several guns and bombs to be shipped to the USA for modification and testing. The equipment was reported as en route to the USA towards the end of December 1944. The US Army had

220   *Defeating the Panzer-Stuka Menace*

identified a need for a short-range weapon that could fire on a high trajectory to hit targets out of line of sight, but which were too close to friendly troops to employ dedicated support assets such as medium mortars. An example of such a situation might be an enemy position on a reverse slope, where the US infantry had occupied the crest of the slope. This seemed to be driven by conditions in the Pacific that US forces were facing, similar to the Arakan conditions that the Commonwealth forces had encountered earlier, and prompted them to look at a Blacker Bombard on a Sherman. The weapons were received and then handed to the Merz Engineering Company for modification. This company was to modify the weapon heavily, first using high-grade aircraft materials to improve the strength of the weapon, fitting a faster cocking system and creating a baseplate that would accept the weapon so that a tree was no longer needed. Finally, and most oddly of all, an adaptor for a time pencil was required. One has to wonder about this last point, as the designated role for the weapon was to be used as a manned, crew-served weapon, so why the need for a timing device, which the weapon already had?

Other modifications that were to be included were to the bomb. The USA decided to change the fuse to one of their own making, which would not have an arming delay, although long-term plans were for a new fuse that would have a 25yd arming distance. Later testing would show that the charge of the weapon could be increased by 50 per cent, which would result in a corresponding increase in range.

Merz Engineering Company seems to have provided examples of two base-plates. One was a custom-designed round plate, the other a modified form

The parts of a US version of a Tree Spigot: A. Screw; B. T-handle with chisel edge; C. Cocking wire; D. D ring to fasten lanyard to; E. Sight; F. Spigot; G. Base.

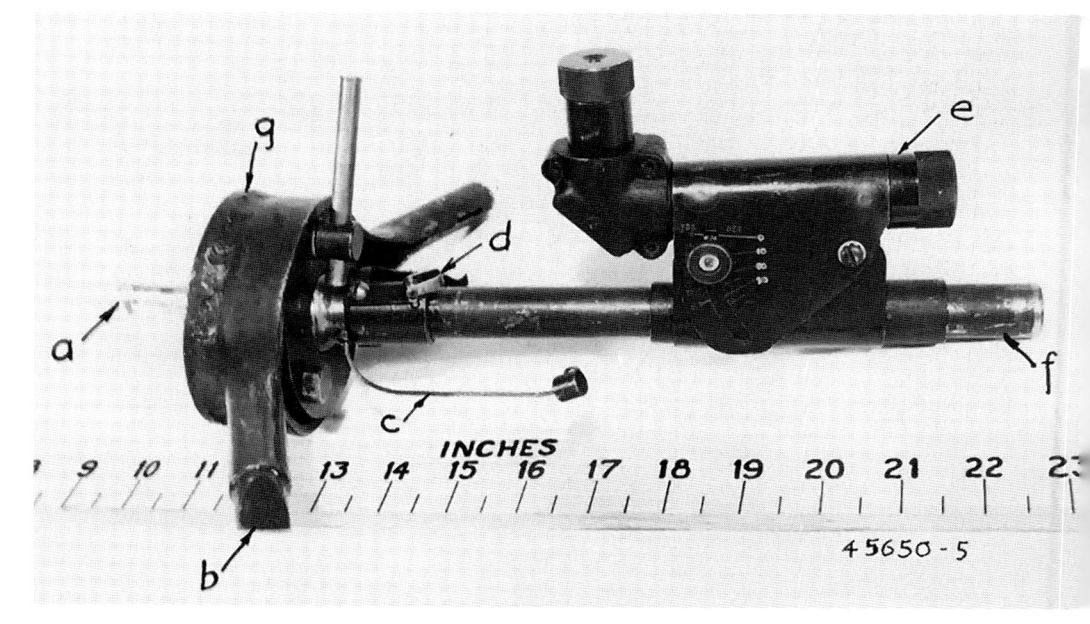

of the M2 Mortar baseplate. The circular one was found to be superior, although when fired from a hard surface such as a road the plate crumpled. Finally, new projectiles were to be developed. These were to be both HEAT and White Phosphorus projectiles, as well as a grappling iron with a line.

At the start of August 1945, the project was terminated. The reason given for this was that US troops in the field had adopted 60mm mortars for the role by reducing the propellant charge. Initially, the fuse had proved to be the weak link, but it was judged that modification of both the 60mm and 81mm mortar fuse would be quicker into service than the entire Tree Spigot programme.

The USA did have a couple of other spigot weapons under development. The first one to appear was first reported on in May 1944. It was designated

The US version of a Tree Spigot on a Merz Engineering Company baseplate. A bomb has been loaded ready to fire.

the Mine Exploder, T12. It came about as there were plenty of other mechanical devices for mine-creating currently under development, however, the USA realized that a 100lb charge would clear a 20ft circle of mines, as long as the angle of impact was between 45 and 90 degrees. The system was mounted on a Sherman, with the turret and turret ring removed. In their place, there was a platform of twenty 60mm spigots. This platform could be tilted by jacks, which were controlled by a pair of handwheels. This tilting ability was to allow levelling of the platform, which could be tilted by +/–10 degrees longitudinally and +/– 8 degrees transversely. Another five spigots were mounted on a bar that ran across the glacis plate of the Sherman. These were geared so they could be depressed down to 20 degrees elevation and used as direct-fire weapons to attack concrete.

The projectile fired by the system was the Shell, HE, Spigot 60mm, 115lb, T13. This was, by now, the traditional spigot-projectile shape with a drum tail. When test-fired, the projectile had a spread of about 1ft laterally and 1yd in range. The spigots were set up to fire their bombs in a line, much like the Hedgerow, and could be fired individually or by a ripple switch. The first bomb would impact 50yd in front of the vehicle and extend backwards. This would clear a lane 20ft wide. There are two sources that state the length of the clear path, however, they both have different values for the length of the cleared lane, one is likely a typo as the first source says 350ft, the other 250ft.

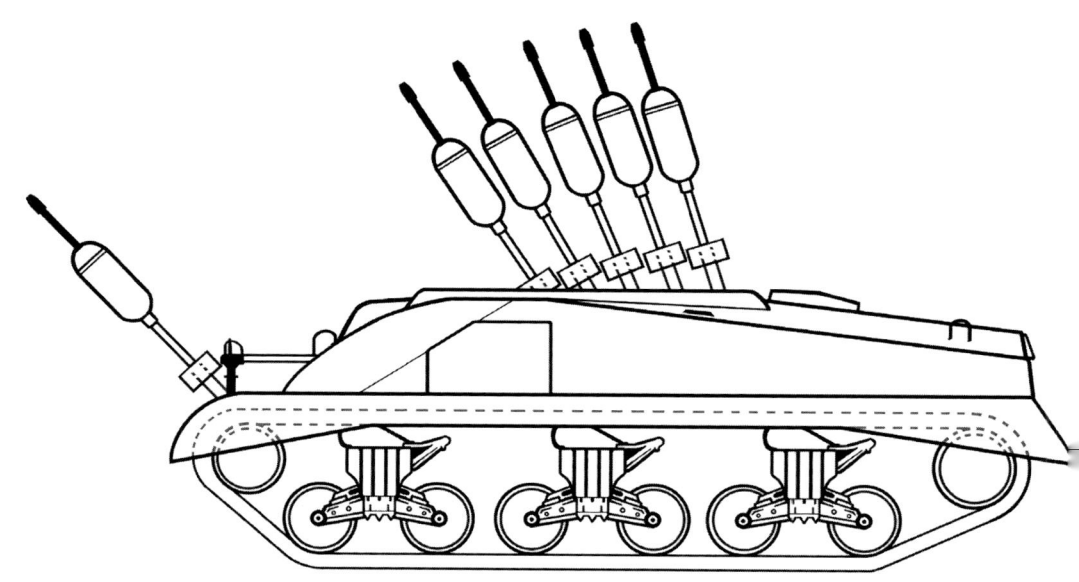

Drawing of the side elevation of a T12 Mine Exploder, based off the sketch drawn in documents. This particular rendition is missing the armour plate around the bombs.

The Other Spigots

The platform could fit a 0.5in thick armoured screen that was 32in in height. With this fitted the all-up height was 12ft 2in. The screen could be removed reducing the vehicle height down to 9ft 6in.

Two prototypes were ordered, along with 500 rounds of T13. One prototype was to be fitted with the armoured screen protecting the rounds on the spigot, the other was to have this left off. It appears that the vehicle was ordered from the York Safe & Lock Co. in York, Pennsylvania. The first prototype to be completed lacked the armoured screen. Firing tests of the weapon were filmed with a high-speed camera. This revealed that the platform was not sufficiently stable enough during firing. Thus the No. 2 prototype was modified with jackscrews to provide additional stability to the platform. This modification was successful when the vehicle was delivered in December 1944. After the firing tests, the No. 2 prototype completed a 100-mile road test while fully loaded and suffered only very minor faults.

At this point a new version was designed, the firing platform was lowered by 28in into the fighting compartment. This restricted the ability of the platform to tilt to only 5 degrees. Additional armour protection was also planned to be included. However, it appears this version was never completed as there are no further reports on it, and the project was cancelled in February 1945.

The next US spigot weapon seems to have started life in about 30 January 1945, when the requirement was discussed. It was termed the Grenade, Spigot, HEAT, T30. The gun to fire it was to be the US copy of the British 6-pounder, the M1 57mm gun. The requirement was driven by recent experience against the Germans and the ineffectiveness of the US Army's infantry weapons. One wonders how much of this was a reaction to the recent Battle of the Bulge, and the events thereafter. The requirement asked for a projectile that was usable with all standard equipment in service, including sights. The maximum weight of the complete round was to be no more than 25lb, with an effective range of 400yd and a maximum of 800yd. Penetration was to be a whopping 12in of sloped armour. The project lasted until 14 June 1945 when it was cancelled. One presumes that this was a consequence of Germany's defeat meaning the removal of the requirement.

The next US spigot weapon was one of the most curious of all spigot weapons. Codenamed Bigot, it was a project to adapt a service Colt 1911 .45 calibre pistol to a spigot weapon that fired darts. This was done by dropping a solid-metal block into the chamber. This held a threaded hole. With the block in the chamber, the spigot was inserted into the mouth of the barrel and then screwed into the hole in the chamber block. The spigot then projected out of the mouth of the barrel. The spigot had a solid firing pin running its entire length. When the pistol's trigger was pulled the 1911's firing pin struck the base of the Bigot firing pin, imparting the movement to that rod, which would then strike the propellant in the projectile's tail tube.

A 1911 .45 pistol fitted with a Bigot. Although it looks like a normal muzzle-loaded projectile, it is a spigot, similar in function to the Clarke design. One can see the collar, mounting the fins and how it would slide down the tail tube. (*Ian McCollum/Forgotten Weapons*)

The propellant, in this case, was a .25 blank cartridge, and it also had a 'sealing wad' like the Clarke spigots. This would make a Bigot completely silent and flashless. The tail tube of the projectile was inserted down the barrel, sandwiched between the barrel on the outside and the spigot. A collar was free to slide up and down the tail tube, onto which were mounted four aluminium fins. As the projectile was launched the fins would remain in place until the back of the tail tube reached them, and then the entire mass would be carried off the spigot.

On 13 July 1945, a meeting was held where the Bigot was discussed and then demonstrated. The minutes make it sound like the weapon was fired across the meeting room! But one presumes this would have been frowned upon. The Bigot performed poorly, the fins came off and the projectile tumbled and made a considerable noise.

The meeting decided that around thirty redesigned Bigots with welded fins would be provided to Lieutenant Colonel Allan Feldman of the Army Ground Forces for further trials.

At first glance, one wonders about fitting such a device to the 1911, as it would surely be much simpler to attach a sound moderator, and then you retain the use of the magazine and have multiple follow-up shots. There is one clue. On the Internet there exists a picture featured in Czechoslovakian magazine *Strelecka Revue*. In one of its issues, it shows an FP-45 Liberator pistol with a Bigot fitted. The Liberator was a .45 chambered pistol designed to be manufactured as cheaply as possible, and it was also single shot. In such a situation a Bigot would make perfect sense being more cost effective to manufacture and supply than a silencer, and would not have the downsides of the 1911 fitted with the device. It is likely, therefore, that the Colt 1911-fitted Bigots were just development platforms.

It will come as no surprise that the Allies were not the only combatants to use spigot weapons, although the British used them in far greater numbers. Germany seems to have had a couple of spigot mortars. The larger of the two was the colossal 38cm *Schwerer Ladungswerfer*. It used a 169mm spigot and was mounted on a turntable. The weapon's entire weight was around 1.76 tons, and it fired a 328lb projectile. From what little is known about this monstrous weapon it was designed before the war, and quickly fell out of use with only limited numbers produced.

The vastly more successful spigot weapon was the 20cm *Leichter Ladungswerfer*. It had an 89.6mm spigot, and fired a projectile a shade over 47lb, filled with 15lb of 65/35 Amatol, and a TNT top layer, and nose fuse. The range of the weapon was 787yd, with a projectile velocity of 288fps. Rate of fire was around eight shots per minute, although the loading drill meant the crews would likely tire quickly. The propellant, and firing system, was possibly the most unique part of the weapon. The mortar was fired electrically, which appears to have been done to minimize the exposure of the loaders to the blast by allowing them time to clear the area once the bomb had been fitted to the spigot. Before loading the bomb into the ready to fire position the propellant needed to be fitted to the top of the spigot. The propellant charge was a steel and plastic cup, designed with two flanges which would fit into the grooves cut into the spigot. The primer consisted of a steel base cup, with a hole in the centre for the primer. Close to the bottom of the cup, there was a groove machined into the steel, drilled into which were several holes that would allow the propellant gasses to escape. Completing the container was a plastic lid, moulded so that the central column fitted down onto the primer. When joined, both were held together by an adhesive tape. A second steel cup was then slotted over the base cup. This second cup was an obturation device. The primer would then be screwed into place and retained the obturation cup. When triggered the primer would detonate the propellant, and the gasses would then create pressure in the grove. This pressure would apply force to the obturation cup causing it to expand, filling the bore of the tail tube, and obtaining a gas-tight seal, sending the bomb on its way. Compare this highly engineered charge with one from a Bombard or Hedgehog and one can easily see that the German version appears to be over-engineered, and significantly more expensive to produce. This applies to even the propellant itself. In British charges the propellant was just a rod of powder, diced into smaller lengths and tipped into the cavity for it. The Germans used much more finesse. Their propellant was formed into very thin disks, with several holes through them. Seven of these disks were then tied together by a silk thread to form what German manuals refer to as 'charges', and the British examining the round as 'ties'. Each tie contained 182 grains of propellant. Three of these ties would be placed inside the charge for the mortar. Two would be at the bottom of the charge, the third would be held in place by a spider nut at the top. These ties were the standard way German mortar rounds were filled, with each round requiring a number of ties as listed in the instruction manual.

The *Leichter Ladungswerfer* was used by engineering units at the start of the war, for the destruction of obstacles. There were high-explosive, smoke and training rounds for it. There was also a round described as launching a grapnel and rope. After about 1942 the weapon was withdrawn from front-line service and ended up arming portions of the Atlantic Wall, with several being reported in the Channel Islands.

Two German soldiers loading a projectile onto a *Leichter Ladungswerfer*.

The final common spigot weapon of the Second World War was the Japanese Type 98 320mm spigot mortar. The weapon had its origins in the mid- to late 1930s for use in China against the Soviets. The mortar entered service in 1938, and used the Imperial Japanese Calendar (*kōki*) for its designation – 1938 was 2598 *kōki*, and thus the mortar became the Type 98. Although the mortar entered service the year before the Battle of Nomonhan (Khalkhin Gol), it was held back due to concerns about secrecy. This seems a shame as a light man-portable weapon, with a considerable payload, would have been exceptionally useful to the Japanese forces in the battle, although it is unlikely to have altered the overall outcome of the battle due to the length of time it took to prepare for action.

The spigot was a large, hollow, brass tube, with a baseplate attached. The spigot then had a wooden platform built up around it and the baseplate. The entire assembly was then placed in a pit dug at the required angle, which was usually 45 degrees. Silk bags filled with the propellant, believed by Allied intelligence to be black powder mixed with nitrocellulose, were loaded into the projectile, then the bomb was loaded on the spigot.

This projectile consisted of three components, a tail section, a body and a nose cone. Construction of a complete round was achieved by screwing the tail and nose cone to the body, all of which were made from thin cast steel. Both the nose and body were filled with picric acid, a primitive high explosive from the late 1800s which had fallen out of use by the middle of the First World War. The nose contained 56lb of explosive and the body 47lb. Both the nose and body had separate fuses, most alarmingly of all, the fuse in the body could only be accessed before the nose cone was screwed in place. Thus, the fuse had to be armed, and the safety removed before the round was finally assembled. The live shell would then be loaded onto the spigot. Manhandling a live, unsafed, fused bomb weighing a total of 737lb, where any rough handling could cause a detonation, cannot have been an enjoyable experience. Each launcher was provided with several rings with handles moulded into them, which could be clipped around the live round enabling up to two people per ring to lift and carry the complete round.

By varying the number or size of the charge bags, and how far down the spigot the round was seated, the required range could be reached. It is likely that as the spigot was brass it would be expanded by the propellant to achieve obturation. Certainly, the spigot was only good for three to four shots before needing to be changed.

At the start of the Second World War, there were five independent mortar battalions, which would go on to fight in several battles throughout the war. The first was at Bataan where around 175 rounds were fired. Later the mortar would be used at Singapore, Okinawa and Iwo Jima in the Pacific Theatre.

The Type 98 was also used in Burma, where a single mortar and two rounds were infiltrated forward of the Japanese lines in the Arakan to be fired at Kohima.

Clearly there were several different approaches to creating sufficient obturation, most of them were along the same lines, to use the gas pressure to expand some form of metal container. In most cases, the spigot weapons were seen as a novelty, and only the British forces adopted the concept in any great numbers.

PART NINE

THE END

Chapter Seventeen

The War after Next

After the war, the spigot weapons of the various nations all but disappeared rather instantly. Only in Britain did they hold on for a while. As has been shown, the Hedgehog remained in service aboard Royal Navy ships for some years, and the Petard continued in service until the 1960s. The PIAT also remained in service for a short time after the war. In the post-war period, the British Army entered a curious phase when they shed huge amounts of manpower and equipment. Indeed, the equipment situation became strangely confused as the army had to undergo a massive restructuring.

The Bombards in stores were likely all scrapped. Large amounts of the produced ammunition had been opened and the explosive extracted for use in the PIAT rounds. Indeed, a power-operated machine for opening the Bombard rounds had been installed in one of the ICI factories and had cost £372 11*s* and 7*d*. This machine was not decommissioned until 1946. The decommissioning of the no-longer needed factories was a point of discussion between the Treasury and ICI, which lasted until 1950. At that point, an agreement was reached for £1,250 to be paid to ICI for care and maintenance of the facilities. These were then decommissioned, however, ICI even charged the government £6 10*s* 5*d* for the electricity the decommissioning teams used during their operation.

The Bombard projectiles that had not been reclaimed were prepared for destruction. The bombs were first inspected for a fuse, and if one found it was removed. Then the protective tubes were cut with a hand saw. The cuts were made near the top of the case, and one between the bomb body and the tail. These cuts were then struck with a hammer to create a wider opening. Finally, the prepared cases were shipped out to sea and dumped overboard.

The PIAT stayed in service, although it appears the ammunition production contract was terminated immediately at the end of the war, with only about 8 million of the planned 10 million rounds being produced. This led to the situation where there were no more rounds being manufactured to refill stocks, and the army needed to maintain a supply of ammunition in case of a war. This led to a ban on firing practice with the PIAT. The exact out-of-service date for the PIAT is hard to obtain. It is certain that almost none, if any, PIATs went to Korea, and the British forces there were re-armed with the M20 Super Bazooka. However, there is the suggestion of an official

232   *Defeating the Panzer-Stuka Menace*

out-of-service date of 1956, but it is unlikely any would have seen combat after the Second World War, at least in British hands.

The PIAT would, however, see combat around the globe in a variety of small bushfire wars with several forces. The sheer flexibility and utility of the weapon, as well as its simple rugged design, meant it was the perfect weapon for these types of conflicts.

The first such war was the battle for Israel in May 1948. The PIAT was often the defending Israelis only anti-tank weapon, and a weapon used by the attacking Egyptians. At the crucial Battle of Yad Mordechai, there was a PIAT with two or three rounds. During the battle, the Israelis managed to scavenge another twelve bombs from the Egyptian bodies heaped in front of their position. On the last day of the five-day siege a Vickers light tank Mk VIB was used by the Egyptians to force the Israeli lines and was taken

A rather bored (and harassed) looking Dutch PIAT operator, surrounded by one of the hazards of peace-time training. This particular incident was during Exercise Crescendo, which was held in March 1951 in the area of Veluwe in Holland.

under fire by the Israeli PIAT, although no hits were scored. The near misses convinced the crew to stop sitting in the open waiting to be obliterated, and they advanced. Once closer to the Israeli lines, and now remote and isolated from friendly infantry, the tank was disabled by explosive charges and later captured.

Another war the PIAT served in was the First Indochina War. In the hands of French forces, it was often used as a mortar or bunker buster. One common sight was a PIAT mounted on a pedestal and with a gun shield on French riverine craft. The presence of the PIAT in the French arsenal does raise a very intriguing possibility that the Vietminh took control of any PIATs they captured, and later, like so many other ex-French weapons, passed them on to the Viet Cong and used them in the opening stages of the Vietnam War. However, this is a possibility based largely on speculation from the similar journey of many other weapons, and there is no evidence this was the case. Although by this point one wonders how the ammunition's shelf life held up in the high humidity and tropical heat.

There is a story that a PIAT was in use in the 1971 Battle of Longewala on the India–Pakistan border, although once again there is no conclusive evidence of its use.

The final and most recent use of a PIAT was reported in 2008! A pair of drug dealers were arrested at an address in the City of Lakeland in Florida. As part of this operation, a PIAT was seized. Several witnesses stated they had seen one of the drug dealers fire the weapon in 2007, discharging it into Lake Parker. One wonders about this, as ammunition for the weapon would have been either horribly toxic or very unstable, depending on the type of filling used. In addition, the propellant would have significantly degraded, meaning there was a decent chance the drug dealer would have blown himself up if the round had been a live one. Or did the drug dealers' jury rig some kind of projectile that would make a loud bang and intimidate the witnesses.

When the last combat use of the PIAT was is difficult to say, as stocks of these were likely sold on to new owners several times over. For example, piles of PIATs were discovered in a warehouse in Iraq in 2006. PIATs will likely continue to turn up, in the most unusual of places, although no ammunition will be available.

During the Second World War all energies were focused on winning, the British adopting the stance that the legalities could be sorted out afterwards. After the fighting had ended a Royal Commission on Inventions was held to sort out these legal matters and to make amends to inventors by awarding payments. Both Blacker and Denovan put in claims, Denovan in respect of the invention of the AVRE, and Blacker a long list of features that made the spigot weapons a success. After the Royal Commission passed judgements it granted Blacker an award of £7,000 and Denovan £1,500. In both cases, this was far below what the applicants had applied for. For example, Denovan had requested $10,000. It should be noted that Blacker had already managed to obtain an award of £25,000 from the Ministry of Supply previously, and this had been paid as Blacker had claimed over £26,000 in out-of-pocket expenses. All these payments were seen as *ex gratia* and meant that the owner of the patent ceded any claim to them. Blacker, it appears, was badly advised over the legalities of this as later he would submit another claim for the use of the Hedgehog by the US Navy, but this was quickly rejected.

But what of the inventors themselves? Denovan returned home to Canada. At the time of his submission to the Royal Commission, in April 1949, he was living in Quebec. It seems that he later moved to Ontario, where, in 1953, aged 37, he gave an interview to the local paper. In 1998 the 5th Combat Engineer Regiment, Royal Candian Engineers, dedicated one of its buildings to his memory, and it appears from the few documents that can be found online that he passed away the following year.

For Blacker things largely carried on as they had since 1942, with him inventing new guns. On his Royal Commission application he does list his occupation as a farmer. His weapon designs seem to have lacked spigots and were much more closely tied to rockets, as well as improving the accuracy of the rockets. There were a few recoilless rifles in his collection of designs. One of these had an angled rear tube, about 150 degrees from the barrel. This would fire a counterweight made up of buckshot at a safe angle. There are pictures of Blacker at his home with the weapon after it was built.

Blacker's grandson, Barnaby, told me a story of these later years, which sums up Blacker perfectly. During a visit Barnaby was with Blacker's wife, Lady Peel, in the kitchen. Suddenly there was an earth-shattering explosion, which caused dust to swirl down from the high surfaces. Blacker lurched through the door, smouldering slightly and somewhat dazed after his latest device for visiting mayhem on someone or something had malfunctioned. Lady Peel sweetly asked, 'Are you ok dear? It's just we heard a bit of a bang.' After collecting his thoughts, Blacker whose ears were still ringing just answered, 'Oh yes, everything's fine.' Then headed back down into his workshop in the cellar. Blacker passed away in 1964.

Blacker, for all his faults, was an incredibly brave and highly inventive weapon designer, able quickly and naturally to come up with ideas off the top of his head. At first glance, he was very much of the 'seat of your pants design school'. However, this is unfair. In many of his works he goes into complicated maths. His work on rocket engines, the aerodynamics and jet efflux show this. Of course, those were all means to an end, and that end was usually causing something to explode. In the case of the rocket aerodynamics, the work was to make the rocket-propelled projectile more accurate.

Blacker's early fascination with spigots and his work before the war meant that the British had an expert who could introduce the concept of a working spigot, and Blacker's work led to four weapons that were part of defeating Nazi Germany and Japan. The Bombard, while arriving a year after it was sorely needed, did establish the idea of spigot weapons, and the concept of man-portable chemical energy anti-tank weapons. This precursor work with the Ordnance Board almost certainly leads to a much smoother introduction of the PIAT. The Bombard also led directly to the Hedgehog. The Hedgehog was possibly the greatest failure of the spigot arsenal, but that was in no way down to the weapon. While the Battle of the Atlantic was won with only assistance from the Hedgehog, the reason the weapon did not play a more significant part was due to the scandal surrounding its introduction by the navy. This disruption was not fixed until after the U-boat peril was already on the retreat. But if training for the Hedgehog had been available at its introduction the Battle of the Atlantic would have been over in the first half of 1942, instead of the cumulative battles in March 1943.

The PIAT, and by extension the Petard, was the outstanding success of the family. Without them the infantry would have lacked weapons capable of killing tanks and providing other supporting fire. The Imperial War Museum has a huge collection of audio recordings of veterans available online in which they recount their stories. Going through that list the ones that mention the PIAT fall into several distinct categories. The most common is receiving instruction on the weapon. The next most common is using the PIAT to blow up something other than a tank. This was the key to the PIAT's success, its flexibility to be used on a wide variety of targets. It gave the British infantry platoon a distinct edge in firepower and flexibility when combined with the 2-inch mortar.

Finally, the Petard, which at first glance seems to have played a limited role. However, the sheer number of pillboxes, fortified positions and field works this gun reduced demonstrates its importance. Imagine D-Day with a vastly higher proportion of the German fortifications still intact. One prime example of that is the Sanatorium at Le Hamel on Gold Beach. This fortified strongpoint remained intact until the later stages of D-Day and split the Allied beaches. The Sanatorium was able to sweep Gold Beach with fire. It remained intact and resolute until an AVRE appeared and cracked open the concrete, allowing the infantry to gain entrance and clear the fortress. The Petard's performance on D-Day alone justifies the weapon, but it went on to do far more throughout the battles that followed.

The longest lasting of Blacker's inventions was the HESH round. In the post-war world, the Soviets used the lessons learnt from the war creating well-armoured tanks. These were enhanced by sloped or curved armour, which made them much harder to kill. HESH was the perfect remedy for this design, actually becoming more effective against sloped armour. In addition, HESH could function as a HE round for the main gun, meaning one never had to make the choice between an anti-infantry or an anti-tank round and run the risk of only having the wrong projectile available. HESH also enabled the arming of many smaller and lighter vehicles such as the Saladin armoured car or the Scorpion light tank with guns that had a reasonably potent weapon for a small weight. The Royal Armoured Corps' love of HESH has continued right up to the present day. It is only a modern reduction in spending on research and development for weaponry that has meant that British guns have started to fall behind in capability. That linked with improvements to smoothbore technology means that only now is HESH being superseded.

While the Second World War would have been won without Blacker's inventions, their presence made the war vastly cheaper for the Allies in blood and treasure than would have been the case otherwise. Battles that would have been very close-run things suddenly appear to be much easier because of the spigot weapons. There is no monument to Blacker today, apart from the many descendants of the people his weapons saved.

Appendix A

Blacker Spigot Weapons Genealogy

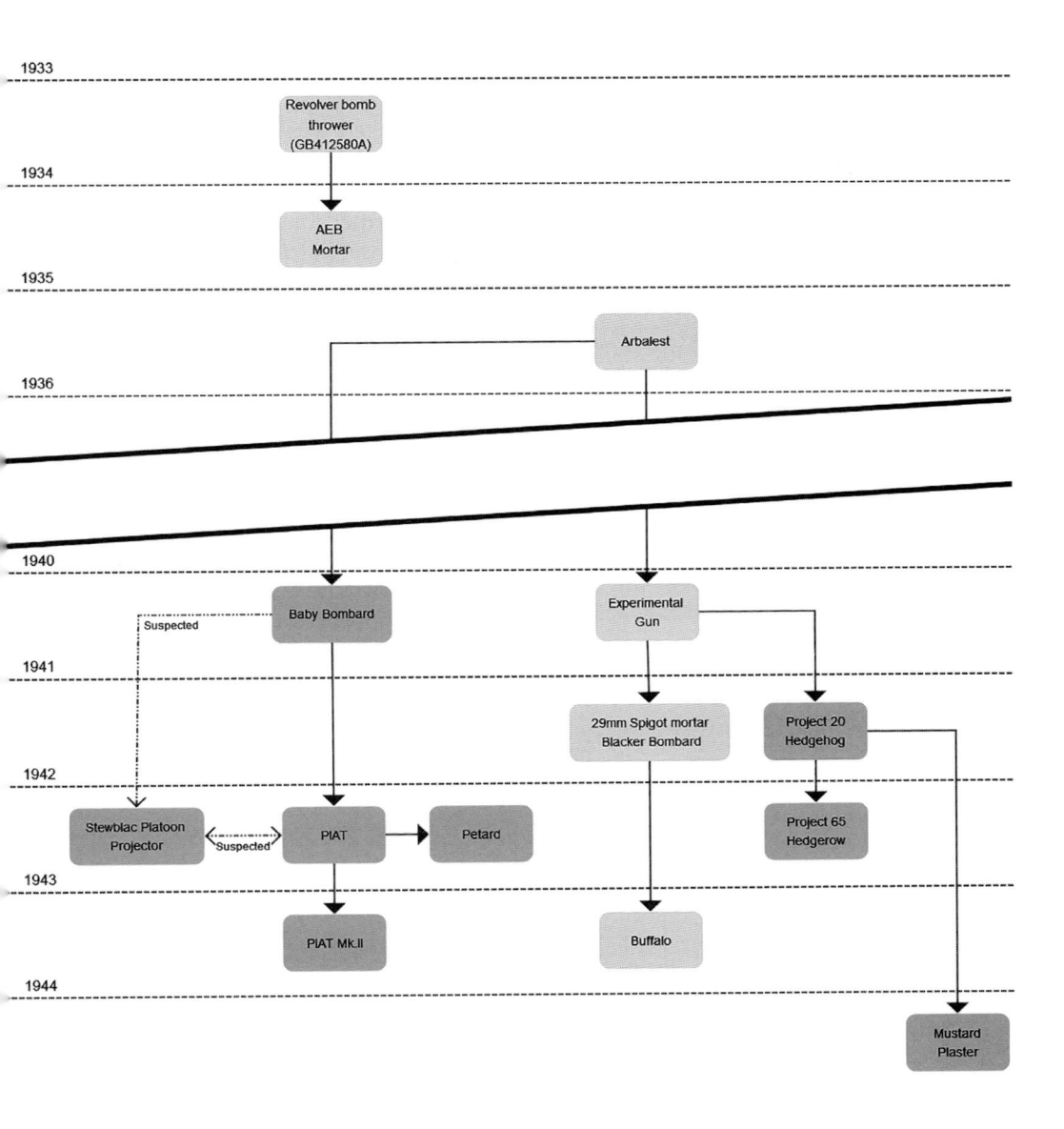

1933

- Revolver bomb thrower (GB412580A)

1934

- AEB Mortar

1935

1936

- Arbalest

1940

- Baby Bombard
- Experimental Gun

1941

- Suspected
- 29mm Spigot mortar Blacker Bombard
- Project 20 Hedgehog

1942

- Stewblac Platoon Projector — Suspected — PIAT → Petard
- Project 65 Hedgerow

1943

- PIAT Mk.II
- Buffalo

1944

- Mustard Plaster

Appendix B

Bombard Ammunition Stores

A colleague of mine, Jeremy Rosenblad, has been looking into the Canadian Archives. Reports were found detailing a number of ammunition types and their stock levels. From these documents Jeremy extracted the data for the Blacker Bombard.

The following data is limited to only rounds that have been released for use. It is very unlikely to be the total supply of ammunition available worldwide, although in some of the smaller areas the numbers given may be the entire stock in that command.

	As of 27 Mar. 1942	As of 11 Apr. 1942	As of 18 Apr. 1942	As of 25 Apr. 1942	As of 2 May 1942	As of 9 May 1942	As of 16 May 1942	Missing, format change	23 Aug.–23 Sep. 1942	23 Sep.–23 Oct. 1942	23 Nov.–23 Dec. 1942	23 Dec. 1942–23 Jan. 1943	23 Jan.–23 Feb.
Home Forces													
20lb AT	15,000	30,000	30,000	20,000	10,000	50,000	15,000		–	163,000	11,000	–	15,000
14lb HE	–	–	35,000	30,000	10,000	20,000	5,000		–	216,000	7,600	–	2,000
Middle East													
20lb AT	5,000	–	20,000	–	–	–	–		–	–	–	–	–
14lb HE	–	–	–	–	–	–	–		–	–	–	–	–
India													
20lb AT	5,000	–	20,000	–	–	–	–		–	–	3,500	–	–
14lb HE	–	–	–	1,000	10,000	5,000	5,000		–	–	2,500	–	–
East Africa													
20lb AT	–	–	–	–	–	–	–		–	–	–	–	1,000
14lb HE	–	–	–	–	–	–	–		–	–	–	–	500

South Africa									
20lb AT	–	–	–	300	–	–	–	–	–
14lb HE	–	–	–	60	–	–	–	–	–
Gibraltar									
20lb AT	–	–	–	–	–	–	–	–	–
14lb HE	–	–	–	1,000	–	–	–	–	–
Prussia/Iraq									
20lb AT	–	–	–	–	–	–	13,000	–	–
14lb HE	–	–	–	–	–	–	–	–	–
DMT									
20lb AT	–	–	–	–	–	1,000	–	991	3,241
14lb HE	–	–	–	–	–	–	–	–	–
War Office reserve									
20lb AT	3,600	78,300	85,300	127,800	130,600	124,800	148,600	473,200	402,800	435,500	487,500	480,000
14lb HE	200	–	–	300	2,900	7,700	19,300	260,500	117,500	130,600	214,600	254,500
Total stock to be retained under War Office control									
20lb AT	6,600	85,300	127,800	130,600	134,800	148,600	153,100	305,600	472,800	480,800	435,000	487,300
14lb HE	200	–	300	2,900	7,700	19,300	21,100	140,500	168,300	162,700	125,900	214,500

Appendix C

Companies in North and South Groups

North Group
- ICI
- F&S (no further details)
- Bruce Peebles and Co., Edinburgh (electrical engineers)
- Blackenborough (no further details)
- Thomas Broadbent and Sons Ltd, Huddersfield (electrical engineers)
- Internal Combustion (no further details)

South Group
- Mellor, Bromley and Co., Leicester (knitting machine manufacturers)
- G.D. Peters and Co., Slough (manufacturer of fittings and components for railway carriages; later worked on the Mosquito)
- Benham Ltd, Battersea (possibly Benham and Co., maker of kitchen fittings)
- Adamant Engineering Co., Luton (manufacturer of steering equipment)
- Tusroke, Luton (motorcycle manufacturers)
- Morris Singer, Walthamstow (no further details)
- E.S.S. Signs Ltd, Hendon (no further details)
- Auto-Dairy Engineers, Wembley (manufacturers of dairy machinery such as bottle washers, made complete Bombards)
- Newman Engineering, Wembley (made complete Bombards, no further details)
- Brown and Tawse Tubes, Bromley-by-Bow (maker of steel tubes such as pipework, made only mobile mounts)
- Dibbin (no further details)

Appendix D

PIAT vs Bazooka – Comparative Trials

When the PIAT first entered service there was a trial held to compare the PIAT andt the M1 Bazooka. This was held in North Africa, and was different to the trial held in the UK mentioned on p. 172. At this particular trial they had no Panzers on hand to serve as a target, so they used a M3 Lee that had previously been knocked out. As the primary objective of the test was to check the PIAT's performance, it was fired at 50yd to ensure it could accurately hit the desired locations. The Bazooka was fired at 70yd. Although this may seem slightly unfair to the Bazooka, this may not be too harsh as the Bazooka may have had longer ranged projectiles.

Shot	PIAT Location of Hit	Effect	Bazooka Location of Hit	Effect
1	Miss	Over turret	Miss	Rocket Malfunction
2	Turret ring	3cm hole, ran alongside the turret ring	Miss	Over turret
3	Hull gun mantlet, 15 degree slope.	2cm hole. Damage to hull door on opposite side and on 37mm	Turret, 15 degree of slope	3cm outer hole, 0.5cm inner. Splatter on 37mm gun
4	Hull, right-hand side of hull door	2cm hole, inside 3cm. Line of damage cutting across fighting compartment	Hit, rear bogie	Tore off tyre over 5cm. Damage to the idler wheel. Track broken before shot
5	Below driver's visor, 30 degree angle	2cm hole. Inside spalling within 20cm of hole. Damage to 75mm gun	Rear hull, above idler wheel	2cm hole, impossible to measure inside hole. Severe splatter to engine
6	Turret	2cm outer hole, 3cm inner. Spalling punctured recuperator of 37mm causing loss of oil	Ricocheted off hull gun mantlet	Exploded behind tank
7	Side hull	2cm hole. Splatter on cases on floor of turret	Side door	2.5cm hole, inside 2cm hole. Inside spalling within 5cm of hole. Splatter all over the hull

Appendix E

Matilda Hedgehog Serial Numbers

by Thomas Anderson

The following table lists the serial numbers of the equipment issued to all six Matilda Hedgehogs.

Tank No.	No. 19 Set	Besa MG	2-Pounder	Very Pistol	Owen Gun
82136	383	C8752	L35483	39532	5998
88344	17072	C14244	26134	2153	803
35307	9963	899	33868	6939	1314
10194	1038	2958	5520	36071	1443
6908	240	C8205	19749	37150	3129
35357	970	C1618	144248	4712	1874

Bibliography and Sources

Extra special thanks to the Blacker family who provided considerable assistance and helped fill in the holes in the official paperwork.

Archives

Canadian National Archives
London Munitions Assignment Board
   4th Meeting – Minutes for Meeting on Monday 30th March, 1942
   14th Meeting – Minutes for Meeting on Tuesday 14th April, 1942
   16th Meeting – Minutes for Meeting on Tuesday 21st April, 1942
   18th Meeting – Minutes for Meeting on Tuesday 28th April, 1942
   25th Meeting – Minutes for Meeting on Tuesday 5th May, 1942
   29th Meeting – Minutes for Meeting on Tuesday 12th May, 1942
   31st Meeting – Minutes for Meeting on Tuesday 19th May, 1942
   90th Meeting – AGENDA for Meeting on Wednesday 7th October, 1942
   104th Meeting – AGENDA for Meeting on Wednesday 7th November, 1942
   9th Meeting – AGENDA for Meeting on Monday 8th January, 1943
   23rd Meeting – AGENDA for Meeting on Monday 8th February, 1943
   36th Meeting – AGENDA for Meeting on Tuesday 9th March, 1943
   British Army Staff Liaison Letter No. 2 prepared by B.A.S., Washington. May 11th 1943.

Churchill College Archives, Cambridge
WEIR 20/11: Anti-tank Weapons and Blacker Bombard (W11)

Imperial War Museum
29mm. Spigot Mortar (Blacker Bombard): Training Instruction (Provisional)
29mm. Spigot Mortar (Blacker Bombard)
The 29mm Spigot Mortar
Assembly Instructions for 29mm Spigot Mortar ('Bombard')
Audio interviews:
   Rose, Stanley Rupert
   Harris, Frederick Leonard
   Tremain, Bert

The National Archives, Kew
ADM 1/13898 Spigot Battery Mortar
ADM 116/5006 Hedgehog Volume 1
ADM 116/5246 LCA and LCT Fitted with Hedgerow
ADM 277/37 Hedgehog, Project No. 20
ADM 1/17565 HMS *Vernon* Meeting

AVIA 22/2921 Manufacture of Bombard
AVIA 22/576 Blacker Bombard
ADM 189/175 Technical History of Anti-submarine Weapons
ADM 277/12 Waterhammer
AVIA 53/43 Royal Commission Inventions LVS Blacker
CAB 66/28/47 Report on Fulfilment of the Moscow Protocol, October, 1941–June, 1942
CAB 120/370 Sticky Grenade and Bombard
CAB 120/378 Anti-tank Weapons
DEFE 15/1449 PIAT HE Filling *vs* 2-inch Mortar
DEFE 15-1442 German 20cm Spigot Mortar
HO 196/18
PREM 3/428/1 Sticky Bombs
PREM 3/428/6 Jeffries Shoulder Gun
SUPP 22/54 Unserviceability of Hollow Charge Warheads in PIAT, 3.7" and 95mm
T 161/1131 Treasury PIAT Requirements
T 166/20 Denovan Claim
T 166/42 JJ Denovan Supporting Evidence
WO 188/1776 Squirts Anti-tank Projector
WO 188/1919 PIAT Smoke Bomb
WO 195/6096 Detonation of Tellermines by Hedgehogs
WO 203/1175 Reports on Infantry Assaults in the Arakan
WO 203/540 Bombard Mounted on a Sherman Tank
WO 291/153 Effectiveness of PIAT Shooting
WO 291/964 Studies on Working Methods
WO 32/11630 Hedgerow Mortar
WO 32/11630 Hedgerow Spigot Mortar
WO 32/9461 23pdr Bombard
Ordnance Board proceedings:
  SUPP 6-349
  SUPP 6-466
  SUPP 6-467
  SUPP 6-468

Nuffield College library, Oxford
CSAC 80.4.81/G.265 'Guns and Ammunition'
CSAC 80.4.81/G.266 'Guns and Ammunition'
CSAC 80.4.81/G.267 'Guns and Ammunition'
CSAC 80.4.81/G.268 'Guns and Ammunition'
CSAC 80.4.81/G.269 'Guns and Ammunition'

US National Archives
472.4-5: Tree Spigot Gun
ETF 550 E-2149: Military Intelligence Division, Great Britain – Visit to the Demonstration Held at Experimental Station No. 6, Knebworth
1822: Tree Spigot Gun 11 July 1945
299): Spigot Gun

Publications

Catalog of Enemy Ordnance, originally published by the US Office of Chief of Ordnance, 1945.
Fletcher, David. *Mr Churchill's Tank*, Schiffer Publishing Ltd, 1999.
Ford, Ken. *Operation Market-Garden 1944* (3), Osprey Publishing, 2018.

Henry, Hugh G. 'The Calgary Tanks at Dieppe', MA thesis, University of Cambridge, 1996.
Kobashi, Yoshio and Ginga Shuppan (with assistance from Akira Takizawa). *Nihon Rikugun no Himitsu Neiki*, 1994.
Milton, Giles. *The Ministry of Ungentlemanly Warfare*, John Murray, 2016.
Moss, Matthew. *The PIAT: Britain's Anti-tank Weapon of World War II*, Osprey Publishing, 2020.
Nachrichtenblatt der Panzertrupppen, Nr. 18, Dec. 1944.
Strelecka Revue, August 2000.
Waffen Revue, Nr. 37.II.
War Department Technical Manual, Vol. 30, Issue 451.

Websites

http://www.pillbox.org.uk/blog/216735/ (accessed: June 2019)

The following sources were used by Thomas Anderson:

Archives

Australian War Memorial
AWM 54, 115/6/1 PART 1. (Bombs and Grenades – New:) Provisional Tactical Doctrine for Matilda Tanks, Fitted with Hedgehogs, Characteristics, Drawings of, Method of Filling Projectile, 1-3/4 inch Hedgehog or Porcupine. Typical Arrangement of Stencilling, Sealing and Labeling, Method of Filling, Primer, Electric QF cartridges No. 13 MRS I and II, Steel Body with Tail – Box, Projectile, 1-3/4" Hedgehog P68, Mark I and III – Wood to H One, Mark II Projectile – Details of Tail for Mark I and II Body Plus Sealing, Tail Tube, 1-3/4" Hedgehog, Mark III.
AWM 54, 115/6/1 PART 2. (Bombs and Grenades – New:) Provisional Tactical Doctrine for Matilda Tanks, Fitted with Hedgehogs, Characteristics, Drawings of, Method of Filling Projectile, 1-3/4 inch Hedgehog or Porcupine. Typical Arrangement of Stencilling, Sealing and Labeling, Method of Filling, Primer, Electric QF cartridges No. 13 MRS I and II, Steel Body with Tail – Box, Projectile, 1-3/4" Hedgehog P68, Mark I and III – Wood to Hold One, Mark II Projectile – Details of Tail for Mark I and II Body Plus Sealing, Tail Tube, 1-3/4" Hedgehog, Mark III.
AWM 54, 115/6/2. (Bombs and Grenades – New:) Papers Giving Details and Description of Projector Hedgehog, No. 1 MKL, Test Instructions, June 1945.
AWM 54, 905/23/6. (Stores and Equipment – User Trials:) Copies of User Trials Reports, Extracts from Ordnance Board Proceedings on Spigot Mortars (Blacker Bombard). Trials of QF 25-Pr Gun (light); Trials of Self Propelled, 40MM AA Gun. Demonstration Projector Infantry Tank Attack, Spigot Mortar for Destruction of Japanese Fixed Defences, Lists of Rocket Kites, Summary of Reports on Trials of PITA.
AWM 54, 21/2/2. (Ammunition – Supply:) Ammunition Mortars, Range Table – Spigot Mortar for Destruction of Japanese Fixed Defences, 1943.
AWM 54, 925/5/4. (Tanks – Types:) Provisional Tactical Doctrine for Flame Throwers Tanks (Frog) – Appendix A to 1 Australian Corps G/6925/SD of 14 March, 45 Provisional Tactical Doctrine for Flame Thrower Tanks (Frogs) Appendix B for Matilda Tanks Fitted with Hedgehogs (C) Bridge Layer Tank (Covenanter Mark II) (d) for Tank Dozer, Australian No. I MK I. A Paper by DTI on Policy for Use of Mobile Flame Throwers; Instructions Concerning the Organisation and Employment of the Flame Thrower Tank Battalion Points of Known Types of Japanese Tanks Vulnerable to Flame Throwers, Matilda Tank Maintenance.

AWM 54, 115/9/1. (Bombs and Grenades – Inventions:) Blast Bombs, Sketch of Grenade Initiated Ammonal Charge, January 1943.

AWM 54, 937/3/36. (Training General – Tropical Warfare:) HQ 4 Australian Armoured Brigade Training Instruction No. 7 – Employment of Tanks in Jungle Warfare, New Guinea

AWM 54, 925/7/5. (Tanks – Reports on:) Armoured Fighting Vehicles Bulletins Nos 4 to 10, 4th Australian Armoured Brigade (n.d.).

AWM 54, 423/13/24. (Intelligence – Technical Summaries:) 4 Australian Armoured Brigade AIF, AFV (Armoured Fighting Vehicle) Bulletins Nos 1 to 14, Equipment, Organisation and General Information.

AWM 54, 759/1/3. (Photography – General:) File of Photographs Showing Various Types of Jeeps – Engineers Trucks – Tank Dozers – Matilda Tanks – Stuart Tanks – Grant Diesels – Machinery Lorries – Ambulance – Covenanter Bridge Layers – Photos of Vehicles on Charge – 4th Australian Armoured Brigade.

AWM 52, 3/1/11/9. (Unit War Diaries, 1939–45 War) 2/5 Australian Armoured Regiment, July–September 1944.

AWM 52, 3/1/30/6. (Unit War Diaries, 1939–45 War) 2/1 Australian Armoured Brigade Reconnaissance Squadron, June 1945.

National Archives of Australia

NAA: MP76/1, 18447. (Inventor/Submitter –) M. Miller – Range Finder for Use in Armoured Fighting Vehicles in Connection with Hedgehog (plans included).

NAA: MP742/1, 215/1/217. Investigation of the Hedgehog Mounted on the Matilda Tank (contains twelve photographs).

NAA: MP76/3, G261. Blacker Bombard 29mm Spigot Mortar.

NAA: A705, 15/17/510. Directorate of Armament – Armament Instruction – AAP 735.0 Section 1 Number 14 – Bombs, Projector Infantry Anti-Tank (PIAT) – Inspection and repair (0.25cm).

NAA: A705, 15/40/167 PART 1. Disposal of Equipment – E7E guns PIAT (Projector, Infantry, Anti-Tank) and Mortars 2-inch and 3-inch, Guns Bofors 40mm Mark 1 (1cm).

NAA: B3138, 43/Z/112 Trial No 125/2 OQF 2 – pounder Mk X v. Japanese 'bunker' (contains seven photographs).

NAA: MP385/7, 52/101/153. Army – Tank Trials Against Log Weapon Pits.

Publications

Bingham, James. *Australian Sentinel and Matildas*, Profile Pub, 1972.

Hopkins, Ronald Nicholas Lamond and Australian War Memorial. *Australian Armour: A History of the Royal Australian Armoured Corps, 1927–1972*, Australian War Memorial and Australian Government Publishing Service, Canberra, 1978.

Ross, A.T. *Armed & Ready: The Industrial Development & Defence of Australia, 1900–1945*. Turton & Armstrong, 1995.

Index

4/7th Dragoon Guards 165
5th Duke of Cornwall's Light Infantry (DCLI) 165, 168
9th Durham Light Infantry 165

Arakan 69, 220, 244, 228

Balikpapan 199, 200
Bataan 227
Bay of Biscay 84, 96
Beaverbrook, Max Aitken, 1st Baron 55
Bernières-sur-Mer 123
Beta C-mag 8
Bizerta 116
Blacker, Barnaby 234
Blacker, Latham Valentine Stewart, OBE 3–5, 7–11, 13, 15–23, 27–30, 33–5, 37–9, 41, 43, 44, 60, 70, 86, 137–9, 141–5, 169, 170, 181, 196, 197, 217, 220, 233, 234–8, 242–6
Bougainville 213
Burma 68, 69, 228
Buxton Bombard training school 60–2

Cardale, Lieutenant Colonel W.J. 180
Carr, Assistant Chief of the Imperial General Staff, Major General Laurence 38, 39
Churchill, Sir Winston Leonard Spencer 8, 10–13, 28, 29, 38–40, 43, 73, 74, 91, 171
Clarke, Major Cecil Vandepeer, MC 217–19, 224
Clarke, Major General Edward Montagu Campbell, Director of Artillery (D of A) 11–13, 19–21, 27, 28, 38, 39, 43, 141, 143
COMLANCRABNAW, US Task Force 116
companies
    Boosey & Hawkes Ltd 27, 32, 35, 37, 86

Thomas Broadbent and Sons Ltd 56, 57, 240
Cocksedge & Co. 186
Cook, Troughton and Sims 56
Dowty Equipment Company 99
Evershed & Vignoles 93
Gale and Polden Ltd 62
I.A. Hodgson & Co. 143
Holmans Ltd 82
Imperial Chemical Industries (ICI) 8, 13, 34, 35, 55, 56, 60, 141, 143, 145, 147, 159, 160, 181, 197, 231
    Ardeer, ICI plant 34
    Kynochs, ICI plant 197
Merz Engineering Company 220, 221
Morris & Walker packing company 197
Nash & Thompson Ltd 44
Rubery Owen & Company Ltd 71
Parnell Aircraft Ltd 17, 19, 44
Thompson Brothers (Bilston) Ltd 120, 125
Thorneycrofts Ltd 80
A. & P. Uscinski 202
Vauxhall Ltd 179
Vickers Ltd 29
James Williamson & Son Ltd 183

D-Day 54, 71, 120–3, 133, 185, 186, 235
Denovan, Lieutenant John James 177–81, 186, 233, 234, 244
Department for Miscellaneous Weapons Design (DMWD) 80, 82, 86, 88, 90, 91, 97, 101, 108, 113, 115, 120, 123
Department for Tank Design (DTD) 177
Department for Torpedoes and Mining (DTM) 91, 93
Dieppe 177, 178
Director of Naval Ordnance (DNO) 92
Dunkirk 8, 11, 27, 32

El Alamein   67, 197
Everest, Mount   7
explosives and chemicals
  amatol   35, 36, 225
  ammonal   35, 36, 195, 196, 245
  baratol   35, 36
  hydrogen cyanide   140
  Minol   100
  nitrocellulose   33, 227
  nitroglycerine   33, 34, 162
  Nobels 704   35, 36
  Nobels 808   33, 34, 49, 55, 73, 139, 143, 147, 162, 183, 184, 219
  Pentolite   162, 183, 184
  picric acid   227
  RDX   100, 121, 147, 160, 162
  Torpex   100, 101, 121, 129

Feldman, Lieutenant Colonel Allan   224

Gabčík, Jozef   219

Hankley Common demonstration   180, 181, 186
Hartnett, Sir Laurence John, CBE   196
Hayling Bay Hedgerow test fire   113, 114
helicopter   137
Heydrich, Reinhard   219
Horam Brickworks disaster   59, 60, 67

Iwo Jima   227

Jefferis, Sir Millis Rowland, KBE, MC   6, 9–13, 27, 28, 32, 38, 39, 43, 82, 135, 137, 140–4
Juno Beach   122

Knox, Brigadier Fergus Y. Carson, 50th (Northumbrian) Infantry Division   123
Kohima   228
Kubiš, Jan   219

Le Hamel   235
Le Harve   187, 188
Lennard-Payne, Sub Lieutenant P.C.   122, 123
Lindemann, Frederick Alexander, 1st Viscount Cherwell, CH, PC, FRS   8, 13, 27, 29, 34

Lingèvres   165
Little, Admiral Charles James Colebrooke   82
Longewala   233

McArthur-Onslow, Brigadier Denzel   200
McNaughton, General Andrew George Latta   70
Macrae, Colonel Robert Stuart   10, 11, 32, 65, 217, 218
Market Garden   165
Melchett, Henry Ludwig Mond, 2nd Baron   8, 55, 154
Mersa Matruh   67
Milner, Major Alan   205
Minqar Qaim   68
MIRc   8–11, 13, 27, 28, 30, 33, 34
Miteriya Ridge   68
Mogg, Major John   165
Murray, R.   122, 123

Neuve Chapelle   5
Nobel, Alfred   33
Nomonhan, Battle of   227

Okinawa   227
Operation Anthropoid   219
Operation Postmaster   74

Pegasus Bridge   169

Quetta staff college   7, 8

Risborough demonstration   150
Ruweisat Ridge   67, 68

Salerno   116, 118–20
ships
  HMS *Enchantress*   99
  HMS *Fowey*   99
  HMS *Graph*   199, 100
  HMS *Himalaya*   3
  HMS *Howe*   116
  HMS *Lotus*   94
  HMS *Osprey*   93
  HMS *Violet*   96, 97
  HMS *Westcott*   85, 90, 91
  Maid Honour   73, 74
  RMS *Lusitania*   77
  USS *Nauset*   118, 120

Index 249

Tel el Eisa 67, 197
Terrell, Edward, OBE 80
Tilly-sur-Seulles 184

vehicles
  A.11 Matilda 37
  A.12 Matilda Hedgehog 201, 208, 211, 213, 242, 245, 246
  Churchill tank 123, 124, 149–51, 153, 177–82, 184, 186–9, 243
    AVRE 123–5, 182, 184–9, 233, 235
    Bobbin 177
    Crocodile 189
  Covenanter 158, 159, 245, 246
  Cultivator No. 6 NLE 'Nellie' 218
  DUKWs 168
  LVT 131
  Porpoise sledge 131
  Sherman Crab 112
  Stuart tank 70
  T12 Mine Exploder 222

Waziristan Campaign 9
weapons
  1933 bomb-thrower patent 16
  AEB bomb-thrower 16–20
  Ampulomet 66
  Arbalest 8, 17–23, 27–30, 38, 39, 43
  Baby Bombard 138, 139, 141–3, 145
  Bazooka 171–3, 241
  Bigot pistol adaptor 223–5
  Bombard, 29mm Spigot Mortar 8, 10, 25, 27–9, 33, 35, 37–43, 45–7, 49–74, 82, 83, 109, 110, 135, 137, 144, 149, 157, 180, 184, 186, 196–8, 220, 225, 231, 235, 238, 240 243–6
  Brandt, 47mm mortar 18
  BSA, 2.5in mortar 18
  Buffalo, demolition projector 186
  Colt 1911 pistol 223, 225
  Denny Gun, demolition projector 181
  depth charge 70, 77–80, 82, 86, 88, 92–5, 97, 101, 129, 202
  Ecia, 2-inch mortar 18
  Fairlie Anti-submarine Mortar 80–2, 86, 88, 90

FP-45 Liberator, pistol 225
Granatenwerfer 16 5, 6
Hay Pocket Howitzer 5
Hedgehog Anti-submarine Mortar 82, 83, 85–8, 90–102, 105, 106, 109, 110, 113, 120, 121, 123, 125, 129, 133, 191, 200–3, 205–13, 225, 231, 234, 235, 242–6
Hedgerow mine-clearance device 103, 112–25, 127–9, 131–3, 155, 222, 243, 244
Hotchkiss, 25 SA-L mle 1935 43
Kangaroo mine 34
Leichter Ladungswerfer, 20cm mortar 225, 226
Mustard Plaster Anti-submarine Mortar 106
Northover Projector 59, 66
O Thrower Anti-submarine Mortar 80, 90, 111
Panzerfaust 171, 173
Petard, demolition projector 43, 70, 180–3, 185, 186, 189, 231, 235
PIAT 10, 14, 15, 23, 43, 74, 135, 137, 139, 144, 145, 147–9, 153–8, 160–6, 168, 171–3, 181, 183, 198–201, 231–3, 235, 241, 244–6
PIAT Mk II (Gun No. 100) 169–71
Porcupine Anti-submarine mortar 82, 83
Projector, AT Portable, No. 1, Mk 1 139–40
Schwerer Ladungswerfer, 38cm mortar 225
Snake line charge 70, 188
split Hedgehog Anti-submarine Mortar 99
Stewblac Projector 145
Sticky Bomb, ST Grenade, Grenade, Hand, Anti-Tank No. 74 11–13, 32, 139, 173
T30, Grenade, Spigot, HEAT 223
Telmera (Scott) 52mm mortar 18
Type 98 320mm mortar 227, 228
Water Hammer Anti-submarine Mortar 108–11, 231

Yad Mordechai, Battle of 232